Ruhmana

The Book of the Soul
Annotated Edition

By: Saparmyrat Niyazov Turkemenbasy

Introductory Notes
By: Andrew S Edwards

"Leader of the Turkmen"- that is the meaning of the name Turkmenbasy, the title endowed upon Saparmyrat Niyazov, the first President for Life of Turkmenistan. This book, Ruhmana, is book one of what translates as "The Book of the Soul" in reference to the fact that it was supposed to represent the Turkmen soul. The book itself shows, just in its existence, the history of what was happening in Turkmenistan at the time, as well as a narrative of its writer. Saparmyrat Niyazov, before becoming President for Life was a leader within the Soviet Union's Communist Party, and had risen in the ranks to lead the Turkmen SSR's Supreme Soviet. With this knowledge of the Soviet hierarchy, Niyazov saw the need for a strong leader with a strong image to control an emerging nation- and with Ruhnama he hoped to become just that.

Ruhmana is not entirely of Soviet personality origin though, as it provides several other uses too, as a book to lead Muslims, a book to create peace, and a book to unite the Turkmen that had not previously been a free nation in the modern age. For the Muslims it did the most though. It showed Niyazov as a devout Muslim, different from the atheist leaders of the Soviet Union, which helped bring in money from the gulf Arab states. Additionally it talked of peace among Muslims, and loving one another, and how Allah dislikes hatred a war- a key principle in keeping Islamic radicalism and militancy out of Turkmenistan. It also drew the Christian minority together with the Muslims, using Jesus and Eve (whom I mentioned in my book "The Force that Acted" are also significant figures in Islam) as an example of parenthood. The religious nature of the book later became more than some Muslims thought was appropriate. In its later years Niyazov stated that Ruhnama was a Holy Book, inspired by Allah, and though not equal to the Qur'an, should be read as much. This even culminated in passages from the Ruhnama being inscribed on the entrance of his home mosque, and some Imam's and Mufti's began to complain.

From a non-religious strictly Turkmen stance, it was the exultation of their existence as a nation and a people. It tells of 5000 years of decent from the Prophet Noah, all the way to Turkish conquerors through narratives of the Turkmen and other Turkic peoples great conquests and kingdoms. As the book was required reading in schools, and tests on the book were given to even get drivers license, it instilled in the readers a nationalist spirit in hopes of keeping the unity that the Balkan nations, and other former communist countries lacked, as evident from the Bosnian War or the Russian invasion of Georgia. Niyazov fueled this great nationalist spirit in every day life, even adding a Turkmen blanket pattern to the countries flag.

The book has been compared to other books such as the Indonesian Pancasila, in that it fueled a pseudo-religious nationalism, and most books by absolute rulers, such a Gaddafi's Red Book, or Hitler's Mein Kompf had this uplifting national spirit that they draw in the reader, but Ruhnama was in fact much much different. It taught peace, forgiveness, and neutrality- which led to Turkmenistan's eventual Neutral status within UN. It did not promote anger towards other nations nor irredentism, as one might expect, but love and happiness, perhaps the cornerstone of what he thought should be of true importance to socialists.

It did however have its down sides and abnormalities, as most ruler's political books do, such as incoherent ramblings and an almost cult status. The book itself became an image of the nation, being taught as a major subject from grade schools to universities, and replacing subjects such as physics. Posters plastered the capital city, and a large monument to the book was even erected that opened daily and played passages from the book. The book was even released out of the airlock of a Soyuz space capsule so that it may "conquer space as well."

All said and done, the book Ruhnama served its purposes of unifying the Turkmen, pacifying the militants, and maintaining the power of Saparmyrat Niyazov Turkmenbasy. The book has been translated into many languages, but struggles to find the resonance that many other ruler's books have. It is my hope that this edition of the book, with its Anglicization of words, and cleaning of text will help readers who seek a greater understanding of ruling political books. It is an excellent look inside the mind of a long serving national ruler, and one of the very few examples of a peaceful neutral political book. Whether you are reading to critique an absolute ruler, or to find knowledge in it's passages, I hope you enjoy the time you have reading it.

THE NATIONAL ANTHEM OF THE INDEPENDENT NEUTRAL TÜRKMENISTAN

TÜRKMENISTAN
MY BELOVED MOTHERLAND,
MY BELOVED HOMELAND!
YOU ARE ALWAYS WITH ME
IN MY THOUGHTS AND IN MY HEART.
FOR THE SLIGHTEST EVIL AGAINST YOU
LET MY HAND BE LOST.
FOR THE SLIGHTEST SLANDER ABOUT YOU
LET MY TONGUE BE LOST.
AT THE MOMENT OF MY BETRAYAL
TO MY MOTHERLAND,
TO HER SACRED BANNER,
TO SAPARMURAT TÜRKMENBASY THE GREAT
LET MY BREATH STOP.

Contents:

The First Section
TURKMEN

IN THE NAME OF ALLAH, THE MOST EXALTED My Beloved People!
My Dear Nation,
This book, written with the help of inspiration sent to my heart by the God who created this wonderful universe and who is able to do whatever He wills, is Turkmen Ruhnama.
Allah has exposed the Turkmen nation to great and difficult problems since the creation of humankind. My people has successfully passed through these hard times. The Turkmen people whose history goes back 5000 years to the period of Oguz Han, contributed to the universal values which emerged in the lands between the Eastern Mediterranean and India, and indeed, cannot be underestimated. In its own lands, the Turkmen people founded more than 70 states including the Anew, Altyndepe, Margus, Parfiya, Seljuks and Kineirgenq states.
The Turkmen people has a great history which goes back to the Prophet Noah. Prophet Noah gave the Turkmen lands to his son Yafes and his descendants. Allah made the Turkmens prolific and their numbers greatly increased. God gave them two special qualities: spiritual richness and courage. As a light for their road, God also strengthened their spiritual and mental capacity with the ability to recognize the realities behind events.
9
After that He gave His servants the following general name: Turkmen.
tirk means core, iman means light. Therefore, Turkmen
means "made from light, whose essence is light." The Turkmen name came to this world in this way.
Allah by his sacred command sent the Prophet Noah scriptures including holy orders. The Prophet Noah distributed these to the people of his time. The essence of these pages was, indeed, beautiful ethics. There were sayings like:
"honor-honesty to young men; virtue to the girls, intellect, sagacity, dignity to the old men and women; nobility to the brides."
Prophet Noah taught his children and youth courage, nobility, keeping their promises, hard work, and spiritual virtue. He made them aware that any small problem in any of these would mean a problem in their honesty in general. Tirk iMAN, that is, Turkmen young men considered verbal attacks on their homeland, their relatives and parents, as attacks on their honor and they did not hesitate to struggle against these.
The Prophet Noah ordered girls, wives and old women to cover their bodies with long, loose dresses, and their heads with head scarves, but left their faces open. "Turkmens faces reflect the light of Allah. For that reason sunlight, which is the torchlight of God, should fall on their faces and this should not be prevented."
Prophet Noah also advised repeatedly that men should not hit the faces of their children or wife. As for the woman's mouth, he ordered them to cover it.
I The original Turkmen word is uyat which comes to the meanings of chaste, innocence, bashfulness and virtue.
10
This cover become the Turkmen traditional cover or yasmak. Later he ordered

the girls to cover their faces with the extensions of their dresses when they made eye contact with a man and to bite the extension when they heard ugly words. Prophet Noah ordered the elders to be careful, patient and wise when educating children and placed on the shoulders of the elders the burden of bringing up children suitably equipped with the necessary skills for conditions in the real world. Prophet Noah wanted the youth to avoid making errors and not to be mistaken. He preached thus:

"If elders make a mistake once, their juniors make it a thousand times. If the father makes a mistake, the son makes a mistake; if the mother makes mistakes, the daughter makes mistakes; if the father-in-law and mother-in-law make a mistake, the bride makes a mistake." For this reason he established the rules of good manners at home for Turkmen.

This rules of good manners are as follows:

1. respect your elders
2. love your juniors

Prophet Noah said, "If you do- not respect your old people, and do not love your juniors then humanity gets lost; and an era of no mercy begins"

3. respect your father and mother

He advised children kindly: "Do not talk to your father and mother while looking in their faces. Do not frown at, make sour face to, them. Do not behave badly to them. If they order something, then do it." This can be internalized by the children easily and in a short time.

4. Wear clean and decent clothes. (Outward appearance)

11

Prophet Noah ordered: "Good clothes improve the external appearance and make people look good. Choose clothes that suit you."

5. Keep goods at your home that have been earned by your own labor and efforts.

Prophet Noah said: "Do not take other people's goods.

Do not bring them to your house, and do not make them

yours," and added, "The home is also a place to visit."

6.The decoration of the home, its order, cleanliness and appearance should be very good.

Prophet Noah repeatedly said: "Each material thing should make the soul feel comfortable and should increase happiness in life. If your house is dirty, then you feel bad, disoriented and uncomfortable."

7. Protect the home and its exterior and neighboring areas and the place you live in.

Prophet Noah ordered: "Remain aware of and protect wholeheartedly your neighbors and your neighborhood. If an enemy attacks your neighbor's home, then you will be the next."

8. Spiritual sublimity

Prophet Noah advised: "Always maintain sublime targets for your spirit. That adds spirit and light to the value of your life, and makes your difficult dealings easy."

9. Women's make up'

"Do not be mean with emerald stones for your daughters and wives. Find them wherever they are and give them to the women. If one upsets his wife or daughter, he is not a Turkmen since they are very pleasant by nature, and

12

their souls are pleasant too. Please them if you want to treat them well. Give them valuable pieces so that they may wear them on their breast, neck, and back. However, never harm their faces; the face itself is more valuable than thousands of emerald pieces. Allah's love in people's heart shows itself in people's faces and enlightens the world. If you do this, they look better, satisfy your soul, and strengthen your spirit." as Prophet Noah advised. He always said: "The decoration and beauty of the home are the daughters and the wives. A rose is beautiful in the garden; a wife, a daughter is beautiful in the home."

More than this, the Prophet Noah said:

"Keep the fire in the stove alight and do not allow your family to perish ' Fire is life and puts an end to problems, frightening evil away."

Turkmens have preserved their religion, their language, and the purity of their nation, and created their own customs and legitimate conduct. These multifaceted positive changes derive from the spiritual wealth of the people. Every Turkmen has this spiritual wealth and up until the 18th century by their labor, honor, courage, and endurance they determined their fate by themselves with cooperation at various levels, in the family, society, people and nation.

If you look at the history, over the last 300 years Turkmens attributes have changed, their power and scope has decreased, conflicts have replaced unity and cooperation. My Turkmen nation with neighboring nations, the clans between themselves, and tribes against other tribes, all fell into different conflicts. The lack of trust reached such a level in our nation that citizens distrusted citizen, brother distrust-

13

ed brother and father distrusted son. They lived without trusting each other or anyone else. I lived in the Soviet era and when I was young I recognized and felt my people's lack of trust in justice and their hopeless view of the future. Our people were not only unable to understand what they were experiencing but also unable to judge their daily life. There was this kind of belief among our people: "Day belongs to the

powerful, and kawurma(2) belongs to those who have canines" They used to believe that whatever you do, you cannot prosper. But why has the fate of Turkmens been so problematic in the last three centuries?

The state was divided, tribes fought with each other, the nation lost its core, was almost led to forsake their religion, its language was simplified, culminating in the loss of their horse, costume, jewelry, and customs which had been gained through a thousand years work. Nothing happens in this universe without a reason; whether it is a natural or man made disaster which afflicts a nation, there is always a reason for it.

Let's leave each Turkmen to think about this question and face this problem in his soul and answer it before God.

By the order of Allah the Most Exalted, as the shadow of the third millennium fell on to us, in 1991, Turkmenistan became an independent state. However, at the outset, this was only on paper. The developing society, state institutions, thinking on national independence, sustainable economy and international affairs shaped by national interest were namely taking shape. The most challenging aspect of this business is to connect individual fate with independence and to understand

2 A roasted or fried meat dish

how our national interest is attached to the independence. The most challenging aspect of this business is that views, reasoning and mental independence are not up to the level of understanding the national benefit and interests that come about as a result of them.

If you do not have a national state organization, a national policy, a national ideal which will enthuse and mobilize people, a national economy, a national civilization, a national army, then your condition cannot be described as full independence. We need time for this. We need at least 10-20 years.

First, people's perception and spirit should change. Each Turkmen is responsible for the nation's fate, national state, society, its indivisible unity, and unification. Each Turkmen should know what kind of path their nation followed in the past, should be able to compare it with their current era and know their future. The general interest of the Turkmen nation depends on each individual Turkmen. Allah the Almighty gave us limitless land and water. He gave us underground resources. He created our nation intelligent and able to judge their own conduct. In addition, he gave us an independent Turkmen state.

Turkmen keep your morale high and keep good work, prosper and make others and your country prosper. Those who will make the Turkmens attain the true level and status of the Turkmen and work for Turkmenistan will be the Turkmens themselves.

My dear Turkmen nation, in order to urge your soul and mind to fulfilll these duties and to raise a strong faith in your heart for self-confidence, and to be a support to you, I have written this book, Ruhnama, for you. I dedicate and present the book I have written to you today.

16

My Dear Turkmen Nation!

You are the meaning of my life and source of my strength. I wish you a healthy and long life. Our Turkmen ancestors were courageous people and they began to educate their children before they came to life. The Turkmen child reached maturity and bravery, and then has a national education and worldview. For that reason, bodily health, intellectual stability, and integrity, and good manners were the special characteristics of the Turkmen.

In our times, the Turkmen should take care in his eating and drinking to preserve his health and endurance. He should not eat greedily. In order to keep his health, strength and productivity, the Turkmen should remember Allah Almighty's order: "Eat and drink but do not waste," and behave according to this order.

The real Turkmen should be careful about the clothes he wears and the way he dresses should be reasonable. His appearance should be pleasing since Allah is beautiful and the Turkmen should be appropriate for His love.

The Turkmens before us continued to read and learn new sciences even though they had reached the highest levels in the sciences. They lived with the accumulated knowledge that had passed from generation to generation and passed it on to the current generation. They thought that the learning of the sciences would end if they made any break in this endeavor.

Today's Turkmens, you will be seen as scientists if you keep reading. If you lose your learning, then you will become illiterates. Every citizen of Turkmenistan should have a knowledge of science. This would be the result of brave souls, poetic perceptions, sensitive heart, and spiritual richness. To read and to learn is to have a deeper knowledge of life. When one reads, new ideas and anxieties emerge in the mind. Thus, to read and to learn is to appreciate Allah Almighty. Intellectuals and scientists have special place in my world and I show them great respect.

The Turkmen man should lead his family efficiently and direct them to goodness.

Intellectual and wise, the Turkmen father should set a good example to educate his children; he should approach his children with love and should choose for them and offer them modesty, happiness, and compassion; he should treat them equally and justly. The Turkmen child should not commit illegitimate acts, and should be both physically and spiritually healthy. Thus, a Turkmen child should have a sense of humor, and be generous and loyal to his/her parents and the country, in addition to having a sense of responsibility. After all these, the parents duties to their children are as follows: first, they should ensure they gain knowledge of a valid science, then help them to have a home and, third, help them to marry. The Turkmen man should be on his own after these aids. We take these three responsibilities seriously in Turkmen territory. In each subject and area, our road be bright.

In societal relations, the ethical values advised in the Qur'an and their strength will improve the Turkmens characteristics and make them more powerful in this Golden Age of Turkmens. Turkmens will be civilized, clean, attractive, and useful individuals.

Turkmens, without distinction, should not deceive, should not lie, should be honest, and should not be jealous. Good morals and honesty are the characteristics which suit

the Turkmen best. The Turkmens who have these qualities should be the citizens of the 21st century. May Allah give us strength and patience on this road. The never ending spiritual source for a true Turkmen, who continuously ponders on his spiritual world, who really worries about his well-being, who is unselfconscious,

alert and careful about enhancing his intellectual, physical and spiritual capacities, should be the Ruhnama, which never lets his exuberant, sensitive, poetic and sublime heart, and longing for spirit, deeply felt enthusiasm and inner feelings, extinguish.

Fate gave me the role of being leader of Turkmenistan at the juncture of the second and third millennia. The burden of the responsibility of taking my people from the last years of the second millennium, in which things did not go well, to the summits of the third millennium fell onto my shoulders.

This position and responsibility, which have been given to me without my asking, have motivated me to call up my spiritual, intellectual and physical strength that Allah granted me with and use them as a societal force to achieve progress in my country. I understand that it is necessary to call up not only my own strength but also all the national spiritual strength given to the whole Turkmen nation.

Indeed, throughout history which connects one generation to the others, there is a law of individual-society relations: the power which has been generated by the society in one era comes to life in an individual matured in the same nation at a later point. This should not be put to keeping people where they are but to come back with a different outlook and raise them to the summits. I dedicate Ruhnama, my desired and expected book, to my people. Although the demand for a book such

19

as this has come from our generation, this is not a problem which has only surfaced in recent history. The Turkmen generations before us, even though they did not make such demands explicitly, felt the necessity of spiritual principles which will not lead our generation to divide and disappear. Each individual comes to the fore with the symbols that constitute its core: the commander holds a weapon, the poet holds a pen, the doctor holds a remedy. The President, as historical character, writes his guidelines and come to the fore with these.

My main guideline is Ruhnama. As a systematic worldview, Ruhnama is the core of all my political, economic and life targets, with civil content and methods of use in different areas of society.

Before beginning to talk about the different aspects of the historical necessity in this book, I would like to draw attention to a characteristic of Ruhnama, which shows that it is one another within life, which is a part of life, integral but not exclusive. The greatest miracle of Allah in the world, the human being, has passed through dark periods, natural disasters and societal fightings, many difficult times. The knowledge and conscious life of the human being begins with the book, namely when human being understood the word and considered it sacred. These miraculous books have been given to the Prophets Moses, David, Jesus Christ and Muhammad, peace be upon them all. The Messenger of Allah, our Prophet Muhammad, peace be upon him, endorsed the fact that the four sacred books, including the Qur'an, were given to the Prophets by Allah, and thus word has gained a highest, exalted, rank.

The Word is the most sacred gift that God gave to human beings.

20

The Word is the fruit of people, but it is given to human beings by God.

With the coming of the sacred books, the era in which human beings worshiped evil forces was ended. The era in which the wisdom of the word has been appreciated began immediately afterward. These eras became the two most significant eras.

Allah, the Almighty, the Omnipotent, in the Qur'an that He sent to Prophet Muhammad, said that Noah, Moses, Christ and Muhammad are elevated spirits. The Turkmens Ruhnama is not a -religious book. The Qur'an, the book of Allah, the Most Exalted, is the first and the most important and the reference book of the Turkmens among other Muslims that guides people to put their life into order. God's book, the Qur'an, is sacred and cannot be replaced or compared to any other book.

We also believe in the books mentioned in the Qur'an. About the Old Testament that was sent to Moses, Allah said in the Qur'an: "We really sent the Old Testament and therein are good ways to take as examples and Allah's light." The Gospel is the book sent to the Prophet Christ.

Allah who created miracles ordered that:

"After the prophets we sent Christ, son of Maryam, and with him it has been endorsed that previously sent Old Testament is real. In addition we gave him the Gospel and with this book gave the shining light that approves what is said in the

Old Testament and the right path."
Allah the Merciful gave the book Zebur (Psalms) to the Prophet David.

Allah the Merciful said: "We gave Zebur to David."
Apart from all these, we believe that Allah sent suhuf (scriptures, pages) to other prophets. If something should be said about believing in the Qur'an, obeying the Qur'an has been ordered in it and it has been placed above comparison to others since it has privileges, given by Allah, that are absent in others. That is why we show extra respect to the Qur'an. We obey the Qur'an and the Qur'an is a sacred book.

Ruhnama should be a source of power and striving to reach the targets of Turkmen's Golden Age. The real Turkmen cannot treat himself badly and does not forget who he is and his real duties towards his own people. The Turkmen's outlook cannot be separated from his inner life. Indeed, the Turkmen should be able to keep the delicate balance between the material judgment of his body and his spirit.

Ruhnama should be a source of power that will keep hearts alert, of intellect, and suitable spirit, and the poetic soul of those real Turkmens who are concerned with their own spiritual world and also their spiritual and physical development.

Ruhnama is the book of unity and togetherness. It is the only source that will connect Turkmen's present and its past. Up until now, there were a number of words, special words, but not a whole word. Ruhnama should fill this gap.

Ruhnama should place in the hands of Turkmens their unique and whole history, and spiritual striving. My philosophy is unity and togetherness. For in the absence of unity and togetherness, there is no nation. If it happens by accident, it does not last long. Spiritual multiplicity, different mental perspectives, and different voices of the soul have been built upon this unity. The unity and togetherness inside becomes the pillars that keeps the nation together. No other nation in the world was divided into so many tribes as the Turkmens. The real unity of Turkmen is blood and language unity.

Unity provides the nation with the means to construct its future. Without unity, it is not possible to understand the Turkmens past. Turkmenistan is one of these nations which has the richest history. There have been so many books written on different periods of Turkmen history, but a surprising situation emerges when one considers the huge number of books: it is not possible to find Turkmens alone in these books. It is also surprising that in the works of historians, and other intellectuals, the bits and pieces of Turkmen history are very different and sometimes controversial. If you believe in one of these, Turkmens are nomadic or semi-nomadic peoples and according to another they are a pastoral people and deal with farming. According to another, they are urban people and live in castles and established some major civilizations. Yet another says from a political view point hardworking, another says humble, even lazy.

Where does this controversy and confusion come from? No one was able to see the Turkmen nation as a whole since it is a very great nation. This historical confusion reminds us of a short story by our great poet Jalaleddin Rumi: A group of blind men wonder how an elephant is. Those who feel the elephant's legs decide that it is a hard column, those who feel its trunk think that it is a weak tree. Likewise each writer saw Turkmen according to his own view and perceptions. From such a perspective, it is not possible to see the reality; only semi-reality can be seen. It is obvious that semi-reality is worse than a lie. Individuality is the biggest trap of our era's way of thinking.

For that reason, anew spiritual approach is required to encompass the whole Turkmen nation and history. Of course such an attempt may not include all historical details. That is the duty of historians. As I said before, we need a measure to decide on unity inside. The spiritual analysis and descriptions of the content of the unrepeatable amount of the coincidences, similarities and differences of the history are needed. In this discourse, unifying and generalizing philosophies play a role.

Ruhnama is the veil of the Turkmen people's face and soul. It is the Turkmen's first and basic reference book. It is the total of the Turkmen mind, customs and traditions, intentions, doings and ideals. It will be our legacy to the future after drawing lessons from the past! One part of Ruhnama is our past that the existing knowledge at present could not enlighten and the other part is our future! One part of Ruhnama is sky, the other part is earth.

We wrote the first pages of Ruhnama during the first ten years of our independent and permanently neutral Turkmenistan, while we improved our working places, established the infrastructure and changed our life.

In those ten years of Turkmenistan's independence and permanent neutrality we wrote the Ruhnama for the soul and mind of Turkmens with enlightening words and with hope.

Where does the greatness of human beings come from? The greatness of the human being begins with his discovery of his own, that is, with his discovery of his inner world. It is

easy to know or measure others, but the real difficulty is to know oneself! For that reason our wise ancestors said: "Those who know themselves become the saints."

Dear Turkmen!

Be your own ruler. If you succeed in managing yourself, then you can overcome all difficulties.

My Citizens! The Turkmen of today and tomorrow should know himself. He should know his weakness and his strength, through and through! The doctor who knows the problem can easily solve it. The people who can judge their problems can avoid the problems! Ruhnama is the Turkmen's book about himself.

Ruhnama is not only our book! Ruhnama is also the book of our brothers and other nations that rejoice at our happiness and are proud of our successes and with whom we are together creating our Golden Age in these lands.

Ruhnama is also the book of our near and far brothers and neighbors. You become friends after you get to know someone. The foreigners who read Ruhnama will know us better, became our friends faster, and the far and the foreign becomes closer to us on our path to being accepted in the world.

Turkmenistan which has been the center of many great transformations and a center of development and progress, had a very special place in the history and expansion of Islam into the world. Turkmen people have made unlimited contributions to the world.

If one wished to create a flag of beauty and perfection, then this flag would be a Turkmen carpet.

If one wants to create a model of endurance, beauty and

25

purity, then one should take the Ahalteke horse as an example.

Dear Citizens!

In a short time, we have established our excellent stable state and taken the first step in our progress. The second step lies in our mind, heart and blood. We shall establish this great transformation with this book entitled Ruhnama.

We have sacred territories that will open the eyes of those who became blind from weeping for their lost lands. We have wonderful songs that open deaf ears. We have beautiful smelling springs that make silence burst into song. We are the owners of these beautiful lands.

Without looking to the opportunities and sources at their hands, Turkmens did not hesitate to go to war, and fighting head-to-head, they won or lost their battles. If this territory falls into danger, we have courageous young men who put their lives into danger, like Girogly, to fight! We have old people like Gorkut Ata who will advise on keeping unity among people. We have diamond-standard, wise people like Magtymguly. In such a country and with people like these, can we not turn the 21st century into the Golden Age of the Turkmen? It would be a shame if we could not change this territory into a heaven and establish a wonderful golden society when we have our people who devote their love, effort and sincerity to the task.

Allah the Almighty created us as humans, we came into this world as humans, and it is our duty to make of our people a noble and trustworthy people, to establish an era of well-being and found a good society.

My Dear People

I feel proud of my Turkmen territory and Turkmen land. This sacred land inspires my heart like a poet's.

26

27

This land is Turkmen territory in which Hydyr walks in beautiful deserts, Kowus walks in shadowy mountains, Kysas walks on the shrinking shore of the sea. Turkmens seek refuge in its territory, so like a laden table. This territory is called Turkmen land which has been made of pearls, diamonds and gold! Its soil is its treasury, its subterranean resources are its treasury, its mountains and its sea are its treasury. We produce crops in this land in all seasons. They are harvested, their seeds multiplied by thousands and returned back to the soil.

This Turkmenistan is trustworthy like the Turkmen's promise, high-ranking in honor, sacred like the Turkmen's home, miraculous like the Turkmen's belief. In the blue sky of this land white geese and cranes prepare for wedding days, beautiful springs and summers come from the sky of this magical land, and clouds with rains and thunderbolts make the Turkmen homeland very green and contented.

The happiness of the Turkmen Spring cannot fit into a Turkmen's soul and the land and sky tell its story, the roses bloom from the stones.

We say welcome and open our arms to those who come to these lands. World travelers, our gate and soul are open. Come and visit us! Come and travel in the lands of Oguz Han, Gorkut Ata, Seljuk Han, Alp Arslan, Meliksah, Soltan Saniar, Gbrogly and Magtymguli.

My fellow countrymen, though you are not travelers, you visit this territory, touch the soil on which many valued people, rulers and your ancestors lived.

This land is a sacred and miraculous land.

Ruhnama is a visit to this land. Ruhnama is a visit to the past of this territory and a visit to the future of this territory. Ruhnama is the visit made to the heart of the Tirkmen. Ruhnama is a sweet spiritual fruit grown in this territory.

No human being who has not experienced what I lived through can understand me.

Your father who is supposed to support you in hard times is dead in an unknown, foreign place!

Your dear mother is lying with your two sisters under Karakum. You are alone in Leningrad. You have no one behind you who is asking about you and writing letter to you.

I was sick and asked my supposedly close relatives to take care of me. They wrote to tell me that they had forgotten about me, let alone helping me.

There was no one other than The One, Allah Almighty, to seek refuge in and no one to ask for help other than my Allah. The whole country was crying that there is no Allah. Oh, Allah!

I used to remember Girogly at that time. His enemies took his head and went away. They did it in order to prevent the Turkmens from ever uniting again under a leader. But Jygalybeg is alive. There is no place in the whole story that says that Jygalybeg died. Perhaps Jygalybeg has been waiting until now for a courageous young Turkmen to come to life. We need courageous, lion-like, tough young men to take care of enslaved Turkmens. We need Girogly Beg.

I tried to express my feelings, which I could not suppress in myself, which became knot on knots on my throat, which

brought me almost to the edge of frenzy, madness, in the following poem:

Jygalybeg

I have powerful Turkmen thoroughbred, would you groom it Jygalybeg ?
I have also a broken and uneased heart, would you groom it, Jygalybeg ?
My bowers are shackled, my Qandybil is a grieved country now,
And our ill-fortune never awakens, unless you, unless you..., Jygalybeg!
Where are the mountain-like variants who rose against the black mountain?
Alas, sorrowing are the stately variants that fought against the bad lot !
Many heroic and wise fell martyred, so that I was left behind lonely, abandoned,
Even the dessert bent double with pain, moaning. Can you hear, Jygalybeg ?
The prosperous wealthy men were collected, suffered, and sent to exile in Siberia,
The lion-hearted brave fell as martyr in the fight and already became graves,
Your orphan cried bitterly, left all alone, no strength, patience, endurance,
All my land weep and my folk bewailed, the country in disorder, Jygalybeg

I have powerful Turkmen thoroughbred, would you groom it Jygalybeg ?
I have also a broken and uneased, heart, would you groom it, Jygalybeg ?
Lend me Girogly's curved sword and your spear to me, Jygalybeg !
No fear! I shall fight to death. Give me your own crown, Jygalybeg I

Attractive surroundings and a good view are wonderful but if there is someone who understands you, then home is better. Heaven-like places are good and pleasant but your own homeland, your fatherland is more appealing and attractive. Run away from that who opens his door but shuts his heart to you. However, forgive that who opens his heart but shut the door to his home because he might have some excuses.

I was born on 19 February 1940 in Asgabat. My dear father went to fight in the Second World War. He struggled against the fascist invaders in Caucasia.

After fighting for two years, in 1943, seven Turkmen, including my father, in a Russian troop were captured by enemy forces at a village, called Thcikola, Viladi Kafkaz of the capital city of the Northern Osetia. I learnt the tragic fate of the hostages after 18 years by chance. Then I was a second year student at the Polytechnic Institute in Leningrad. All the students went home during summer time. Dormitories and classes would remain empty for some time. I was missing my motherland, language and Turkmen song since I had not been to Turkmenistan for the last two years. I also missed my school friends and other friends. If you do

not have parents and relatives, then there is no one watching over you, and caring for your health, sentiments and wishes. The false concern of some people does not convince an orphan. You have to make your own decisions and decide on critical situations regarding your fate. Your only friends are your ideals and your spiritual world.

I have thanked God a hundred thousand times since I was five years old that I inherited honor, nobility, patience, highness of spirit and objectives-ideals from my parents in my body and soul. My character has not been weakened through times of both success and failure but rather strengthened. This become a fountain that will never dry up for my Turkmen people, my sacred land, my motherland, for the past and present, for its future generations, which started as a spring but turned into a river.

When I was studying at the university, I used to go to the library. I read not only books about my lessons, I found rare books about Turkmen history and read them patiently.

Once I was reading a book in the library. An old Russian, wearing glasses, stared at me from both my left and my right.

I did not pay attention and thought that he was confusing me with someone. But he came near to me and looked again. I am usually a calm person but his stare disturbed me.

"Father are you confusing me with someone else?" I asked politely.

"I thought you resembled someone, my son. However my eyes are not good enough."

I was looking at this old person and even though I do not forget anyone even if I have only seen them once, I could not

remember having seen him before. I learnt much about this man on a train journey later.

The old man said: "If I am mistaken, my heart will break. If I am not mistaken, then my heart will also break. May God help me!" He tried to calm down and raised his right hand:

"Whoever you are , you must be the son of Catamaran Annany'az."

I felt like a bucket of hot water had been thrown over me. I felt waves run inside me on hearing my father's name from a stranger.

Then we introduced ourselves and talked. This professor, lwan Semyonowic, had been my father's friend during the war and they had fought shoulder to shoulder against the enemy forces and even shared their last food when they were at the front. We talked a lot about the problems and the tragedies of that period and the wartime.

He said that he had written two letters to Asgabat and asked for information after my father's death. In response to the letters, he had received the reply that Catamaran Annanyyaz's wife and children had died during an earthquake. He was surprised and delighted to see me alive.

"Your father was tall with high cheekbones. Your appearance and movements are like Atamyrat's. When the fighting was not heavy, we used to gather around your father when he sang. He was able to play all instruments and was a very good conversationalist, and when he danced he was the master of the dance. He astonished the Caucasians.

My Dear Saparmyrat, your father was like a bullet fired

33

from a rifle. He was sometimes braver than necessary. When I said to him 'Catamaran you have children, so take care of yourself," he used to answer, "And if I save myself, who will save my children?'He fought like a lion."

The old man also told the whole story about the tragic end of the troops that were captured by the enemy forces during the war.

We had to surrender. We did not decide on this but our commanders ordered us to do so. In the war this kind of situation occurred. This was not the fault of the soldiers. Even though this was so, it is still not possible to describe your father as a prisoner of war. He was immediately shot as a communist. He did not lose even the smallest part of his courage. Betrayed by his countrymen he went his death, like Christ sold to his enemies by Judas.

Your father was a hero, a real hero. I wrote a piece about his courage. I am not a writer but I could not prevent myself from doing this. I wrote it since I wanted to tell my friend's story to the world. Since I felt obliged to do this, I sent it to a friend of mine in the Moscow cinema for his consideration. He liked it and said at the last moment:

"We should make the hero a Georgian because if we do not do this, no one will know who this Turkmen is."

lwan Semyonovic took a breath. He cleaned his glasses and continued:

"I understand them... It was the Stalin era. But I refused the change of hero and withdrew my script. Dear Saparmyrat, my son, your father was a real hero, learn about his fate in war and his heroism."

My fellow citizens, there are so many people who have

34

held these high spiritual values since Turkmen people entered the historical arena. I am only one among those, since these sentiments are widespread among Turkmen people, and the Turkmen nation is stable and lasting.

In 1963, 1 missed my homeland and went to Turkmenistan via Moscow. At that time, I met with another person who had known my father closely. My fate gave me a surprise, and I met a friend of my father's from the military after 18 years. It happened like this. At that time, the Asgabat-Moscow train would wait for some time at each station.

There are some people who do not like train travel. However, it is a particular pleasure to enter the world of ideas and to get to know new places.

The conductor on the train was sary Aga, who was from Yalkym village near Asgabat. He was a courageous and hard working Turkmen and we met on our way to Turkmenistan.

Human beings are different from each other. Some people you feel close to, you want to meet and know them better. Sometimes you see a person and decide to stay away from that person. I leamt something certain about Turkmen people in my early childhood, that Turkmens like to be asked questions. Cary Aga was a curious man:

"My nephew, some people feel uneasy if you ask a few questions. They say, 'Who are you, a prosecutor or a judge?' Our Turkmen said that humans know each other through speech, animals recognize each other through smell. We had a very big village but it disappeared during eras of the civil war and the Bolsheviks. When repression increased, many people fled to other places. If you ask carefully the Turkmen

35

population was fairly small, and each and every one always knew one the other, a fact which is well-known.

I learned that Qary Aga had known both my father and grandfather.

"Dear Saparmyrat, you should only be surprised if you meet someone who did not know your grandfather, Annany'az Artygy. There was no one who did not know Annanyaz Artygy in Gypjak, G6kje, Bagyr, Herrikgala, Yalkym and Biizmein. Annanyaz Artygy was an able man who used to invite others to eat at his table. They sent your grandfather into exile in 1932 since he had a private place and shop and had workers working on a salary.

The reason that I know these facts in detail is that my

I

mother and uncle were neighbors. of Annanyyaz Aga. "Qary Aga, did you meet my grandfather?" He smiled with pleasure.

"We had so much in common. I met him in many different places, village, markets, town center, you name it. Once I took two bags of barley and went to the city. I was very young. At that time, on Sundays, the city was very crowded and it wasn't possible to find a place for donkeys, horses, camels and vehicles. At that time we did not have vehicles that we have now and there were a limited number of Turkmen in the city.

I was walking with my bags and there was a poor man in front of me riding on a donkey. The idle young people of the city were hitting him with sticks and he was close to falling off. The poor man was not sure what to do and was shouting and cursing at the kids. Their parents were on both sides of the road and were watching heedlessly the kids

36

attacks. A man wearing a special black Turkmen hat (silkme telpek) came rapidly and ran into the street. He began to whip the people standing heedlessly around and these people ran away because of the sharp lash of the whip. Then an old man said to the crowd:

--You struck the right people, Turkmen, you struck true. If a child does something wrong, then his parents are guilty.

--Yes, Dear Saparrnyrat, I remember when your grandfather Annanyaz Artygy became chief of the village for the second time. When my father heard this he said:

-- The people of Kipqak did not do the right thing; the government did not arrest people like Annanyaz A-rtygy since they are rich! The government is afraid of Turkmens like Annanyaz Artygy.

Fate brought him a bad day in August 1937 when he was accused of committing a crime. He was declared an enemy of the people and sent to death row in prison. Your grandfather knew that such an end would come. But he did not refuse the ordinary people's demand.

Dear Saparmyrat, when your father entered the city both young and old would look at him. He rode his horse with pride. He was very good looking and created a very good impression. He was like a beg or han. He always looked for the goodness in others but these kind of people were annihilated in the Stalin era."

Qary Aga walked around for a while and directed a train out of the station. He came back to my side.

"Our relations were good with your father. He was three or four years older than me. I was living in Yalkym near Aigabat and used to visit my uncle frequently. They sent your grandfather into exile in 1932. If they would send even your 53 year-old

grandfather into exile, no one could feel safe. His friends advised your father Catamaran to move to another area. He moved to Kerki city in this way, where he worked as a teacher. Later he lived in the village of G6kdepe from 1935-36. In 1937, he bought a house in Aigabat and settled there and began to work there.

At that time we were really close friends. Saparmyrat, I remember your father's face; he was always a pleasant, attractive, forward-thinking, patient and finemanly person."

I did not led him go on but asked: "When is the last time you saw my father?"

From 1941 onwards we fought against the German invaders in the same troop. Another day I will tell you how we saved our country. There is no such thing as a sweet war and, indeed, in this bloody war, there were times we won and times we were defeated. In 1943, near to Wiladikavkaz in North Ossetia after an intense battle, we were taken prisoner by the enemy. The Germans were trying to control the situation and shouting to each other while holding the automatic weapons. Russian soldiers were collected in one place after throwing away their weapons. There were five of us from Turkmenistan, four Turkmen and a Russian. At that time, a friend of ours, took out a piece of tobacco and wrapped it with old newspaper. We were taking it in turns to smoke it. When the cigarette came to Catamaran, there was a Russian on his right, and a Turkmen friend said 'Catamaran do not give it to the Russian. The Germans are going to kill us now. Give it to me and I will have a smoke before dying.'

'No, friend, this friend also fought with us and put his life in danger to save the country. He should smoke when his turn comes. There is God and we should not lose our hope even to our last breath.'

Then a German began announcing something over a loudspeaker and another translated into Russian, 'Line up" and over a hundred captured soldiers lined up. Then they announced:

"Any communists present, step forward".

In front of the line, there were German soldiers with automatic weapons at every ten paces. All of a sudden I was startled when a Turkmen near to me said: 'Can't we push forward that Catamaran who gave the cigarette to communist?' (implying that you prefer giving cigarette to a Russian rather than to us so you are also like him, a communist then, so you should step forward)

They grumbled: 'Now do you understand who you should have given that cigarette to?'A German soldier who had heard and seen this event came running up and then they took away Catamaran by poking him with their guns, fifteen paces away to the edge of a hollow. Then, having gathered several more men, in front of our eyes, they executed them by shooting them by a machine gun and threw the dead in the hollow."

Qary Aga added, 'May Allah full their graves with Divine Light' and wiped his eyes with a handkerchief taken from his pocket. He looked at me quietly. No, he made no mistake; there was no tear in my eyes. He did not see my sadness. He guessed that I had not believed what he had said. 'My son, at that time Hitler ordered that whenever the German soldiers took a communist captive from among the Soviet soldiers then they were to execute them there and then. There was permission for the exchange of other captives for German captives. 1, like all the others, benefited from the exchange of prisoners and I returned rightly to my homeland," he said and again stared at my face.

"Qary Aga, thank you very much for what you have said. These are matters of fate," I said and I stared out of the window of the train. Through the window it looked as if gray sand was flowing past. The train passed Turkmenabat and went on towards the Repetek Desert. It was as if my dear father, straight and brave, was visible in front of my eyes in his last appearance to me. Moreover, his pure thoughts: "No, I do not die. I have three young sons and their beloved mother, my Gurbansoltan, living in my homeland and they are my descendants." His words were in my ears.

Iam pleased with the fact that neither my grandfather nor father left any inheritance to me. In fact they left me instead something as valuable as a great inheritance. Everybody who knew my father and grandfather praised them: "Your father was a very great man." Like this, they extolled and glorified them and these expressions filled my heart with joy. What greater wealth can there be than that?

Many years later on, I wondered what had happened to the men who had shared the cigarette. They had been freed in an exchange of prisoners and the three of them had returned to their villages. But, they encountered many troubles in their fate. Two of them were from the villages in the area around Aigabat. In the 1950's, the first one had a stroke, lost his mind and tongue and died. The second one committed suicide by hanging himself at home. The third was from the village of G6kdepe. After the war he had committed suicide by throwing himself on the railway.

40

We sometimes say that there is no need for you to settle your accounts in this world. Whatever you have done, the world will settle your account for you. War, look at it! Such horror! The 20th Century has been a bloody and brutal century in which mankind, in his lifespan burdened with disasters, has rendered many losses and sacrificed many lives. There have been two World Wars, and tens of border wars and inter-state wars have occurred. Our Turkmen citizens have participated in those wars too. Sometimes it was against their will and sometimes voluntarily. In the Second World War alone, 740,000 Turkmens died at the hands of the German invaders. Tens of thousands of men were injured and maimed. To measure the loss of our citizens materially and financially is impossible. We have given the name of the hero of the Turkmen state to all the martyrs in this war. May their place be in the heavens and their graves fulled with divine light!

The war ended, the veterans returned to their homeland and it was as if a bright light had been ignited in the hearts of the people. But, it was not to last. God once more tested the Turkmen province. On the night of 6th October 1948 Aigabat was devastated by an earthquake which left our beautiful city in ruins. In one night, out of a population of 198,000 people in our capital city, 176,000 were martyred, the majority of the rest were injured or disabled. Our family also suffered in that disaster. When we went to our beds, there were four of us. My dear 33 year-old mother, my 10 year-old elder brother Nyy'azmyrat, and my 6 year-old younger brother Muhammetmyrat all were martyred that night. The next day, when I broke down and wept over the

3 because those who are killed in such disasters are recognized to be martyrs in Islam ruined house, although I had not yet completed 8 years old, I knew I was alone. In this way, I sat through 6 lonely days and nights. On the seventh day, they came and carried away my dead mother and dear brothers to bury them in Ymam Kasym graveyard.

In those six days, I had understood that this was the end of my childhood. My tears dried up for ever. The last time I looked upon my dear family and the places where they lay under the ruins, in their presence I vowed to myself silently:

"My Dears, your spirits and that of my dear father will live in my heart for ever. They will lend me effort and power to achieve my aims and on your behalf I will realize your purposes and the dreams which you were not able to live out. May Allah help me!

Our Ancestor Oguz Han is the forefather of the Turkmen people, whom Turkmen people assume to be a prophet. From the ancient civilized heritage of Turkmen soil and from the Oguz Han era, Golden Cow sculptures and many other valuable relics have been found.

You cannot convince Turkmen people that Gorkut Ata is a man without saintly miracles (karamat)!

Turkmens in history founded the great Parfia State. ,&rsak ah established relations with the Romans. During his era he was known as The Holy &rsak ah. In the history of the Turkmens, there have been many men who have been believed to be like prophets and described as godly, holy. We have never tried to force other people to believe that these are men who have prophecy, however, we do believe that those were not ordinary people but worked saintly miracles (kararnat), which we do not let others abuse our beliefs, either.

D6vletmdmmet Azady said: "The richest of all richnesses is sagacity, the most precious heritage is breeding and training, the most beggarly of the beggarly is regret." For us, the heritages derived from our ancestors, Oguz Han, Oguzs, Persians, Seljuks and Harzemahs are unsurpassable honors and priceless treasures.

The beauty, fineness, of the human being lies in the truthfulness of his words. Unfortunately, it was not really that

some sections of the Tilirkmen society were corrupted and derailed. Between the 14th and 16th centuries, because of internal conflicts within the Turkmen nation, it ceased to prosper. The principalities and the Hanates could not agree and made great wars among themselves, a prelude to the perishing of the Turkmen themselves. The esteem, power, strength and spiritual credit of Turkmen was in decline.

Brave Turkmen! In this world, in the history of humanity there is nothing true and eternal except our Exalted, Eternal, Allah. Within the Seljuk State, after the 14th Century, because of the central state, we began to be divided into kingdoms, Hanates and principalities. The Turkmen dynasties of Akgoyunly (Whitesheep) and Garagoy'unly (Blacksheep) had started to fight among themselves.

After the 17th century, following the Russian expansion around the Caspian Sea, and the establishment of relations between Russia and Persia, the Turkmens were excluded, their settlements decreased. History witnesses that external forces settled and regulated the tribal conflicts of Turkmen people, and their territorial and water disputes with neighboring countries. Between 1879 and 188 1, the Turkmen nation's economic, political, and social life was destroyed by the harsh impact of the G6kdepe Wars. For this reason the Russian state was able to establish a pro-Russian puppet authority that expanded its cultural and religious propaganda in Turkmen lands.

This is not a history book. Though if we do not know the past, then the destiny of our future generations will lie in obscurity or darkness. In addition, their spiritual belief will diminish and Turkmens will lose their fundamental principles.

Therefore, it is necessary to be cognizant of these things. Between the 17th and 19 h centuries, some states diffused wicked propaganda in pursuit of their own national interests. They falsely represented the nation of Turkmens as pillagers and merciless slaughterers, and described them as a wild community who kill each other, living in tents, an ignorant, uneducated and nomadic nation.

These kinds of unjust and aberrant assertions are the political tricks which aimed to erode the legendary past of Turkmen people and their contribution to the history of the development of the world through many centuries, to justify their invasion of its land and to take the Turkmen nation captive. In fact, these sorts of untruthful and fallacious statements severely degraded the place and the honor of Turkmens in world history. For the sake of God, it is necessary to say that for 74 years under Soviet rule we lived as if we accepted those opinions, Dear Turkmen, whoever thought differently was declared the enemy of the people. For this reason, hundreds of thousands of our citizens were executed, and millions of them were expelled or migrated to foreign countries.

The remaining three million Turkmen citizens, in their homeland, mislaid their identities by saying that we were Soviet people. Not only that, they started to forget their language, religion,

nation, national feelings and emotions. Inciting and provoking differences and conflicts between the tribes, polarization, diversity, and promotion of anarchy were the basic, systematic, methodical games our enemies played against us.

My dear Turkmen, look back in the history take heed and also repent. Because of commands and ideas of others nation should one renounce his own core, self and identity?

In fact, there are 24 clans and more than 40 tribes of Turkmen.

My wish from the Great Allah is to convert the Turkmen to his essence or main identity! Beginning from Oguz Han, to the end of the medieval age with the solidarity and unity, the courage, the patriotism, the equity, the indulgency, the religion, the language, the culture of the tpeople known for their great spiritual belief, on into the 21 century, may you give continuity to my unique nation, my one and great God! Preserve and save us, Allah, so each Turkmen shall win again the ethics and customs of our ancestors who were on the true path!

In the communist Soviet Union, which was founded at the beginning of the 20th century by force, torture and blood, from 1987 on conflicts occurred between various parts of society. Conflicts between the different nations and injustice reached an unbearable level within the state, and so government and its rule failed, and order tended to disappear. In this historical period I felt that the politico-economic position of the Soviet Union was deteriorating. On 22 August 1990, 1 made a declaration that we would establish Turkmenistan as an independent, sovereign stable state having equal rights and status and independence in foreign relations with other countries as all the world states.

Within the two preceding months, our relations with the Soviet Union's systems had almost ceased, and we saw that life necessitated further new improvements. It became obvious that we could not go far or progress and make our people happy and prosperous within that existing Soviet System with a status independent within its borders but dependent on the Soviet System.

Dear Turkmens, it was the point in history that our ancestors had longed for. At that time, together with my colleagues, it was necessary for me to work to establish an independent state by day and night without tiring, and troubles Ih

were not able to deter me. On 26 October, we called a convention of the Turkmenistan High Council. In the convention, the historical resolution of Turkmenistan, we explicitly and definitively declared the independence of the State of Turkmenistan. This is the content of the declaration:

THE CONSTITUTIONAL LAW ON THE INDEPENDENCE OF TurkmenISTAN AND THE STRUCTURE OF THE STATE

On 26 October, there was a meeting of The High Council of Turkmenistan; on the agenda of the meeting was the people's notice of their will and wishes. The Council made the essential decision to put into effect the expression of the independence of the Soviet Socialist Republic of Turkmenistan. In this resolution, certain crucial issues were resolved.

1. The State of Turkmenistan, within the borders of the

46

USSR, is declared an independent, democratic state. The independence of Turkmenistan is based on great ideals - To establish the real national state of the Turkmen people, to provide basic rights and freedoms complying with the charter of the Universal Human Rights Declarations in the Constitution of Turkmenistan, as well as the other nonns of international law, to establish a humanist democratic state respecting the principles of the rule of law. It does not discriminate between individuals or citizens according to their nation, race, social origin, or their religion.

2. The political regime of the State of Turkmenistan is a republic. In this republic, state sovereignty belongs to the people. The republic exercises its own sovereignty through the direct vote and by means of representative institutions.

3. Inside the borders of Turkmenistan, the Constitution and Laws of Turkmenistan are applicable.

The Constitution of the Former USSR and laws are applicable only under those circumstances in which there is no explicit law related to the matter within the Constitution and Laws of Turkmenistan; and it is valid until the completion of the reform and regulation of state relations and legal relations in the legislation process.

4. The borders of Turkmenistan within the borders currently drawn are inviolable and indivisible.

5. The state sovereignty of Turkmenistan is executed by means of the division of powers into legislative, executive and judicial powers.

6. Complying with the Constitution of Turkmenistan, the High Council of Turkmenistan exercises the legislative powers.

47

7. The highest ruler of Turkmenistan is the President who is the Head of State. The President of Turkmenistan also holds the rank of Chairman of the Executive.

8. The courts of Turkmenistan are independent and subject to the law.

9. Inside the borders of Turkmenistan, Turkmen citizenship applies. The constitution and law of Turkmenistan regulates the matters pertaining to the laws on obtaining citizenship of Turkmenistan and citizenship relations with other countries. Turkmenistan protects and assists its citizens inside and outside its borders.

The constitution and laws of Turkmenistan, in accordance with interstate treaties, recognizes the rights and freedoms of foreign citizens and stateless persons in Turkmenistan as in the norms of international law.

10. Within the borders of Turkmenistan the surface and underground resources, air zone, water and natural resources, sea and continental shelf are the people's national wealth and property, which all serve as material bases of Turkmenistan's independence.

On the general possessions of the USSR, there is the share of Turkmenistan in the USSR's diamond, foreign exchange and gold reserves.

11 Turkmenistan, in its economy, establishes a functioning free market economy. It controls state possessions in all their forms and equally protects them.

12. Turkmenistan independently determines its fiscal and monetary system; the state determines the structures of banks.

13. Turkmenistan recognizes the independence of the

48

adjoining republics in the USSR, the definitiveness of their borders, and their territorial integrity and indivisibility.

14. It is as an independent state that Turkmenistan is a member of the world community, having equal rights to determine and execute its foreign policy. Turkmenistan joins the United Nations Organizations and other international organizations as a direct member, establishes diplomatic relations, open embassies and other competent agencies and makes international contracts.

15. Turkmenistan resolves independently its military policy, protect its territorial integrity and independence and establish military capability. Turkmenistan declares that there are no nuclear, chemical, biological, or other weapons of mass destruction in the territory of Turkmenistan.

16. Turkmenistan is concerned for the national and cultural advancement of Turkmen people, the rise of national consciousness, the revival of the traditions

of the people and is committed to the expansion of the use of the Turkmen language, which is the state language.

The Republic of Turkmenistan is the guarantor of all the living nations which have the right to live and to flourish freely with their national and cultural values in the territory.

17. Turkmenistan claims its own state signs, flag, regalia and national anthem.

18. Until the admission of the new constitution of Turkmenistan, Turkmenistan's USSR constitution will be applicable, so long as the previous laws do not conflict with the new Constitutional law.

19. The Independence Day of Turkmenistan is declared

49

a general national holiday; it will be celebrated on every 27 October and it will be a day of vacation.

20. The formal constitutional law, when accepted, will be put into effect.

The arrival of this event, one more state in the world, the date of the establishment of the Republic of Turkmenistan has been written in golden letters in history.

That date was the worthiest, most defining, and happiest moment of my life. That event will never be forgotten and it will always be one of the most inspiring and touching historical moments, and not only for me. For the destiny of the Republic of Turkmenistan is the delight of all its people.

Good luck in the matters which concern you now. May the deeds you attempt be the best and most needed, my independent homeland of Turkmenistan!

My Dear Turkmen People!

On 8 December 1991, the USSR State collapsed and we had to tackle what it left to us without Quarreling..

After the demise of the USSR, the newly independent countries, with the help of international, financial institutions, settled all accounts mutually. Finally a very important agreement was made not to fall into land occupation and border disputes between the CIS countries. In this agreement, the most important matters were clearly solved as below:

The separate countries of the former USSR admitted the current borders existing from the era of the former USSR borders between the republics.

The possessions established within the border of every 50

state in the time of the USSR were claimed by the independent states as their own state possessions.

The quantity of the wealth and the shares of the debts and credits of the independent states were ascertained by calculating the USSR's exchange funds and adding the gold in the gold reserves.

The credits of Turkmenistan on separation from the USSR, up to 4 December 1991 were fixed as I billion 87 million US dollars. The debt Turkmenistan owed to the USSR was 707 million US dollars. The final account was fixed such that USSR owed Turkmenistan 380 million US dollars.

This debt had to be paid by the Russian Federation, heir of the USSR.

I understood the fact that these were notional credits and that we would not get our credits because of the tight economic borders of the Russian Federation.

That's why I thought that it would be better for us to separate peacefully. I put my idea to the first president, Boris Yeltsin, and he supported my proposal to donate our credits. We made a contract between the Republic of Turkmenistan and

Russia, preparing a proposal for a treaty complying with International Law. The content of the treaty is below:

The AGREEMENT, between Turkmenistan and the Russian Federation, is to regulate the legal matters succeeding from the debts and credits of the fon-ner USSR to foreign states.

Turkmenistan and the Russian Federation confirm the memorandum, dated 28 October 1991, on the mutual agreement regulating the debts of the USSR and its legal successors to the foreign creditors and the contract, dated 4 December 1991, regulating the legal matters succeeding from the debts

and credits of the USSR to foreign states, and also agree on the solutions to the matters relating to both sides on the legal matters succeeding from the former USSR's debts and credits as below.

Matter I

What is meant by the purpose of this agreement on the former USSR State's debts and credits is the interpretations which are valid in the Articles l(a) and (b) of the contract, dated 4 December 1991, concerning the legal matters succeeding from the debts and credits of the USSR to foreign states.

Matter 2

The parties confirm that the share of debts determined for Turkmenistan is equal to 0.70%, a ratio which was fixed by one indicator in the former USSR's debts and credits to the foreign states.

Matter 3

Because of the position of the former USSR on I December 1991, Turkmenistan transfers its responsibilities for payment of its share of the debt to the Russian Federation, and the Russian Federation accepts those responsibilities.

Matter 4

Because of the position of the former USSR on I December 1991, the Russian Federation accepts the share of Turkmenistan from the state credits. Turkmenistan transfers the stated credits to the Russian Federation.

52

Matter 5

After this agreement comes into effect, it will be accepted that all conflicts between the parties related to the debts and credits of the former USSR to the foreign state have been

resolved by the contract of 4th December 1991 regulating the legal matters succeeding from the debts and credits of the 'b

USSR, in addition to the agreement of 6 July 1991 on "the share of the full estates of the USSR in the foreign states".

Matter 6

The stated contract will become effective when it is signed on 31st July 1992, in Moscow, in two copies in the Turkmen language and Russian language, both of which

have equal legal force.

Turkmenistan

The president

S.A. Niyazow

Russian Federation

The president

Boris Yeltsin

After that, Turkmens, like newly weds, had to establish their home, struggle for a living, regulate their life, cultivate and occupy themselves with good business... For thousands of years, Turkmens, in the face of extremes of cold and heat, considered it very important and took great pains to train new members of the household properly, respecting society's values and participating in society.

We were a newly emerged state. Therefore, we needed everything from pins to planes, medicine to computers. In the past, we produced tea in Nusay, but to make tea we had to bring wood to boil the water for it from Russia, we cultivated cotton in Merw but sent it to Europe to be made into cloth.

53

Our ancestors did not say in vain, "If your brother has much wealth, you are rich, too; but if you are able to live by your own means then you are also rich."

We have maintained our friendship with the former USSR, and we have not aroused its enmity.

We are very close to our former friends, and we make new friends; we have no grudge against anybody, and we have no foe burning with a great passion for revenge. So, when the general situation is like that, where is the logic in us entering and founding various political, economic, and military unions?

The Tirkmens, in an historical process over thousands of years, constituted a great nation under the name of the Turkmen. We call ourselves Turkmen with pride! What is it that gathers us in one home, collects us around one dining table, builds one body, and bears us quickly towards the future? Have we matured only by convening around one language and religion? What are the other elements that make us a nation?

In the 20th century, humanity progressed by exploring nature and all lands; by researching the details of the animals and plants of the earth, by flying into space, they advanced to a new and progressive age.

Since creation, human beings have considered themselves the only thinking, constructing, creating beings, and the only intelligent rulers of the earth. Finally, they have begun to realize that this thought was wrong.

The human is not the only interacting, communicating and thinking living creature in the world! All living things and animals are able to perform some mental process or communicate in the world! All plants can interact among them-

54

the universe and the heavens!

The human being feels he is alone.

This is because people, by becoming too deeply involved with material things, have lost their connections with the spiritual and heavenly realms. They have lost their ties with embracing nature: mountains, oceans, seas, rivers, forests, deserts and living things. They have lost their spiritual connections with their ancestors who have lain buried for thousands of years.

In the past, people saw God as the wind, rain, lightning, moon, sun and the sky, until at last they came to believe in Allah, the One and the Only!

The Turkmens witness that Allah alone is great. The Turkmens have always held and defended the belief that Allah maintains all the climatic regions and geographical divisions of the whole world, the universe, and every comer of life; the Turkmen sees the signs of the power of His disposal in every case in the universe; and he often mentions and praises Him and asks for tolerance.

The history of the Turkmens is very glorious, too. The spirit of the Turkmens who comprehend this history will soar!

But the history of Turkmens, has been written as they wish by everybody except Turkmen historians.

No one should show contempt for the Turkmens by writing a false history because they have a great history!

No one should defame the Turkmens by writing a false history because they have a very pure and clean nature!

The story:

When Soltan Sanjar was returning from hunting, he met a farmer working in his field. Upon the signal of the Soltan,

selves; they know how to process messages in some way conveyed to them too!

After the ruthless attacks Jengiz Han, the Turkmens spun a circle of development from East to West. Turkmenistan was the most developed country in the world. The first type of carriage was devised by the Turkmen. It served to make much of the work of the army and the state easier.

In early days Turkmens discovered the art of making various tools with molten ores. "The epic of Ergenekon" shows the ancient of Tirkmens. This epic mentions the melting of ores from a huge mine, which has a metaphorical meaning, that is, exploring and stretching out to the new territories and world. It conveys a perfect example of the Turkmen sword to the current era. On this sword was engraved, "The Tirkmen never unsheathes his sword against his neighbor."

Today, this sword is in a museum in Iran. The making of various tools and materials made of iron and steel spread from the Turkmen plateau to the world. The ancient historians wrote that the best cloth was woven in Merw and Nusay. In their books the Turkmen plateaus are well-known for silk cloth and silk carpets.

Inventions increased day by day.

Turkmenistan became the home of scientists, scholars, intellectuals, philosophers, artists and poets.

So the egg has cracked and the chick has hatched; but this fledgling must now develop the strength of wing and the mature judgment to fly in the heights.

Mankind, by exploring the universe, lost his belief in

the universe and the heavens!

The human being feels he is alone.

This is because people, by becoming too deeply involved with material things, have lost their connections with the spiritual and heavenly realms. They have lost their ties with embracing nature: mountains, oceans, seas, rivers, forests, deserts and living things. They have lost their spiritual connections with their ancestors who have lain buried for thousands of years.

In the past, people saw God as the wind, rain, lightning, moon, sun and the sky, until at last they came to believe in Allah, the One and the Only!

The Turkmens witness that Allah alone is great. The Turkmens have always held and defended the belief that Allah maintains all the climatic regions and geographical divisions of the whole world, the universe, and every comer of life; the Turkmen sees the signs of the power of His disposal in every case in the universe; and he often mentions and praises Him and asks for tolerance.

The history of the Turkmens is very glorious, too. The spirit of the Turkmens who comprehend this history will soar!

But the history of Turkmens, has been written as they wish by everybody except Turkmen historians.

No one should show contempt for the Turkmens by writing a false history because they have a great history!

No one should defame the Turkmens by writing a false history because they have a very pure and clean nature!

The story:

When Soltan Sanjar was returning from hunting, he met a farmer working in his field. Upon the signal of the Soltan,

56

57

his servants took the farmer away to a place and honored him with various kinds of food and drink. The Soltan, after carrying him away, threw a sack in front of him and said, "Take as much as you can carry away from the treasury."

The farmer thought and took a very small amount of gold in his hand. When the Soltan asked him why he didn't take a sackful, the fanner replied, "I don't need so much gold that I would carry it as a heavy burden now and after, but I need enough gold to help me carry out my deeds and duties efficiently."

We have stepped into the Golden Century. We have to tackle our current duties successfully for the sake of our great past and the future of the fortunate young generations. We should comply with our Turkmen nature, original principles and historical mission.

Tirkmen are loyal to their promise and principles!

The word of the older is an order (like a stately decree) for the younger Turkmens! It is obligatory for the older to respect their rights and esteem the young.

The way of Turkmen is the clean way.

In the war of Da-ndanakan fewer than forty Turkmen Hans defeated the army of Soltan Masud, the son of Soltan Mahmyt of Gazna of the strongest Turkmen state, not only in Asia, but in the world. They declared the new Turkmen state by meeting around a dining table. At this meeting was the saint in Islam, Abu Se'it Abyl- Ha'yr (Miine), who wore the y

dervish's cloak twice and who gave permission to Qagry Beg (ruler) and Togrul Beg (his brother) to establish a state. The Golden Throne was

erected on the site of the battle of Da'ndanakan. However, there were some people who said, "There can't be a throne. Today is not a day of good omen."
I

Abu Seyit said:

"Just as there is no bad place to be found on this Earth, as all places were created by Allah, so there can be no day of bad omen in the days created by Allah! Your state is the people's state. Rise up and as long as you do not deviate from the way of great Allah, and the honesty, justice and equability of the Turkmen, then there is no obstacle which you cannot overcome and there is no castle you cannot conquer"

We established the Turkmen people's state by building the throne in the homeland of the Turkmens, who have spread through the world. Our way is the way of ancient Turkmens! Our way is the way of the Oguz Han, his prophet-like way!

Our way is the way of justice.

Our way is the way of welfare.

Our way is the way of unity and solidarity.

Our way is the way of friendship and brotherhood.

Our way is the way of free conscience.

Our way is the way of free labor.

Our way is the way of national integrity.

We cannot go any other way. No Turkmen should go any other way because our independent state of Turkmenistan is the people's state. The way of the people is the way of Allah.

59

My purpose in writing Ruhnama is to express explicitly how the nation has contributed much to the sciences, literature, civilizations, and development of the world and in every area of life. I describe our good fortune at the beginning of our history, which affected the world, but in the last seven or eight centuries our nation has shrunk. She is measurably smaller but still not an insignificant nation. Though her name is often not recalled among the great, in fact, she is a very great nation, in her mind, in her spirit, in her blood, in short, in all her entity. I want to show that the great legacy of our ancestors remains. The Turkmen nation has traced marks as magnificent as those of Great Britain, of the Great Indian Nation and of The Great Chinese Nation.

The flag of the Turkmen nation is her pure honor.

The greatness of every Turkmen is the greatness of her nation.

The Turkmen nation gave these to the world:

pure Turkmen horses, perfect Turkmen carpets, magnificent Turkmen ornaments, wonderful Turkmen clothing and finery, pure white wheat, and the species of the yellowish sheep.

During the era of the Gaznaly Mahmyt, the Seljuk Kingdom, Kbneiirgeny states, Turkmen was the leading nation in the science, literature, and art in the world. Turkmens introduced the Turkmen civilization to others.

60

After the collapse of the Harzemah state, which had supported science, literature and the spiritual world, the Turkmen's eminent philosophers, scholars, literati, artists and craftsmen spread not only through Turkey, but also, by another route, to Caucasus, Anatolia, Arabia and from there passed though Egypt to Spain. In this way, the scientific achievement of the Turkmen nations became the ferment of European scientific advancement. The Turkmen wheel precipitated the scientific progress of the world. The life-style of the Turkmens made a great contribution to the improvement of science, production and industry. Later those issues will be analysed in depth.

Ihave written the Ruhnama to enable my nation to perceive our past and to envision our own dignity. And the content is not only related to the past. The book is based on the spiritual features peculiar to the Turkmens that developed in the past. From this aspect, I would like to draw to your attention to the fact that the Ruhnama is different from the other historical 'titles written in the past. In the light of the writing tradition of the "Oguznama", which has been held in high esteem by the Turkmens since ancient times, I am writing Ruhnama within the same tradition. Apart from this, the "Epics of Oguzs" were composed from poor history, knowledge and historical events. Despite containing some of the basic concepts of philosophy and historical experience, they were accepted as distinct from the books of philosophy. The reader himself must think, evaluate and mature this philosophy in his mind. By in his mind, what is meant is something outside the content of the epic of "Oguzs". The Ruhnama deals with the new form of national consciousness.

61

Philosophy is a tool of wisdom, and we can use it to analyze the features of the Turkmen spirit. In the epics of "Oguznama", the historical events are ordered chronologically. The spiritual and moral dynamics which make a nation into a nation are not considered at length in them. The Epic of "Oguznama" is the writing related to the reputations of the ancestors in the past. By means of this writing it is intended that later generations feel proud of their ancestors and, in other way, own their awareness of history. Thus, the information or knowledge functions as the source and spring of the heart.

In the period in which I was writing "Ruhnama", the spring of my mind and heart was philosophy. I also wrote in the "Ruhnama" style so as to feel proud and get pleasure from the greatness of our ancestors. But this goal is to be reached not only by giving information related to historical events but also by explaining their underlying moral meaning and philosophy. This refreshes the past and in particular the historical memory.

The past, unrepeatable events traced in history, is no more. Memory is the essence of the flow which combines the happenings of the past, the present and the future within the realm of the historical unity of the past.

As human beings are mortal, remembering can be taken as a spiritual habit which can combine and integrate spiritually the generations that are separated from one another.

Looking at ourselves, we see gulfs between the various generations and eras. Moreover, here and there past generations did not know each other, did not understand each other's languages, as if all of the Turkmens regarded each other as strangers. The ties between them had been broken.

62

love of the mother-earth and the protection of the fatherland. This person begins to view his own personality as a stronger link in the chain of the generations, as if he has been released from moral loneliness and alienation. If Allah wills it, the generations who drink deeply from the clean water of the spring of philosophy of the "Ruhnama" may grow into beautiful, moral people.

Life trains people and history trains the character.

The "Ruhnama" is a book opening the spring of the mind and meeting the thirst of the dry intellect. In our recent past the number of thirsty intellects has increased and the thirst for those springs in the clearings of the morals of Turkmens. As we have changed our outside world, the clear water fountains and red and green rose gardens in our inner world must be increased. We say Turkmenistan, day by day, is more and more pleasing and beautiful public buildings are being constructed.

I have been witnessing the heart of my nation growing into its own beauty. I agree with the principle that, "Beauty, primarily, must be within the heart of the people". I am honored by the current successes.

Secondly, turning back to our early comparison between "Oguznama" and

Ruhnama, we can say that Oguznama is a book which is only related to the past. In these books the future is not living either as an idea or a target or a sign. On the other hand, the basic feature of the "Ruhnama" is that I can analyse and present the past from the perspectives of the future. In my view the past is the possibility of the future coming into being. When I was wondering in the past I sought the future.

It is impossible, however, that they should not have been aware of each other, the Seljuks and Magtymguly, the Ottomans and G6rogly.

A break in memory leads to the generations regarding each other as strangers. The reason for the break in memory is the movement away from the frame of national solidarity, caused by heavy foreign domination of the moral values of the generations. This causes the nations to be spiritually and morally divided and fragmented.

The real power lies in the heart of the people. After the collapse of the heart, however, man starts to decline in strength because the heart is the spring of national pride. After the spring has dried up, to discuss facts becomes nonsense. There was no Turkmen streak in such people.

My basic aim in writing "Ruhnama" is to open the dwindling spring of national pride by clearing it of grass and stones and letting it flow again. I hope to enliven the heart with the medication of Philosophy. It is like replanting the and land of the past, which has become unproductive and useless, with the pine trees of the Turkmen plateaus. In this way I wish to rid us of the disease, trouble and anxiety of insensibility.

But if the memory of the past awakens in someone's mind, then, he, like before, becomes the continuation of history. This person's moral life and capacity to live start to bubble again like a life-giving spring. His mind and heart transform and become the area for the continuation of the historical and moral. In this person, his ancestors are resurrected with their spirit, their memory, even their capillary blood vessels again. This person is capable of living, feeling the

love of the mother-earth and the protection of the fatherland. This person begins to view his own personality as a stronger link in the chain of the generations, as if he has been released from moral loneliness and alienation. If Allah wills it, the generations who drink deeply from the clean water of the spring of philosophy of the "Ruhnama" may grow into beautiful, moral people.

Life trains people and history trains the character.

The "Ruhnama" is a book opening the spring of the mind and meeting the thirst of the dry intellect. In our recent past the number of thirsty intellects has increased and the thirst for those springs in the clearings of the morals of Turkmens. As we have changed our outside world, the clear water fountains and red and green rose gardens in our inner world must be increased. We say Turkmenistan, day by day, is more and more pleasing and beautiful public buildings are being constructed.

I have been witnessing the heart of my nation growing into its own beauty. I agree with the principle that, "Beauty, primarily, must be within the heart of the people". I am honored by the current successes.

Secondly, turning back to our early comparison between "Oguznama" and Ruhnama, we can say that Oguznama is a book which is only related to the past.

In these books the future is not living either as an idea or a target or a sign. On the other hand, the basic feature of the "Ruhnama" is that I can analyze and present the past from the perspectives of the future. In my view the past is the possibility of the future coming into being. When I was wondering in the past I sought the future.

64

1, by means of the "Ruhnama" string the past, present and future on a single rope. The past is the mark of the future, the present is the consequences of the past and the future is the marriage of the past and the present. Thus, the form of the future, what might be, depends on the degree of our understanding of the past. The possibilities of the future depend upon our capacity to perceive which realities of the past are to continue in the future, which are to disappear gradually, and how to overcome them. So, the degree of reality of the future is the degree of the reality of our mind and will.

There was no place for the future in any of the "Oguznama" written in different eras because there was no discussion about the problems of the era in them. The writers of the stories did not view themselves and their epoch in historical perspective.

The era of "Ruhnama" and the interpretations of the world of Ruhnama are the contrary of this because the perspective of the world of "Ruhnama" is different. While acknowledging entirely God's order, will and decree in history, it is necessary to mention the view that we build the future with our own hands. This is a confession. To refuse to do this would be the same as to refuse our responsibilities for our past, present and future works. I have no notion of becoming haughty and slinging mud at my ancestors. Allah forbid! Besides, the era of "Ruhnama" is different from the era when the "Oguznama" epics were written", not the age of being formed by history but the age of forming history. Whatever approaches we may use there, we need to admit one thing: we ourselves are forming our history, present and

65

The most immediately visible aspects of our nation are the striking material values: the horse, the carpet, our musical instruments (dutar), jewelery and ornaments, local/native breed/species dog (alabay), the yellowish breed of sheep and the genus of white wheat. It is obvious that there is no need to find evidence to prove that these belong to the Turkmens. They are there in full view for all to see. Moreover these values are all pure values which have reached the zenith of their maturity in their areas. In short, these are unique and inimitable values without compare.

Perfection and uniqueness here is the main measure of the value. These kinds of values clearly demonstrate the perfection and uniqueness of the free development of Turkmens as one nation because in its perfection the work shows the craftsman's mastery. The measurement of the perfection of the work is the measurement of the skill, the physical and moral powers, and the quality of striving which have been given to the master by Allah. These are one dimension of the matter.

We also try to evaluate the historical value and the age of the production of such material values. Thereafter, not only the experts but also the ordinary people can know that the ages of such invaluable things are in thousands of years. Afterwards, the matter of their age is a matter of the age of the nation because it is impossible for the age of the work to be greater than the age of the craftsman. So, the real truth is that thousands of years ago, the material value, as an example of perfection, became mature.

There was white wheat five thousand years ago, too.

The same must be said of the Turkmen horse of Ahalteke, the Turkmen iti (dog), the carpet and the other artifacts.

From all this there arises the inevitable conclusion that these values are precisely the proof, clear to the naked eye, that the Turkmen nation is a nation with a history of five thousand years. So this is not a frivolous, vain, fabricated idea. So, our national honor is far above blackening others with the false accusations others used against us. Hence our national honor cannot be put into the same scale with others. Our national honor has been established on principles as strong as the Turkmen soil.

Of course, at certain periods when Turkmens lacked complex and well-founded spiritual and philosophical methods and descriptions, there were stages in which Turkmens were weak or in decline. We cannot understand fully now from the existing knowledge and proofs, the exact reasons why it should have happened so. There have even been periods of interregnum, but even those periods were not totally useless or
unproductive, as, in general, it can be seen that the moral values and the creative capabilities of Turkmens were preserved in some way and even rose to the highest levels. This is because hard, grievous and complex historical opportunities incite the inspiration and moral creativity which lie at the basis of the nation.

The wonderful Turkmen epics of "Oguznama", our unique poetry and poetic style, Turkmen Sufism and Turkmen music, all comprise profound meanings in which are embedded moral values which have formed over the course of thousands of years.

It is very important to analyze these types of moral values along with their historical context, meaning and significance, and to comprehend and express these as the Turkmens way of life to others. This is necessary, not only to establish and achieve once more the greatness and fame of our ancestors, but also to understand the principles and basis of our future.

In "Ruhnama" the Turkmen people's historical consciousness, matured over thousands of years, and their moral power and strength are drawn together.

"Ruhnama" is a ship. This ship is chartered to bear the news of the past to the future over the vast sea of Turkmen history.

Ruhnama is a courier. This courier transmits the past's secret and necessary news to the future.

Therefore, I say:

If the spirit of Turkmen is the universe then "Ruhnama"

68

cannot replace or fully represent it. At least this is impossible in terms of its breadth.

Nevertheless, "Ruhnama" must be the center of this universe. In this universe, all the current and the future cosmic matters should go on spinning, in Ruhnama's attraction, centripetal force and orbits.

My Dear People!

Now, I want to mention my private and personal reasons for the writing of

"Ruhnama" and the other causes which led me to begin this work. What is the meaning of the Head of State writing on philosophical matters? This has to be explained in the light of the features of the era and the duties borne on my shoulders. Of course, had we lived in another epoch, I would only be occupied with state and political affairs and these would be enough. As it is, our era falls at the turn of the new millennium. In this period, five- or ten-year programmes are not sufficient for the needs of our state. At this time, it is necessary not only to establish a state but also to create a nation, for a nation needs far-reaching moral values and criteria. We have to seek and find ways in which these kinds of criteria can be provided through moral work and traditional and moral philosophies.

Eras in which great changes happen always demand that we take on responsibilities and liabilities much heavier than an ordinary president's normal burdens. The whole foundation of society must be built to the same blueprint because a nation needs a set of complete and up-to-date criteria. "Ruhnama" offers a simple example of this kind of scale.

69

My beloved Country, My Dear People!

These fruitful lands, on which our grandfathers blood flowed, should be our dining table.

Our ancestors left to our state a treasury full of moral wealth. Let this be a national ideal for us.

Every state needs a national ideal. The train cannot move except on rails. The religions which have been spread throughout the world by prophets are an ideal. The people's traditions, principles and particular customs which were composed over thousands of years, also represent an ideal. The state must be a school conveying the rules of good manners and ethics for life.

History has proved what are the consequences of making one nation superior to another or of one nation humiliating another. The maxim say that one who bums his mouth with hot milk becomes cautious and even blows his cold yoghurt, so as not to bum his tongue again. Alas, ... however, some politicians are still making the same mistake, and it seems that they are not getting wise enough to avoid repeating their errors.

If one person shows hostility to another, it proves that someone's interest is at stake. If one society shows hostility to another, then a third society will benefit from that conflict, and turn it to its own interest.

I believe that the Turkmen nation is a great nation. The nation of Turkmens is a great nation but it is not greater than other nations. The Turkmen harbors no such base thought. Every Turkmen must bear this advice in his mind throughout the span of his life.

70

My beloved Country, My dear People!

It is now ten years since the establishment of independent and eternally neutral Turkmenistan. In these ten years the Turkmen has totally changed; he believed in his being a great nation and this state is his state. He possessed his own freedom, sovereignty, land, water, state and his country. In these ten years, we have developed economically and gained a place among the leading countries in the world. This is a significant and honorable achievement of ours. This is the warranty of the industriousness of our people and their brilliant power.

The Republic of Turkmenistan has surpassed in a month the distance which would normally be crossed in a year. It has been observed that Turkmenistan is progressing towards being a rich and developed country. All have seen this, friends, foreigners, even the blind! Although, in the beginning, there were some people with bad intentions who mindlessly criticized our ways, even they have now understood the rightness of our path. Now we are proud of how Turkmenistan has joined the top ranks of the developing countries, in terms of social and economic advancement.

Ruhnama is truly the "Oguznama" of the third millennium. If we try to express it using the name of our nation, which will be widely known along with its achievements, Ruhnama will be our nation's "Turkmennama" of the third millennium. I wrote this book as a generalization of the history and moral experiences of Turkmen people as handed

71

down over five thousand years. This is the viewpoint of our nation in the third millennium.

After completing the Ruhnama, I re-read it, looked at the content once again ' and it confirmed the feeling in my heart: I realized that I had carried "Ruhnama" in my heart all my life. I realized that "Ruhnama" was the fruit of my aspirations and writing it was my task in life. That is why today I dedicate to my nation these aspirations and works in the form of this book.

Thus "Ruhnama" is not only a way of understanding my nation and people, but also my method of perception. It is my belief that the reasonable man's perception of the world depends upon his ability to perceive himself.

When a person enters the ocean of the historical memory of the nation, he is at the same time diving into his own ocean. When it is impossible to take two directions at one time, you have to understand clearly that perceptions and philosophy are not good enough by themselves.

You cannot approach reality using only thought and intellect. Reality also requires the use of the whole heart. It demands that you include your whole self and see your fate and destiny as a whole.

It was my good fortune to involuntarily comprehend that what I write as my understanding, perceptions and feelings in the Ruhnama are in fact what I have been holding as feelings and aspirations in my heart for a long time. These feelings lived in me during my youth when I understood the spirit, mercy and value of the homeland. The reason for the

72

intimate connection between my fate and the fate of my homeland is the similarity between them. When, after leaving my family and brothers, I was left feeling isolated and bereft, the homeland was afflicted in the same way. I was deeply affected and became as homesick as the soldiers and heroes separated from their homeland.

When I walked the route from the village of Gypjak to the city of Asgabat, between Bizmeyin and Ymam Kasym graveyard, I would sense the loneliness of the homeland, its homelessness and its spiritual desolation.

The bleak steppes, the desolate plains, the shriveled fountains, the bowed cypresses, the disintegrating buildings, the lonely homeland, in their entirety, all these do not exist only outside me but live too in my internal realm, where they cause my heart to ache.

The homeland reminds me of a woman who has been slapped and abandoned in the street.

The resemblance between my fate and that of my homeland almost pushed me into philosophical inquiries. For the first condition of philosophical inquiry is emotional exploration.

The human is like an instrument created by Allah to detect the passage of time. The human differs from other living beings in that, as a result of having mind, he possesses the ability to know time.

In our era, the 20th century, people only perceived the passage of time too late when they realized they had not done what they ought to have done. They regretted the chances they had missed and the things they had neglected to do.

73

Their regrets pushed people to re-evaluate the past and present, and this reevaluation became in turn a spiritual accounting, which eventually helped to bring about the collapse of the state and the establishment of the new state. It is necessary for the human being to struggle with time. Perhaps this necessity is the good fortune of human beings. The only tool with which we may struggle with time is memory.

The human dies, his corpse blends with the soil, but his heart by the means of memory reaches the mind of the following generations. It is in the moral area of my heart and memory that Oguz IIan, Togrul Beg and Gbrogly Beg and many of the others live.

It is my aim to transmit by means of my own heart the spirits of the brave men living in this moral area to the hearts of all Turkmens so that Turkmens who receive the powers from this endless moral fountain may rise again in the next millennium. In this way, the Turkmen attains all the necessary strength and transform himself into all that is his potential.

So, Ruhnama, in all its uses and purposes, is a book about the lessons of philosophy and the moral experiences of past generations, rather than a history book. If we were to compose an accurate history of the Turkmens covering thousands of years, then it would make a very large book. We are only now starting to write anew the history of the Turkmen, the chronology of events and information about them.

Ruhnama is not a history book. This book explains the world anew and the moral principles on which national history is written. The history itself is simply an additional aspect to this. One of my main ends is to express the worldview of Turkmens in the new millennium. For that reason, 'Ruhnama' contains some history and personal views too.

74

The intellectuals of Turkmenistan must carry out more extensive research on the matters expressed in 'Ruhnama'. The essential thing in your reading of this book and the recognition of the ideas in it is not to take too narrow a view of its meaning and issues. Where history is mentioned, it is not as my main objective but as a tool to express efficiently, reveal and demonstrate my thoughts. It is a tool to indicate the greatness of Turkmens.

Moral climates do not form suddenly or by coincidence. The last seventy-five years we have lived and the burdens which many of us could not bear rendered us Turkmens almost unable to gather any moral resources. This was a result of the fact that others aimed to use the Turkmen territory merely for the production of raw materials and in order to do so they intended to bring Turkmens into the position of a society which would be forced to import their all values from abroad.

The greatness of the time, since the day we got our independence to the present day, lies in the fact that Turkmens transformed themselves from a consumer nation to a producer nation. I assert that the transformation from being a consumer nation, either materially or morally, to being in the position of producer nation is a great historical transformation.

Ruhnama is a book which will awaken our nation's capacity for moral productivity and will make them the most industrious. In this historic task, it will be the unseen moral catalyst of great material advancement. In this, the power which is our helper is our pride in our past and our respect for our future.

The philosophy of the Ruhnama is the basis of this hon-

75

our and respect; the emotional aspects of Ruhnama are the essence of this honor and respect.

No book can be written without inspiration. The historical opportunities and new duties facing my nation gave inspiration to my heart. I have always been a poet. Since my youth I have written poems in my diary. The responsibilities resting on my shoulders now force me to move on up from poetry. Nevertheless, the basic condition of being fruitful or productive requires that we do not discard the poetic inspiration of the heart.

The fountain of inspiration of my emotions, The Turkmen nature,

The fountain of inspiration of my ideas, the history of the Turkmen,

The fountain of inspiration of my philosophy, the memory of the Turkmen.

76

The Second Section
The Turkmen's Path

The Beloved Turkmen people!
The Beloved Turkmen nation!
The Turkmen people has a history of five thousands years, a history of victories, defeats and heroism. We are proud of this glorious history, which is the legacy of our ancestors. Our glorious history, as we gain our independence and neutrality, will last forever.

Our history is like a light that excites the spirit of every member of our nation. Inherited from our ancestors, our past is sacred and precious. For thousands of years, our ancestors have protected their self-identity and their consciousness of being one nation, and they have perceived this mission as a sacred value. It was not easy for them to overcome the great impediment of history. This love, for our glorious homeland and our history, gained by fortitude, sacrifice and sincere enthusiasm, has marked the heart of every member of our nation. In its every comer, village, and city the members of our nation live warmly united.

With its cloudy mountains that reach the sky, this land is Candibil, Turkmenistan. This sacred land with its mountains, fields, seas, deserts, and rivers is of God's grace and favor to our nation. If it was said, "You are free. Travel around the globe and choose wherever you want as your homeland," the sons of this nation could not find a more beautiful and beneficial land. Our nation, founder of more than seventy great states, principalities, and Soltanates, after roaming the globe, settled in these lands.

Words lack sufficient power to tell of the fatherly mercy and motherly compassion of this land.

During the last millennium, the love of our nation penetrated the depths of this land. It seems the love of homeland became an inseparable part of our nation's spirit. Truly, our nation and homeland are like body and soul.

For us, this land is splendid. Those brave men who sacrificed their lives for this land are buried here. In this land you find Mdne Baba (Abu Seyit Abyl- Hayyr), who influenced the whole Islamic world and traveled every inch of our land praying to Allah and shedding tears for the goodness of all people. You find sincere concerns and pleas of Magtymguly, who traveled all through our land, the mountains and valleys, keeping long vigils during the late hours of the night and the early hours of the mornings praying for the salvation of all people. You find the spirit of Girogly riding his horse all through our land at a gallop for the defense of all the oppressed, ill-treated and innocent.

In this land, if you plant the stick in your hand it will bud as green as a forest, or bloom like a rose garden; if you shoot an arrow into the soil it will turn into a golden ear of grain! In this land, the words which fall from your mouth become wise sayings. These lands are no less than a blessed source of bread and abundance for those who live here!

Like the breath of Gorkut Ata, Hoja Ahmet yasawy, Bahaweddin Nagyibendi, Nejmeddin Kubra, Salar Baba, Mdne Baba, this fertile and powerful land is a remedy for thousands of ailments and problems. When you touch the soil of this land to the face of a miserable exile who has become blind through weeping over his loneliness, he will surely see again. This soil will cure him. This land will open his eyes.

Our ancestors! Gin[4] Han and Ay'[5] Han are like the golden thread of the Sun always watching over us

Our ancestors! Gok[6] Han and yyldyz[7] Han like the silver-colored nights watch over us!

Turkmen Dag[8] Han stands on your right; De'niz[9] Han stands on your left!

The head of our generation Oguz Han greets our nation from five thousand years ago.

As our brave nation is thirsty for a state, this land has a thirst to rise, for real progress!

Would it not be as exalted as the Mountain of Kipet, as exciting as the river of Jeyhun, and as beautiful as the heart of Sumbar, to live in such a land?

This land which Allah, the most Exalted, protects is

called Turkmenistan: Free and Impartial Turkmenistan.

The history of the Tijrkmen nation can be traced back to the Flood of Noah. We go by the name of Tirk-iman, that is 'o

asli nur[10]. We originated from Oguz Han.

4 Gun means day. 7 Asli Nur is made of light

5 Ay means moon.

6 Gok means sky.

7 Yildiz means star.

8 Dag means mountain.

9 Deniz means sea.

10 Here, the term Turkmen is explained in a different etiological method, that is as follows: Turkfaith-divine light essence.

79

Oguz Han had several sons, named Gtin Han, Ay Han, Yyldyz Han, Gbk Han, and Dag Han. Each son also had four sons.

The 24 clans of Oguz originate from the 24 grandchildren of Oguz Han. Each of these clans has a different name and reputation. The Oguz people all around the globe are of these 24 clans.

BOZOK

This is the right branch.

GFJN HAN

He is the eldest son of Oguz and he has four sons:

The first son: Gaya, which means strong, well built, and undefeatable like a rock.

His seal is Bird falcon, siyik (a portion of meat); right segment, right shinbone, neck.

The Second Son: Bayat, which means imperial, highbom, magnanimous and blessed.

His seal is y Bird falcon, siyik (a portion of meat), right segment, and right shinbone, neck.

The Third Son: Akevi, which means they are everywhere, progressive and they are successful everywhere.

Its seal is Siyik (a portion of meat), right segment, and right shinbone, neck.

The Fourth Son: Karaevli, which means their house is black.

" Gray-affow

Its seal is Bird. Siyik (a portion of meat), right segment, right shinbone, neck.

I

AY HAN

He is the second son of Oguz Han and he has four sons.
The first son: Yazir, which means he has a lot lands.
His seal is . Bird, eagle. Siyik; anklebone and hipbone.
The second son: Dijger, which means they go somewhere to gather.
His seal is . Bird, eagle, siyik; anklebone and hipbone.
The third son: Dodurga, which means he has property.

4

His seal is Bird eagle, siyik; anklebone and hipbone.
Thefourth son: Yaparli.
His seal is Bird eagle, siyik; anklebone and hipbone.

YYLDYZ HAN

He is the third son of Oguz Han and he has four sons.
Thefirst son: Aviar, which means agile and good hunter.
His seal is Bird rabbit. Siy4ik; right hipbone and rib.
The second son: Kizik, which means strong, systematic, order-oriented.

His seal is Bird rabbit. Siyik; right hipbone and
rib.
The third son: Begdill, which means speaks succinctly like a prince.
His seal is Bird rabbit. Siyik; right hipbone and
Thefourth son: Karkin, it means helper, serving food.
His seal is Bird rabbit. Siyik; right hipbone and rib.

UCOK12

This is the left branch.

GOK HAN

He is the fourth son of Oguz Han and he has four sons. The first son: Ba'yndyr, which means he is rich and y
His seal is Bird a white falcon. Siyik; left stomach, neck
The second son: Becene, which means he is hardworking
His seal is Bird a white falcon. Siyik; left stomach, neck
The third son: Cavul, which means honorable and known.
His seal is Bird a white falcon. Siyik; left stom-
The fourth son: Cepni, which means it gains no matter where it is.
12 Three-arrows.

His seal is . Bird, a white falcon. Siyik; left stomach, neck.
13

DAG13 HAN

He is the fifth son of Oguz Han and he has four sons.
The first son: Salyr, which means his sword is victorious everywhere.
Its seal . Bird, Uc. Stiyik; coccyx and rib bone.
The second son: Eymur, which means he has many wives and he is rich.
His seal . Bird, Uc. Siyik; coccyx and rib bone.

The third son: Alayunt, it means he has horses.

His seal . Bird, Uc. Siyik; coccyx and rib bone.

The fourth son: Uregir it means he is ready to help, useful.

His seal . Bird Uc. Siytik; coccyx and rib bone.

DENIZ HAN

He is the sixth son of Oguz and he has four sons.

The first son: lgdir, which means goodness, completeness, bravery.

His seal YI . Bird, Cakir, Siyik; coccyx and rib bone

13 Dag means mountain.

83

The second son: Bugduz, which means he has respect for everyone.

His seal Bird, Cakir, Siyik; coccyx and rib bone

The third son: Yiva, which means his rank is above them all.

His seal Bird, Cakir, Siyik; coccyx and rib bone

The fourth son: Kinik, which means he is the most beloved

His seal is Bird, Cakir, Siyik; coccyx and rib bone

Having subordinated the banks of the Mankishlak, Seyhun and Jeyhun and the foot of Mount Kipet, Oguz Han returned to his homeland. On his return he invited all his sons and grandchildren for a large banquet. Oguz Han gave gold, silver, and precious fabrics as gifts. Then he said:

"Oh my sons, I am now old. Death is approaching for me. Listen carefully to my advice! See my advice as wise words on the way of truth and live your life in accordance with my advice. Pass my advice on to your children and your tribe! And may they also follow my advice forever! May they also pass my advice on to all their descendants. If your tribesmen conform to my advice, forever and ever, you will be the masters of the world; no enemy will be able to overcome you! Follow my advice, and you will not change your religion. Obey my advice, and you will be prosperous in this life and in the next. If they do not keep their word and do not follow my advice and orders, they will certainly fall out with each other. Each tribe will find itself in a different climate, a different region.

84

Oguz Han then said to his six son and twenty-four grandchildren:

"Oh my sons! Give me an arrow."

He was given an arrow. Oguz Han took the arrow in his hand and broke it. Then he said to two of his sons:

"Oh my sons! Give me two arrows."

He was given two arrows. He broke them again. Then he took three arrows from thee more of his sons, held them together and broke them as well. Next, he took six arrows from six of them and he tried to break all six arrows at the same time. He failed. Oguz Han then requested twenty-four arrows, one from each of his grandsons and tied the arrows together. Then to his children he said:

'Try with your all your will and might to break all these together. Are you able to do this?

His sons replied:

"We cannot break all these arrows."

Oguz Han said:

"Take a lesson from this example and support each other. According to my wish, following my death Gin should be your new Han. After him his son Gaya should be your new Han. As long as there is a Han from Gaya's tribe, Bayat should not be your Han. Ba'yat should only be the ruler of his tribe. As long as Gaya is the Han, Bay'at should be the ruler of the right part of our land. The ruler of the left part of our land should be Bayyndyr. Follow these arrangements; do not take the younger brother as your leader as long as the elder brother lives. Gaya Han can be the Han of all of the twelve tribes to the right and left.

86

In accordance with the order of Oguz Han, they then divided the people into three groups. Their duties were to be divided in this way: it was to be the duty of scholars and learned people to collect taxes and flocks of sheep. The duties of budgeting, governing expenditure, the vizierate, and the chief stewardship belonged to the same group.

Those who were brave and stout-hearted were to be assigned leadership roles. Those who were agile and nimble were trained to use the lasso.

Those who were uneducated and ignorant were to be given sticks to be shepherds of camels, cattle, and sheep.

If a captain or another commander should die, one with the best capacity for grooming the horses and for cultivating the land, was to take over. After the death of the chief of the tribe, if there should be no son to represent him after his death, whoever might be the bravest, the most experienced, the best informed on military affairs, with a good record of war bravery was to be the new chief of the tribe.

You should not keep moving from one place to another, nor staying in one place. You should stay on the mountain pasture during the summer. You should stay in sheltered seaside places during the winter and in warm places during the autumn. If you follow this advice your cattle will not waste away and their milk will not diminish. You will thrive. No matter how many years go by, no matter how many generations pass, as long as you follow my advice your offspring will be blessed. They will live in abundance. Allah will help them and send his grace upon them. Their state will be everlasting, their lives will be long and the nations of the world will pray for them.

87

After this age, there will be many kings, Hans and many sons from them. If their advisers, and the wise people with them do not protect the order, the Hanate and the Soltanate will be shaken. When their order is shaken, they will long for the return of Oguz Han but it is impossible.

There will always be many captains, commanders, and generals. Are those who do not abide by the advice of Oguz capable of leading armies? Those who do not listen to our advice in their own land are like those cast into great seas who cannot swim, or they like an arrow shot into a great forest. Such people cannot be leaders. A man who can order his household can lead ten people. He who leads ten people can govern fifty people. Whoever leads fifty people has the right to govern a hundred people. He who governs a hundred people can be the leader of one thousand people. Whoever controls a thousand people can be the leader of an army division. And he who can control an army division is easily able to be the ruler of his tribe. One who can be a ruler can also be the leader of a province.

Whoever keeps his household in order can safeguard his property and country from liars and thieves.

If a corporal cannot control his household, it is obvious that his son and wife share the responsibility. From his army unit of ten men a new corporal should be elected. The same method should be applied to other rulers, such as commanders, ruler of divisions and so on. If a man commits a crime, the commander of the division should request from the major the identity of the man. The major should request the name of the criminal from the captain. Finally, in this way, the criminal should be found and punished. The perpetrators of theft and robbery should be caught and punished in the same way.

88

If there is a consensus of three learned men over an issue, this opinion can be declared and repeated everywhere. Otherwise it is impossible to consider an opinion to be true. Compare your own and others opinions with such learned people's opinions. If it is in accord with such blessed opinions you can adopt it. Otherwise do not speak of it.

If a horse which can gallop when it is fat can also gallop when it is thin, it is a good horse. If a horse is not good in both cases, it is not a good horse.

Great rulers who are leading and waging war or hunting with friends show their horses. They pray to Allah all the time and they trust in Allah; they wish for victory and blessings from Allah, the Truth. You should be as brave as a young steer when serving in the military, and you should be like a hungry white falcon ready to hunt when taking part in a war.

A brave man is not always visible like the sun. If his wife keeps the house clean and tidy and is hospitable to visitors while he is absent because he is hunting or at war, she will undoubtedly enhance his position in society. Her own fame will also spread like her husband's. A good man can be recognized by the actions of a good woman. If a woman is not competent in her own home, this problem influences her husband.

Traders are happy, exuberant and hopeful when they come with their decorated fabrics, and their goods for the bazaar. The commanders of armies should teach soldiers archery, grooming horses and wrestling. The commander should test the soldiers in these things. Those who are brave and lionhearted will be happy and exuberant if they can trust in their abilities and skills.

If a man from our people fails to comply with orders, he must be warned first. If he fails for a second time, he must be threatened and

punished. If for a third time he fails, he must be exiled to a remote place like Hotan, where nobody lives and which hunters rarely visit. But he must be allowed to return after a while. If he complies with the order of the community, there is no problem; this is good. Otherwise he must be jailed. If he is still far from complying with the order of our community, his brothers should meet to consult about him. According to this consultation a decision should be taken about what to do with him.

Whenever you see old people who need help remember this saying: "He who does not help the poor, cannot be the leader." So help all poor and old people.

The ruler is the father of the orphans and the homeless. The ruler must show a father's concern for them. As there is a difference between a poor father and a rich father, the ruler should behave like a rich father.

It is a great task to govern the land and the people. The ruler must always be farsighted

and intelligent, and he must be aware of every development. He must pray to Allah, The Great. He must carry out all his duties in the way of Allah so that from his works, knowledge and actions, the generations may be raised that will be beneficial to this world and the next.

The ruler should assign important jobs to capable and experienced advisors. He will regret it if he assigns important duties to bad people.

All thieves, traitors and criminals should be punished since no one should attempt to violate rules and prohibitions. Those who are suffering tyranny should be helped in order to reduce the numbers of tyrants and merciless people. As it is

90

said, "The ruler who does not punish the criminal and thief strikes his own caravan and people with his own hands." If a ruler does punish crime, he gains absolute legitimacy.

ASTORY

Anuiirwan Adyl, died as an infidel. A man from the community saw him in dream living a very good life and asked him:

- How did you manage to reach such a rank?

Anuiirwan Adyl replied:

-I had no mercy on criminals and I never offended the innocent!

If a man treated with kindness by another man feels indebted to him and respects him and replies cordially to him, he is one who respects justice and equity. Truly, tie fame and the reputation of rulers originate in their armies and states. If there is no army and state, there is no governance. For this reason the importance of army, state and land should be known and appreciated. Those who have no such respect are merciless.

Giving power and authority to cruel people, even after they have been punished, is like setting a wolf as shepherd after it has taken an oath to be kind. Theft, criminality and wickedness are intolerable. Killing a man whose tyranny is clear is better than sending him into exile. Putting a snake from your house into your neighbor's house is not legitimate.

When a ruler gets angry, he should not be hasty because a living thing can be killed, but the dead cannot be brought back to life. A thing which has been mended can never be as strong as it was, but the undamaged can be broken easily.

91

The property of the deceased should be given to poor and homeless people. The blessed hands of the ruler should not be polluted by taking the property of others. Nothing is to be left in this world other than good remembrance and fame.

Never try to damage the friendship of two men. On the contrary, try to make friends with both of them.

An unjust ruler is like a farmer who plants corn and expects wheat.

Good but weak people should not be injured. Ants united can defeat a tiger or a lion.

The history of a nation rises like a river from a small spring. However the golden periods of our glorious history illuminate the world. Oguz Han armored in pure gold and bearing his quiver on his legendary horse waits at the beginning of this glorious history. The Turkmen people, the heirs

14

of Oguz Han, holding green flags wait at this point at the beginning of another Golden Century. The green standard is the symbol of spring, revival and rising! The famous historian Riza Nur writes as follows on Oguz Han, the origin of the Turkmen: "Oguz Han is the national prophet of the Turkmens. But his name is not among the names of the prophets. He is indicated only by the word Torg in the old Hebrew books like the Torah." In another of his books, "General Turkish

History", written at the beginning of the 20th century, Riza Nur writes as follows: "...It was Oguz Han who named the five Turkish tribes

14 The current Turkmen flag, which is on a green base or background.

as the masters of the earth. He reigned for 116 years. However this 116 years should be understood in the old Turkmen calendar."

Oguz Han, the ruler of great lands, conquered them with words inspired by Allah rather than with his sword. He requested that we should be merciful and compassionate:

- If I am asked, I have never said no. I always give what I am asked.
- I waited for the end of good and bad, and I reached my goal.
- I explained all my wishes to my people and I convinced them.
- Without a sword, I govern the people with good words.
- I govern with justice and have organized my own state.
- I never oppressed people, never attempted to kill innocents; I was always patient even though I had been oppressed.
- He who follows the path of truth, never finds evil.
- If your nation does not appreciate your way, you will never see good.
- He who oppresses his own subordinates, he will prepare his own grave.
- He who oppresses his own subordinates is doing what his enemies want. His enemies will be happy about this.
- A way other than justice never suits a ruler

In the age when the Egyptian pharaohs declared themselves the sons of God, Oguz Han came into this world. After he had grown into an adult and a brave man, he trained his own people to be the same. Finally he taught all the other peoples of world in the same manner

Soldiers without the fear of death wage war in their iron armout. Great ideas live forever illuminating the people. The Egyptian pharaohs were mummified and buried in their PYTamids made of huge stones in the wish that they might be eternal. Our forefather Oguz Han wanted to be eternal in a different way, in the hearts, in the spirit of our nation. He preferred to live in the opinions of our people. Opinions and ideas are more permanent than stones and mummified bodies. Oguz Han knew well it was not people but their opinions which are eternal and lasting. The treasure of Oguz Han's opinions, which we have inherited from him, has thrown a light on us from 5000 thousand years ago.

Next

One day its time will come and Oguz Han's opinions and ideas will illuminate not only us but also everyone on earth who has respect for reason and opinion.

The man who knows Oguz Han knows the wisdom and richness of his words and opinions. Each of them opens new horizons for us. His words are meaningful like those of prophets. These words cannot be understood without a deep, careful study.

Man should solve the two most important questions of his life during his youth. The first is to find a profession which will make his life meaningful. The second is to find a beloved who will make him happy.

Our Prophet (peace be upon him) also tried to reach two targets during his life. The first was to convince all people of the unity of God and the second to gather humanity around this idea of God's unity.

Oguz Han also tried to achieve two targets during his reign. The first was to become the ruler and the second to establish his order and rule in the community in order to create a new community.

There exist nations where the persons who live in them should exalt the dignity of their nation.

There exist nations where persons should try to exalt themselves to be part of this nation.

The Turkmen nation is the second type; it is a great nation. Its members should work hard to exalt themselves to the level of their nation's dignity.

The lover who is as exuberant as the tumbling river Jeyhun, does not believe that there is another sweetheart as beautiful as his sweetheart. He sees his darling as an angel sent from heaven. We are the lovers of our nation. However we are not lovers who have totally lost their reason over their beloved. We are trying to understand our nation by trying to understand our nation's ideas; we are proud of our nation's dignity. Let us think about the captivity and the unfortunate situation that we have experienced within the last hundred years. We have been part of a nation in which it was prohibited to say 'I Jove my nation', in which it was prohibited to say 'my nation'. For this reason we should love our nation twice as much now.

We love our nation, our homeland, our state. Love

becomes much when it is shared. Fire becomes fierce when it is fed with firewood. Prayer becomes acceptable if it is frequently repeated.

We first listen to our minds before commencing a task. The mind of man never deceives him, because Allah is enthroned in our hearts. Listen your own heart.

It is difficult to remain pure and clean on earth. Even the light that illuminates everything around blackens whatever the fire touches. Be careful not to cause harm when you are trying to do good.

Words, though they may resemble each other, have different meanings. The arrows we fire are similar as well, but only few of them hit the target.

When a dog barks his owner checks what is happening around him. Listen. Know how to listen. Even animals listen. You are human, so listen with your heart.

We say months and days pass so quickly. No, in fact months and days pass so slowly; what passes quickly is life.

... The treasure we have inherited from fifty centuries of our past is nothing but ruined cities and old buildings. It is not enough to be learned to understand this legacy. In order to understand the meaning of this legacy, you should read it as you read the Qur'an. You should decipher the deep meaning behind each word.

Oguz Han's name means sky and earth.

The names of his six sons denote the six great things in this world.

Kyat, who was killed by Oguz Han, was a totem of the previous religion!

Gik Bbrij, who came to the world with a thunderbolt from the sky, is a totem of the second period!

"He who knows himself is a saint". The human becomes human by knowing himself.

Recognition of the nation is the duty of brave men and of clever men!

Idesire to talk with our ancestors who rode on horseback in the depths of history. I

try to talk with them, with their fame. However they are busy with their important problems. Suddenly you hear Giroylv's enthusiastic voice from the mountains:
0 lads! Let's feast and drink,
And relieve our hearts for a while,
Let's push our enemies off and clear the way As our ancestors did.
Thy Girogly says, "You, guys! Fill the bowls full!
I am proud of the Turkmen!
I love you all!"
You shout, "Girogly, Girogly Beg, I am here!" Girogly does not hear you!
However, you hear his voice, the hooffalls of his galloping horse, as they are close by you. Tears fall from your eyes. The mountains where Girogly lived became misty...
97
Until the third decade of the 20 century, the Turkmen traditionally rode on horseback in heavy armour. This was not a sign of rank or status, but a tradition. This tradition was part of Oguz Han's legacy to us.
The big states founded by Oguz Han lasted thousands of years. The alphabet he prepared was also used for thousands of years. Exactly when this alphabet fell out of use is not
Ih
known, but there is an 18 century lamentation for it named "Beautiful twenty five" by the poet Sheydai:
How pleasing sounds to ears,
15
Saying all the beautiful twenty-five
Some with tuneful voice, the vowels,
I followed all the beautiful twenty-five.
Seven were made of voice,
And eighteen contained noise,
After three thousand years of life
Why let yourself go, all the beautiful twentyfive?
Oh, Sheydayy says, Worse happened,
Alas, all the folk moum, lament for you,
Now they scom you,
Thus vanished, all the beautiful twenty-five Oh my beloved people!
15 The ancient, now forgotten, the alphabet of Oguzs, with 25 letters, 7 vowels and 18 consonants
98
We, as the heirs to the great Turkmen legacy should respect and know the historical legacy of our ancestors, and we should study our cultural richness. This fidelity to our past is our historical duty.
The style of our nation's culture and life originates with Oguz Han.
We know the wise stories of the prophets and their tales, lessons for us from Oguz Han. The source of the great states we founded in the past is also Oguz Han.
"He who has respect for the elder becomes the ruler; one who has respect for the ruler becomes glorious." "Sell your street to your neighbor so that you can come back later." "He who has no elder has no youth!" "He who has no old has no new!" "My fellow countryman is my brother." "I have a brother so I never worry." "I have a brother, I have a supporter." "See yourself as milk, and see your friend as

cream." "neighbor on doomsday!"

Oguz Han ordered us to obey our brothers even they are older by one day. By saying, "If there are no elders, there are learned people", he ordered us to obey our learned people if there are no experienced old people among us.

The absence of Oguz Han who illuminated humanity with his opinions and ideas was felt on his demise. Then the old vizier of Oguz Han, Erkil Hoja summoned a consultative group of learned and experienced people.

They gathered for a special session to discuss how to govern state affairs after Oguz Han. The decisions taken in this special session then became a book. In a chapter of this book it says:

99

"If you cut up a sheep or ten sheep or a hundred sheep, share the meat as follows. Each of you shall eat the meat with his sons or friends". "When a man close to the ruler commits a crime, during his punishment none of the ruler's relatives or sons shall help the man who punishes the criminal. But anyone who says "This criminal protected me" should be taken to the presence of the ruler and punished severely. Then this shall be an example for all!"

Aman from Bozoks of the Oguz generation shall be the ruler. Two persons shall never be your rulers at the same time. If there is one Han it means order, but two Hans means disorder. Old, wise people said, "A sheath cannot handle two swords". "A woman cannot be engaged to two men." "Two customs cannot live in a land!"

Oguz Han's chief stewards on the council said, "We shall never think of going against this advice! If our sons from our lineage are on the truth path, they shall follow this book and principles. If they say 'We shall go by the illicit way,' they will never consider the principles of this book". Then the chief stewards all signed the book and it was kept in the treasury of Gin Han.

Gin Han at that time was seventy years old.

The descendants of Oguz Han, following this covenant-book, reigned for long years. The names of several tribes cited by Oguz Han, such as Gaya and Bayat, even survive today, having passed from generation to generation.

Oguz Han illuminated the path of the Oguz people, our ancestors, for thousands of years.

Another advice our forefather Oguz Han left for us was to assume a task according to who you are! Big tasks for

100

big people, small tasks for small. If you are the husband of your household, your duty is to protect your family; if you are the chief steward of your tribe, your duty is to govern your tribe; if you are the ruler, your duty is to govern your land; if you are the leader your duty is to govern the whole homeland!

Once upon a time, a very poor old man who had lived a very unfortunate existence, was approaching the end of his life, coming close to Allah and destiny. Upon the order of God a wise man approached the old man and asked him about his problems and life. The poor man complained about the conditions of his life. The wise man sent by God then said:

-I will give you a fixed period of time for the next month. Go and try to find the best life you can. I will change your life according to your choice and give you the life you most desire.

The poor old man after watching the rich men whom he had envied before found out that there was nothing to be happy about in their life. After a month the wise man sent by God came again and asked the old and poor man:

-Will you take such and such a person's destiny? He is both rich and wise. There is no one else like him here.

The rebellious man replied:

- No, I do not want his life! He has no son!

-All right, so take this one's life and destiny. This man has four sons like lions and he is the Han of a great country.

-No, I cannot! I am not mad enough to wage- a war if it happens.

101

The wise man sent by God offered several alternatives, one after the other. In the end the poor man understood that his life was the best one for him.

Everyone's soul is so sweet for him; everyone's destiny is blessed for him. Oh my people! Be content, be happy. Complaining only makes you unhappy and unsuccessful.

Instead of complaining, try to find a solution to the problems you are facing. There is no problem without a remedy. Allah, who gives the problems, gives the remedies and solutions with them. The one whose soul is supreme finds the better way.

The reign of Oguz Han was a golden age. His ideas and opinions were not limited to one country and land, but were so great as to contain all the earth. He was such a great man, whose opinions illuminated all the nations of the world.

Anew nation was born with Oguz Han and the fortune of the Turkmen nation was exalted with him.

Our ancestors said, "It is not only the reader who benefits from the reading; the listeners also get the benefit." It was Oguz Han's eminence and humanity which led him to adopt the sons of war martyrs as his own sons.

The Hans who came after Oguz Han also followed his path.

Our path is such a great path. On this great path, our duty is to accomplish great things, my dear nation.

102

After Oguz Han's death, as he had requested, his son, Gin Han, ascended to the throne. Oguz Han's vizier, Erkil Hoja, became the vizier and advisor of Gin Han. One day Erkil Hoja said to Gin Han, "Oguz Han was a great ruler. He conquered all the lands on earth. He had countless treasure and property. He died leaving all those to us. According to the will of Allah, each of you has had four sons. May God protect your sons from conflict over the throne. It is only by assigning a name and a symbol to each tribe and group that unity and peace can be preserved in our homeland. They shall each define their own treasure, lands, domestic administration, cattle with their own signs and official seals. Then none shall complain of another. All shall know their way and symbols, and this is the basis of the perpetuity of the state."

Gin Han accepted the truth of these words and Erkil Hoja continues as Gin Han's advisor and vizier. After this event, the titles of Bozok and Cqok were given to the six sons. The tribes of the left and the right were named with different names, and they were each given a different reputation, seal and sign. A specific animal's name was given to each of the 24 grandchildren as a title. According to this tradition, no tribe kills the animal which represents their tribe's name; neither do they eat its meat, because this animal bears their sign and name.

Erkil Hoja in order to prevent conflict among different tribes during meals given on specific occasions defined the share of each tribe beforehand and distributed each tribe's meat before they started eating. In this way the names of the 24 grandchildren of Oguz Han came out of this sharing. These names later became their official names.

The basic reason for the strength of the state founded by 104
Oguz Han is that it rested on strong and wise customs. As long as rules and order are respected, power and strength are enhanced. We too should maintain and preserve the customs of Oguz Han.

There have been many rulers from the descendants of Oguz Han. In every century there have been many powerful and fortunate rulers from the 24 Oguz tribes. The Oguz lineage reigned for a long time. For example, the Salyrs reigned for a period, and after them there came several other famous rulers. In this way, through the stories of each ruler, the history of the offspring of Oguz lasted.

We know from which tribe or son of Oguz Han each ruler or beg comes. The Soltans of Seljuk and their fathers were also great and famous rulers. Rulers from the Oguz lineage reigned in the lands of Iran and Turan, and even in the large area from Egypt to China for more than four hundred years. In Ruhnama, their history is briefly told within the context of the history of the people of Oguz.

Gorkut Ata of the Bayat clan lived in the age shortly after the Prophet (peace be upon him). Gorkut Ata was the wise man of the Oguz people. What he said happened; he foretold the future. Allah inspired his heart.

One day, Mahy 'a, the ruler of Merw, was given a letter confirming his position as ruler by the Caliph Ali. In the letter it said, "In the name of Allah, the Great and Merciful, may the works of those who follow the just be easy. Oraz Mahyya, the ruler of Merw, came to me. I am very pleased at his visit." This was after the Muslim army had entered these lands and stayed in the region and Turkmens and other clans
105
and tribes had started discussions and formed relationships with them, and as a result they had converted to Islam in groups without any fight.

Why did the Merw people do such an unusual, even unique thing and open the doors of their city to the armed enemy without putting up a fight?
Gorkut Ata the spiritual leader of his nation was among the first to accept Islam. He visited Mekka and Medina and performed his duty of pilgrimage there.
Anyone with sense who reads the Book of Gorkut Ata can understand how farsighted, successful and wise Oguz Begs worldview was. In the book of Gorkut
Ata it can be seen that Oguz people had a great wealth of literature and cultural diversity in festivals and holidays. Could a society with such a wealth of literature, art and cultural range be close to the primitive culture of fire-worshippers? The religion of fire-worshippers was perpetuated by certain narrowminded philosophers of the ancient times, such as Mazdak and Mani. These philosophers by modifying the religion of fire-worshipping suggested new practices such as the sharing of property and even of women. Their ideas and practices do
,h
not resemble our opinions and ideas. The 10 century historian Ibn-i Fadlan wrote about the Turkmen as follows: "The Turkmen people do not cover the faces of their women and girls like their neighbors. Their women are free. However, they do not know what it is to be unchaste. Turkmen women throughout history have

lived without the slightest stain to their honor."

The enemies of Lady Burla, mother of Oraz Mahyy'a, wanted to make her drunk in order to seduce her. When they

came to the place where the women were held captive, they asked, "Who is Lady Burla, here?" All the women in one voice replied, "I am Lady Burla." However, her devious enemies said, "Force all of them to eat the roasted body of her son, Oraz. The rest may all eat of it but his mother cannot." And they attempted to kill the son of Gazan. Aware of what was happening, Lady Burla asked her son, "How can I choose between eating your flesh or dishonoring your father's name?" Her son angrily replied,

Mother! Let your mouth dry up,
Let your tongue rot away,
Were not your rights of God's rights
Then I would force myself to rise against you,
And grip you by your collar and throat,
And bring you down under my coarse heels,
And kick your white face against the dark soil.
Let them slice my flesh and fry it on the fire
And put it before the daughters of the forty beg,
And eat from it two if they eat one,
But never will you defame the honor
Of my father, Gazan!

The religion of Islam penetrated deeply into the spirit of the Turkmen people. After reading the Qur'an or after performing the prayer, they open their hands and pray to God sincerely with their purest feelings.

Since they followed the religion of Gbk Tann/ the God of the Skies and they believed God was in the heavens before

Islam, it was easy for our ancestors to adopt Islam as their religion.

Oguz Han said to the girl to whom he was engaged: "They have engaged you to me now. I will accept you as my wife and love you wholeheartedly if you accept that Allah is one." The girl replied, "I do not know anything about the real god, but I will carry out your orders and words." Oguz Han this time said, "My only desire is this. I mean I order you to believe in Allah, the One and Only." The girl replied, "I consent to all your words and orders." After this, the girl became a real believer with a real faith, serving God carefully.

Oguz Han then took the girl as his wife and loved her wholeheartedly and forgot his former wives.

The Turkmen were already rich in treasure, great cattle, great amounts of property and trust in their own people and country. After converting to Islam, they severed their connections with other religions. It was for this reason the ruler of Merw opened the doors of his city to the soldiers of the Islamic army.

Could it have been possible to bring the people of Oguz, such as Ddli Domrul and Ddli Garcar, to the straight path by any other method?

An apprentice after learning his master's skills can change masters.

Astudent after learning the sciences of one school can enter another.

After becoming adult, young people can move and set up their own homes.

With the flag of Islam waving everywhere, the Oguz

people abolished their former religion and sought a new light which would illuminate them.

Reading the book of Gorkut Ata raises the spirit, relieves the body, and calms the soul. You will be exalted and close to your past.

What is told in the book of Gorkut Ata is the religion and his wise ideas and advice to people.

The ideas of Gorkut Ata ruled over the land of Turkmens for five hundred years. After this, in the third period of our history, Seljuk Beg, from the lineage of Gorkut Ata, became the ruler

The Seljuks reigned around Merw. This reign expanded towards the West, towards Asia MinOL

Many Seljuk Turkmen Principalities were founded during the Middle Ages. These are:

- Turkmen Tuluni State 868-905
- Turkmen Ihsid State 935-969
- Turkmen Symirnia Caka Principality 1081-1098
- Turkmen Dilmachogullari Principality 1085-1192
- Turkmen Danishmentliler Principality 1092-1178
- Turkmen Oguz Yabgu State 7th and 9th Centuries
- Turkmen Karahanli State 840-1212
- Turkmen Ghazneli State 916-1187
- The Great Seljuk-Turkmen Empire 1040-1194
- Turkmen Syria Seljuk State 1092-1117

- Turkmen Kirman Seljuk State 1092-1307
- Turkmen Anatolia Seljuk State 1092-1307
- Turkmen HarezmShahlar State 1097-1231
- Turkmen Yazirs 11th and 13th Centuries
- Turkmen Salyrs 14th and 16th Centuries
- Turkmen Akgo'unly State 1350-1502
y
- Turkmen Garagoyunly State 1410-1468
- The Turkmen- Ottoman Empire 1299-1922
- Turkmen Memluk State (in Egypt) 1250-1323
- Turkmen Halacis (in India) 1202-1323
- Turkmen Delhi Soltanate (in India) 1206-1414
- Turkmen Tugluklular Principality (India) 1414-1555
- Turkmen Safevids State 1501-1736
- Turkmen Avshar Dynasty 1736-1796
- Turkmen Kacar Dynasty 1779-1924

Many principalities survived as dependent or semindependent entities within the Seljuk State. The vacuum which existed after the end of the Seljuk State was fulfillled by Harzemsahlar State.

- Turkmen Sallyklylar Principality 1092- 1202
- Turkmen AhlatShahlar Principality 1100-1207
- Turkmen Artukogullari Principality 1102-1048
- Turkmen Inalogullar Principality 1098-1183

- Turkmen Mingflcikler Principality 1072-1277
- Turkmen Begteginler Principality 1146-1232
- Turkmen Cobanogullari Principality 1227-1309
- Turkmen Karamanogullari Principality 1256-1483
- Turkmen Inanyogullari Principality 1261-1368
- Turkmen Sahipataogullari Principality 1275-1341
- Turkmen Pervaneogullari Principality 1277-1322
- Turkmen Mentesogullari Principality 1290-1382
- Turkmen Candarogullari Principality 1299-1382
- Turkmen Karesiogullari Principality 1297-1360
- Turkmen Germiyanogultari Principality 1300-1423
- Turkmen Hamidogullari Principality 1301-1423
- Turkmen Saruhanogullari Principality 1302-1410
- Turkmen Aydinogullari Principality 1308-1426
- Turkmen Tekeogullari PrincipalitY 1321-1390
- Turkmen Eretnaogullari Principality 1335-1381
- Turkmen Dulkadirogullari Principality 1339-1521
- Turkmen Ramazanogullari Principality 1325-1608
- Turkmen Doburcaturk Principality 1354-1417
Turkmen Kadi Burhaneddin Ahmedi S. 1381- 1398
Turkmen Esrefogullari Principality 1326
Turkmen Barcemogullari Principality 12th Century
Turkmen Taceddinogullari Principality 1348-1428
Turkmen Yarlikogullari Principality 12th Century
111
- Turkmen Emirogullari Principality 14th Century
- Turkmen Boruler Atabegligi 1117-1154
- Turkmen Zenniler Atabegligi 1227-1259
- Turkmen IlDe'nizler Atabegligi 1146-1225
- Turkmen Salyrtar Atabegligi 1147-1258
Next
If we pay close attention, we can see that the Oguz people at the beginning used similar names to the Seljuks. each clan took the name of their ruler. If we look at their dates of establishment and termination, it will be clear are small principalities founded just after the destruction of the Seljuks and Harzemsahs. Many of them were Ottoman State by Osman Ghazi.

THE GREAT SELJUK TurkmenS
In the third period of Turkmen history (in the third decade of the I lthcentury), there occurred several new and developments in our history. The Seljuk commanders Togrul Beg (993-1063) and Qagry Beg (991-1061) founded The other name of Cagry is Davud, the other name of Togrul is Muhammed. Both Togrul and Qagry Begs were foremost commanders. The metaphorical meaning of their names is eagle. If the spirit of the Turkmen is accepted fifth period, then it must be 'eagle' in the third period. For this reason it was very normal for the Turkmen commanders named in such way. Qagry and Togrul Begs were the sons of Mikhail. They were the grandchildren of Seljuk Beg.
112
The boundaries of the Seljuk State extended from the Great Wall of China to Egypt, Asia Minor and the Caucasus. his sons waged war against Samanogullari, Ilek

Hanate, and Mahmyt of the Gazneli State.

The Seljuks are from the Kinik clan of the Oguz people. In 1040 in front of the Dafidanakan citadel, 70km from they defeated Mahmyt of the Gazneli state from the lineage of Oguz. The state founded by the two brothers grew this victory.

Akhutba (sennon) was delivered in the name of the two brothers in all lands under their control. Cagry Beg, "Soltan of Soltans", ascended the throne in the city of Merw; Togrul Beg ascended the throne in the city of Nishapur. time span, many places and cities such as Belh, Curcan, Taberistan, Harezm and then Cibal, Hemedan, Dinavar, Isfahan were conquered.

In 1055, Togrul Beg went to Baghdad and was declared Soltan in the city, which was under the control of the named "Soltan of the seven climates" by the Caliphate.

The land of the Great Seljuk Empire expanded greatly during the era of Alp Aslan, Cagry Beg"s son. It started from tens of countries and principalities.

THE SOLTANS OF THE GREAT SELJUK TurkmenS

Islamic Calendar Gregorian Calendar

429-552 Rukneddin EbuTalib Togrul Beg 1308-1157
429 Adudeddin Ebu yuca Alp Arslan 1038
455 Celaleddin Ebul Feth Melik Shah 1063
113
465 Nasreddin Mahmyt 1092
487 Rukneddin Ebul Muzaffar BerkyaruklO94
498 Melik Shah 11 1104
498 Giyaseddin Ebu Suca Muhammet 1105
511-552 Muizeddin Ebul Haris Sancar 1118-1157
433-583 THE KIRMAN SELJUK STATE 1041-1187
433 Imameddin Kara Arslan Kavurt Beg 1041
465 Kirman Shah 1074
467 Huseyin 1074
467 Rukneddin Soltan Shah 1074
477 Turan Shah 1085
490 Iran Shah 1097
494 Arslan Shah 1101
536 Mugiseddin Muhammet 1 1141
551 Muhyiddin Togrut Shah 1156
Bahrem Shah (the era of conflict)
563 Arsian Shah 11 (the era of conflict) 1168
Tirkan Shah (the era of conflict)
583 Muhammet 1187
487-511 SYRIAN SELJUK TurkmenS 1094-1117
487 Tutus bin Alp Arslan 1094
488 Ridvan bin Tutus (in Aleppo) 1095
488-497 Dukak bin Tutus (in Damascus)
114
507 Ali Arslan Ahras bin Ridvan 1113
508-511 Shah bir Ridvan 1114-1117
511-590 IRAQI SELJUK TFTRKMENS 1118-1194
511 Mugiseddin Mahmyt 1138
525 Giyaseddin Davut 1131
526 Togrul 1 1132

528 Giyaseddin Mesud 1133
547 Muineddin Melik Shah 1152
548 Muhammet 1153
554 Suleyman Shah 1159
556 Arslan Shah 1161
573-590 Togrul 11 1177-1194
470-700 RUM SELJUK TurkmenS 1077-1300
(in Asia Minor)
470 Sileyman 1. Bin Kutalmis 1077
479 (Basli-Baratlik) 1086
485 Kilic Aslan Davut 1092
500 Melik Shah 1 1107
510 Mesud 1 1116
551 izeddin Kiliq Aslan 11 1156
584 Kutbeddin Melik Shah 11 1188
588 Giyaseddin Keyhusrev 1 1192
115
597 Rukneddin Suleyman 11 1200
600 Kilic Aslan iI 1203
601 Keyhusrev I (for the second term) 1204
607 Izeddin Keykavus 1 1210
616 Alaeddin Keykubat 1 1219
634 Giyaseddin Keyhusrev 11 1236
643 Izeddin Keykavus 11 1245
655 Rukneddin Kilic Aslan IV 1257
666 Giyaseddin Keyhusrev iI 1267
682 Giyaseddin Mesud 11 1283
696-700 Alaeddin Keykubat 11 1296-1300
THE PRINCIPALITY OF DANY$MENT TurkmenS
(In Sivas, Kayseri and Malatya)
While the Seljuk commanders were expanding their control in Asia Minor, Gumus,
son of Turkmen commander conquered Cappadocia, Sivas, Kayseri and Malatya.
Gumus defeated the Franks, who invaded Anatolia up to Malatya. The Danishmends
became dependent on the State after a short time.
The Principality of Danishmendliler
Circa 490-560 (Sivas, Kayseri, Malatya) Circa 1097-1165
Muhammet I Gumus bin Tilu Danishment
499 Gazi bin Gumus 1105
it6
529 Muhammet 11 bin Gazi 1105
537 Zunnun bin Muhammet 11 1142
Yagi (Yakup) Aslan bin Gazi
560 Ibrahim bin Muhammet 11 1165
THE ATABEG TurkmenS (12th and 13'h C.)
The education of the sons of commanders and important personalities had been aimed
at teaching them science order to prepare them for public service since the era of
Oguz Han. Those learned and experienced people who in this way then were called
Atalik, Ataliklar, and Atabegs.
The Atabegs started the education of the sons of Soltans at a very early age. Atabegs

were carefully chosen from soldiers.

The children of the Soltans were taught foreign languages, military knowledge and command. The Soltans educated could speak the languages of other nations, understand world literature, and utilise the technology of war.

This education must have been the secret of how Seljuk Soltans with a smaller number of troops defeated great soldiers.

From the start of the era of Oguz Han until the Middle Ages, the countries where the Oguz people lived were science, wisdom, and education. Many students from China and the Byzantine Empire were sent here in order art of war and related knowledge. Those students who were taught by the Atabegs became masters everywhere with their wide worldview, knowledge, bodily health and their skill at command.

With the growing weakness and decline of the Great Seljuk State, the Atabegs in their lands started declaring founding free principalities.

Imameddin Zenni was the slave of the son of Meliksah, who was the third Soltan of the Seljuk State. The Seljuk Azerbaijan came from the lineage of Mesud, who was the ruler of Iraq and came from the Gypjak Memluks. grandfather of the HarzemShahs was a servant at the palace of MelikShah.

BORI TurkmenS

479-549 According to the Islamic Calendar 1104-1154 According to the Gregorian Calendar

Atabeg Tug educated the younger Seljuk princes. Soltan Tutus set Atabeg Tug free in return for his services.

his own son Bori as well.

Atabeg Tug conquered Damascus. After this event, his dynasty started. After his death, he was replaced by his Islamic C. BORI TUJRKMENS Gregorian C.

479-549 1104-1154

497 Seyfilislam Zahireddin Tug 1104

522 Tajimilk Bori 1128

118

526 Semsulmulk Ismail 1132

529 Sihabeddin Mahmyt 1135

533 Jemaleddin Muhammet 1139

534-549 Mucireddin Abak 1140-1154

(or Anaz 1, + 564)

Bdri Turkmens Family Tree

ZENNI TVRKMENS

(Mesopotamian and Damascus Atabegs) 521-648 According to the Islamic Calendar 1127-1250 According to Calendar

Atabeg Imameddin Zenni was the son of Hacip Aksungur, who was the slave of MelikShah. Aksungur became between 1085-1094 (478-487). Upon the order of Tutus he rebelled against MelikShah. Zenni was appointed Mosul in 1127 (521) upon the order of Tutus. Baghdad, Sincar, Cezire and Harran were under his control. Later, Aleppo and other cities related to Damascus in 522. Zenni, thanks to his struggle against the Crusades and his protection of the Muslim lands against the Crusades, was compared with Zenni's death his lands were shared among his sons, the ruler of Damascus, Nureddin Mahmyt, and the ruler Mosul, Seyfetin. Both of his sons at that time were waging war against the Crusaders. Later the Damascus seg

However, other two segments appeared from Sincar and Cezire. Sincar came under the control of Eyyubis in others came under the control of Lulu, who was the vizier of the Mosul Zennis. None of them fell to the Moguls.

Islamic Calendar Gregorian Calendar

521-648 Zenni Turkmens 1127-1250

(Mesopotamia and Damascus Atabegs)

521-631 Musul Turkmen Atabegligi 1127-1234

521 Imamuddin Zenni (Also in Aleppo) 1127

541 Seyfeddin Gazi I It 1146

544 Kutbeddin Maudud 1149

565 Seyfeddin Gazi 11 1170

576 Izzeddin Mesud 1 1180

589 Nureddin Aslan Shah 1 1193

607 Izzeddin Mesud 11 1211

615 Nureddin Arslan Shah 11 1218

616 Nasreddin Mahmyt 1219

631 Bedreddin Lulu 1233

657-660 Ismail bin Lulu 1259-1262

120

541-577 Damascus Turkmen Atebegs 1146-1181 541 Nureddin Mahmyt bin Zenni 1146

569-577 Salih Ismail 1174-1181

566-617 Sincar Turkmen Atabegligi 1170-1220

566 Imamuddin Zenni bin Maudud 1170

594 Kutbeddin Muhammet 1197

616 Imaduddin SahinShah 1219

616-617 Mahmyt (or Omer) 1219-1220

576-648 Cezire Turkmen Atabegs 1180-1250

576 Muizeddin Sancar Shah 1180

605 Muizeddin Mahmyt 1208

6xx-648 Mesud 12xx-1250

BEGTEGINLER

(Erbil Turkmen Atabegs)

539-630 According to the Islamic Calendar 1144-1233 According to the Gregorian Calendar

In 1144 (539), Imameddin Zenni appointed Zeyneddin Ali Kucuk Beg, one of the army commanders, as the Mosul. In 1149 (544) he came under the control of the ruler of Sincar. Later he took over Harran, Tekrit, Erbil

other lands as ruler. After Zeyneddin's death at Erbil in 1168 (563), his son Muzafareddin Gbkboru, because of his fear of being murdered, escaped to Harran. Consequently, Erbil entered the control of the younger

Zeyneddin, Zeyneddin Yusuf. Emir Mucahiddin Kaymaz supported him. After Yusuf's death in 1190 (589), of Damascus and Mesopotamia appointed Muzaferridin Gikbori as his successor in Erbil and Sahrazur. Gi

cities and lands, which had been under his control, such as Harran, Ruhan (Eldessu) and Sumeysat, to his nephew Omer. Gikbori died in 1233 (630). Since he had no son, he requested that Erbil should be given to the Abbasid Islamic Calendar Gregorian Calendar

539 Begteginler (Erbil Atabegleri) 144-1233

539 Zeyneddin Ali Kucuk bin Begtegin 1144

563 Zeyneddin Yusuf bin Ali (in Harran) 1168

563 Muzafereddin Gikbori bin Ali (in Harran) 1 168
586-630 Muzafereddin Gikbori bin Ali 1190-1233
(in Erbil)
ARTUK TurkmenS
(in Diyarbakir)
495-712 1101-1312
Islamic Calendar Gregorian Calendar
Tutus, the ruler of Damascus, conquered Jerusalem and appointed one of his most
trustworthy commanders, governor of the city.
123
Sokmen and Ilgazi, the sons of Artuk, were the victors in the war that they waged
against the Ruler of Palestine. Ilgazi replaced their father in 1091.
In 1101, the Seljuk Soltan Muhammet appointed Ilgazi as the governor of Baghdad.
In the same year, Sokmen Diyarbakir as the commander of the Hisn-i Keyf fortress.
Sokmen in the next few years annexed Mardin to Diyarbakir. Mardin was given to
Sokmen's brother Ilgazi. Consequently Artuklular prevailed as two clans in Hisn-i
Keyf Artuklular (Artuklus) was recorded in history as a generation with a great
respect for science. Artuklular had contributions to the development of science.
Gregorian Calendar
495-629 A. Hisn Keyf Artuklular 1101-1231
495 Muineddevle Sokmen I 1101
498 Ibrahim 1104
circa 502 Rukneddevle Davud 1108
circa 543 Fahreddin Kara Aslan 1148
570 Nureddin Muhammet 1174
581 Kutbeddin Sokmen 11 1185
597 Nasreddin Mahmyt 1200
619-629 Rukneddin Maudud 1222-1231
502-712 B. Mardin Artuk Turkmens 1108-1312
124
Islamic Calendar
502 Mecnmeddin Ilgazi 1108
516 Husameddin Demir Tas 1122
547 Necmeddin Alp 1152
572 Kutbeddin Ilgazi 11 1176
580 Hisameddin Yuluk Arslan 1176
circa 597 Nasreddin A-rtuk Arslan Mansur 1200
637 Necmeddin Gazi I Seyit 1239
658 Kara Arslan Muzaffer 1260
circa 691 Semseddin Davut 1292
693 Necmeddin Gazi 11 Mansur 1294
712 Imaduddin Ali Alp Idil 1312
765 Ahmet Mansur 1363
769 Mahmyt Salih 1367
769 Davut Muzaffer 1367
778 Mecdeddin Isa Zahir 1376
809-811 Salih 1406-1408
TurkmenSHAHS IN ERMENISTAN
493-604 According to the Islamic Calendar

1110-1207 According to the Gregorian Calendar
Sokmen-el Kutbi was the slave of Kutbeddin Ismail,
who was a Seljuk Turkmen and the ruler of the Azerbaijani city of Maranda. His
name originates from this (493), Sokmen-el Kutbi took the city of Helat in Armenia
from Merwaniler. The city of Helat was under the 125

126
Sokmen-el Kutbi's descendants until 1207, that is,. the conquest of the Eyyubis.
Islamic Calendar
493-604 ErmenShahs (Ahlat-Shahs)
1110-1207
493 Sokmen-el Kutbi 1100
506 Zahireddin Ibrahim Sah Enuen 1112
521 Ahmet 1127
522 Nasreddin Sokmen 11 1128
579 Seyfeddin Begdemir 1183
589 Bedreddin Aksungur 1193
594 Mansur Muhammet 1198
603-604 Izeddin Balaban 1206-1207
Gregorian Calendar
127
ILDENIZLILER (Azerbaijan Turkmen Atabegs)
450-560 Islamic Calendar 1097-1165 Gregorian Calendar
Semseddin Ilde'niz was originally a Gypjak. He was great man of science. Thanks to
his successful years as ability to educate Soltans from among his sons, he was held in
high esteem by all.
Ilde'niz was an Atabeg who gave great importance to teaching his students political
knowledge in state administration.
added Azerbaijan to his control and he enhanced his position in the region. Since his
son Muhammed was not current borders, he conquered the Iraqi Seljuk lands.
After Muhammet, his brother Kizil Arslan, "the emir of emirs," became the new ruler.
However he was killed the independence of his lands. His two relatives who then
declared themselves rulers after his death were also arrogance.
SALYR TurkmenS (The Persian Turkmen Atabegs) 543-686 Islamic 1148-1287
Gregorian
After emigrating to Horasan, Salyr, after many campaigns became a commander in
the army of Togrul Beg, Seljuk State. Togrul Beg appointed him as a commander in
his own army. In 1148 (543) Sungur b. Mevdud after conquering the Persian
province, enhanced the Salyrs rule there. This rule of Salyr atabegs lasted half a lost
the war
128
ncrainst HarezmShah Muhammed. (p.128) He handed over Istahr and Eshkevan to
HarezmShahs. As a man Ebubekir felt the forthcoming danger of the Moguls and sent
an ambassador to Ogedey Han to declare his dependence loyalty to the Han. The last
ruler from the lineage of Salyr was Abis Hatun, 11, Sa'd's daughter who was the the
death of Seljuk Shah. Abis
Hatun married Mengu Timur, the son of Hulagi. The worldrenowned
Poet Sadi was brought up in Atabeg Ebu Bekir's
palace.
543-686 Salyr Turkmens 1148-1287 (The Persian Atabegs)

543 Sungur 1148
557 Zenni 1162
571 Takla 1175
591 Sa'd 1195
623 Ebu Bekir 1226
658 Muhammet 1260
660 Muhammet Shah 1262
660 Seljuk Shah 1262
662-686 Abis Hatun 1263-1287
129

LURYSTAN (HAZARASP) TurkmenS

The founder and the commander of this Soltanate was Ebu Tahir Atabeg. Ebu Tahir with the Salyr Turkmens the Great Lurystan in 1148 (543). The areas under Ebu Tahir's rule expanded rapidly, after he had captured Huzistan, offered to him by the Mogul Han. Ebu Tahir later took Isfahan, after the death of Afrasyyap I Argu. However, this after a short while. This small state lasted till 1339 (740) and its capital was Idaj. Some historians also noted 11 took Suster, Huweyza and Basra under his domination. Another family of these Atabegs ruled over Small end of the 12th century to the beginning of the 16th century.

543-740 Lurystan (Hazarasp) Atabegs 1148-1339
543 Ebu Tahir bin Muhammed 1118
circa 600 Nasreddin Hazarasp circa 1203
circa 650 Takla circa 1252
circa 657 Semseddin Alp Argu circa 1259
circa 673 Yusuf Shah I circa 1274
circa 687 Afrasyap 1 1288
696 Nasreddin Ahmed 1296
733 Rukneddin Yusuf Shah 1333
740 Muzaffereddin afrasyap 11 1339
756 Semseddin Hushen (or Nuraliverdi) 1355
circa 780 Ahmed circa 1387
circa 815 Ebu Seyit 1408
circa 820 Huseyin circa 1417
827 Giyaseddin 1423
130

KONEURGENJ T(JRKMENS (HAREZMSHAHS)

470-628 Islamic calendar 1077-1231 Gregorian

The HarzemShahs were the descendants of Anuitegin, who was first employed as a servant by Bilge Tegin a member of the palace staff during MelikShah's reign. As a result of his services to MelikShah and the state, governor to Harezm. Among his descendants, the first person to declare his independence was Atsyz, whose the Soltan Sanjar in 1338 (533). However, he was punished for it and driven off from Koneurgenj. After his granted forgiveness, he was re-assigned to his former position. He gained his full independence in 1156 and up to Jend along the river of Seyhun.
131

Later, Soltan Tekey included Horasan Rey and Isfahan into his land in 1193-1194 589-590). His son, Alaeddin fought fierce battles with the Gurlu Turkmens in Horasan and in consequence conquered a great majority of and also took Buhara and

Samarkand later. After campaigns on the land of Gur Han of Garahytay, he took the fought bloody battles against Jengis Han but was defeated and later took refuge and died on an island in the (617).

His son, Jelaleddin, continued his resistance against the Mongol expansion and proved himself a hero unprecedented was the first to defeat the Mongols who had been invincible until then. However, internal conflicts within his prevented him from reaching his goals. After his stay for two years in India and many interesting adventures established his sovereignty in Azarbayjan from 1225-123 1. There are many commentaries about his ultimate which says he was killed by a Kurdish person. Though the HarezmShah state once stretched to the same borders that of the Great Seljujks, it did not survive.

470-628 HAREZMSAHS 1077-1231

circa 470 Anustegin circa 1077

490 Kutbeddin Muhammet 1097

522 Atsiz 1128

551 11-Arslan 1156

568 Soltan Mahmyt (+589) 1172

132

568 Tekes 1172

596 Alaeddin Muhammet 1200

617-628 Jelaleddin Mengubirdi 1220-1231

133

GUTLUG HAN TurkmenS (In Kirman)

619-703 1222-1303

Barak Hacip, who was one of the servants of Alaeddin of Koneurgenj (HarezmShah), declared his rule in Kirman They came from Garahytays and established their rule just after Jengiz Han attacked Koneurgenj. The Mogul acknowledged Barak's rulership and gave him the title of Gutlug Han. Thereafter, Gutlug leaders always remained

Moguls. Two of the leaders married Mogul wives, and the daughter of the last ruler married Muhammed, the Muzaffars in Iran.

619-703 Gutlug Han Turkmens (In Kirman) 1222-1303

619 Barak Hacip Kutlug Han

1222

632 Rukneddin Hojatilhak 1235

650 Kutbeddin Muhammet 1252

655 Kutlug Hatun

(Kutbeddin Muhammet's widow) 1257

681 Jelaleddin Suyurgatmis 1282

693 Safveddin Soltan-Hatun 1293

694 Jelaleddin Muhammet 1295

701-703 Kutbeddin Sah Jihan 1301-1303

134

135

THE HEIRS of the GREAT SELJUK TurkmenS in the WEST

14th - 19th Centuries

It is widely known that the atabegs and the principalities after the demise of the Great Seljuks Soltanate ruled Iran to Mesopotamia and Syria. As they were unable to establish very powerful sovereignties or Soltanates they by the Monguls and later helped produce the Ottoman dynasty, which would become the inheritors. to the Seljuks.

Togrul Beg, Alp Arslan and MelikShah were the rulers of a powerful state. After MelikShah's death, his sons,

136

Berkyaryk and Muhammed Tapar, started disputes and clashes between them, and that led to the establishment of the new small states. Only during the reign of Soltan Sanjar did the state manage to reorganize itself and to and vitality till his death. Soltan Sanjar's reign remained limited to Horasan. However, other Seljuks states continued existence in Kirman, Irak, Syria and Anatolia as independent states.

The Ottoman Empire

(The Ottoman Turkmen's State in Turkey)

Islamic Calendar 699 Gregorian 1299

Next

In 1299 Osman Ghazi founded the Ottoman State, which lasted 622 years, during which 36 Soltans reigned. He was born in 1258, the third son of ErTogrul Ghazy, who was one of the Turkmen Begs (principals). Due to external, hostile pressures, the Turkmens who settled in Sogut, Anatolia, in 1277 asked for help from ErTogrul Ghazi, who lived in their homeland, Horasan. As a result of meetings held in Merw, ErTogrul Ghazi decided to go to Anatolia and to support Turkmens there with his 400 horsemen. These 400 horsemen were composed of the atabegs and the cavalry who had completed their fighting and commanding training with flying colors and who were able to fullfill the will of Oguz Han, who had said, "Each and every Turkmen soldier is equal to one thousand enemies."

Osman Ghazi was one of the atabegs who received training in fighting and commanding and would establish a very powerful state in Turkey after 20 years.

137

GARAGOYUNLY TurkmenS

Islamic calendar 780-874 Gregorian 1378-1469

The Turkmen clans and tribes, which carried the name of Garagoyunly up to the end of 14th century, were named after their flags which had a figure of a black sheep. The Garagoyunly Turkmens captured the land from the Van Lake, in the eastern part, to the western part of Turkey. They established a Hanate which included Armenia and Azarbaycan in its territory by concluding an agreement with Soltan Huseyin.

Garayusuf, the second ruler of the Garago'unlys, was defeated and expelled by Timur (Tamerlane) a couple of times but he managed to return. After the death of Timur, Garayusuf recaptured in 1405 (807) all the lands he had formerly ruled. He took the Jelayirs under his rule in 141 1. However, in 1469 (874) the Garagoyunly Turkmens accepted the rule and sovereignty of the Akgoyunly Turkmens, whose leader was then Uzun Hasan.

780-874 Garagoyunly Turkmens 1378-1469

780 Gara Muhammet 1378

circa 790 Gara Yusup circa 1388

802 Timur's Decline 1400

808 Gara Yusup (conflict) 1405

823 Isgender 1420

841 Jahanshah 1437

872-874 Hasan Ali 1647-1469
THE AKGOYUNLY TURKMENS
Islamic calendar 780-908
Gregorian 1378-1502

The Akgoyunly (Whitesheep) Turkmens captured the land of their rivals, the Garagoyunly Turkmens in Diyarbakir and Azarbayjan. Their reign lasted only 30 years, because Shah Ismail, the Safavid ruler, defeated the Akgo'unlys in a battle in 1502 (907) and ended their rule.

Islamic Calender Gregorian
Calender
780- 908 The Akgo'unly Turkmens 1378-1502
780 Gara yilik Osman 1378
809 Hemze 1406
848 Jahangir 1444
871 Uzyn Hasan 1466
883 Halyl 1478
884 Yakup 1479
896 Baysunkar 1490
897 Ristem 1491
902 Ahmet 1496
903 Myrat 1497
905 Elwent 1499
906 Muhammet 1500
907-908 Myrat (conflict) 1501-1502

GAZNALY TCJRKMENS
(the Gaznalys in Afganistan and Punjab)
Islamic calendar 351-582 Gregorian 962-1186

Gaznaly Mahmyt, who was the son of Sebuktegin of the Gaya Boyu (tribe) of the Turkmens, was one of the great rulers in Islamic history. He accomplished great services for Islam in spreading and protecting Islam. Gaznaly Mahmyt

first defeated his own brother, who had risen against him, and he brought Eciz Hukumdar of the Samanids under his rule. He got the Abbasid Caliph in Baghdat to acknowledge his rulership of Horasan and Gazna and to declare by written decree that the Caliph himself was no longer the sovereign in those regions.

Gaznaly Mahmyt made an agreement with the Ilek Han and the weakened Samanids and thus made joint military expeditions with that powerful army to India. He entered India seventeen times between the years 1001 and 1026. He expanded his borders, captured well beyond Kashmir and Punjab, and added Kanuj and Mutturun in 1018, and Anhalwar - the capital of Gujarat - and Somnat into his lands in 1024 (415). With all these campaigns, he not only became rich but also aimed to eliminate robbery, pillage, injustice and idolworshipping.

He was renowned as the 'idol-bringer down'and returned to his land with wealth and treasure accumulated from those temples. The effect of these expeditions on India was enormous: Punjab completely submitted to his rule and Gujarat conceded the amount of the tax to be paid to Mahmyt. Apart from in India, he also ran military campaigns against Ilek Han and his land, and captured Gur in 1010, Murgap in 1012, and Samarkand and Buhara in 1016. Towards the last years of his reign, he realized that Togrul and Cagry Begs, whom he had protected, were starting to become a threat to him. Togrul and Cagry Begs remained loyal to and dependent on the Gaznaly State till 1027 (418). After the death of Mahmyt, their names become heard louder and more frequently.

Mahmyt's interest in science, literature and art and his patronage of scholars and scientists were no less than his statesmanship and commandership. He hosted and protected poets, such as

Firdewsi, in his palace. His land, particularly the city Gazna, was far ahead and superior to others with respect to its mansions, mosques, water canalets, ygation networks and facilities needed for health and social life.

His land stretched from Lahore to Samarkand and to Isfahan. However, within a short period he started to lose the provinces in the North. A few years later, in 1040 during the battle of Daidanakan near Merw, Mahmyt's son Masud was defeated by the Seljuk Turkmens and in consquence, their sovereignty and ownership of Horasan came to an end.

Islamic Calender Gregorian Calender
351-582 Gaznaly Turkmens 962-1186
351 Alp Ruler 962
352 Yshak 963
355 Bilge Ruler 966
362 Piri 972
366 Sbbik Ruler 977
387 Ysmay' YI 997
388 Mahmyt (yemineddiwle) 998
421 Muhammet (Jelaleddiwle) 1030
421 Masut I (Nasreddin-Ala) 1030
432 Maudud (yyhabaddiwle) 1041
440 Aly Abul-Hasan (Behaaddbwle) 1049
444 Togrul 1053
444 Farruhzat (Jemalladdiwle) 1053
451 Ybrayym (Zahyraddiwle) 1059
492 Masut iI (Alaaddiwle) 1099
508 yirzat (Kemaleddiwle) 1114
509 Arslan (Soltaneddiwle) 1115
142
1
511 Bihrem Shah (Yemineddiwle) 1118
547 Hysrow Shah (Muyzzeddiwle) 1152
555-582 Hysrow Mdlik (Tdqeddiwle) 1160-1186
THE GURS - THE GURLY TurkmenS
(in Afganistan and India)
Islamic calendar 543-612 Gregorian 1148- 1215
There had always been a few independent Hanates in the province of Ur, a mountainous place between Herat and Gazna. The Gur Turkmens had abode in the citadel of Firuzkuh. Gaznaly Mahmyt captured this city in 1010 (401). It was Muhammed Suri who was ruling there at that time. Suri's grandfathers were

ruling over Firushuh and Bamiyan when the Gaznalys reign was at its most powerful. The Gaznalys and Gurs also inter-married. However, Kutbettin Muhammed of the Gurs killed his own father-in-law at the
143
behest of the Gaznalys. Upon this, Suri's brother conquered Gazna in 1148 to take revenge for what happened. A year later Behram Shah recaptured the city and tortured Seyfettin Suri to death. This ruthless act perpetrated for the second time against their family strengtheed the will for revenge in Aleaddin Huseyin, the brother of Seyfetin Suri. Aleaddin attacked Gazna, set fire to it and put all to death by the sword. For this reason he is known as, "the man who set the world on fire." He left Gazna in ruins in utter disgust and hatred for Gur. Aleaddin died in Gur in 1161 shortly after he was taken captive by the Seljuks Soltan Sanjar. Around this time, the Turkmens-Guzs (Oguzs) took Afghanistan and eventually destroyed the states of Gur and Gazna.

Within the last two hundred years the Turkmens have been accused of being robbers, raiders, and pillagers, and from the 1930's this was changed to invaders. These are only the accusations of those who wish to raid and invade the Turkmen land and of those who cannot find any other excuse to do so. My High and Beloved People, we should learn to take lessons, to draw morals, from the past. For this to be so, the Ruhnama in your hand will support you!
My respected people!
The historical road of the Turkmen Nation is one of glory and difficulty. This road is the one which has led us to independence and enthused us -Or the Golden Century of the Turkmen. I have briefly drawn your attention to the history of our ancestors. We should learn about our past and the states established in the past very well. History is for us the most valuable school of experience. And, what falls to us is the duty to learn our sublime historical values and to protect
our moral values.
146

The Third Section
Turkmen NATION

My Beloved Turkmen People!
My Dear Turkmen Nation!
Living as a nation is a great pleasure. The most important condition of being a distinct nation is to be -an independent country. Turkmens have yearned to become an indivisible nation for the last seven or eight centuries. Becoming an independent nation gave us the opportunity to attain the centuries-old aspiration of Turkmens. Since the Turkmens attained this independent and neutral nationhood, it has become necessary to write this book in order to review our heritage, which comes from the Prophet Noah, and to support our life in the golden century, golden spirit and golden life.

In 1889, stone tablets and epitaphs, on which there were ancient writings, were discovered on the shores of the Orhon River in Siberia. The scholars studied them and concluded in the year 1893 that the script used in these epitaphs was the old Turkmen alphabet and the texts were written in the old Turkmen Ian uage. Thus, through these studies we came to know the old Turkmen alphabet that is composed of 38 letters. There is a sentence in the epitaphs: "Oh Oguz Rulers! Halt and listen! Who can disturb your tradition and your country unless Allah annihilates us or the earth splits?" This indicates the continuance of the Oguz, that is the Turkmens, and emphasizes our wish to be and remain independent. The saying "as written on stone" illustrates this fact much better.

I have thought over my past many times. I have thought a great deal about writing this book, Ruhnama. Every time it was as if the souls of

Oguz Han, Gorkut Ata and Gbrogly were appealing to me. The soul of Oguz Han said:

"Write! The place where your nation came into existence will be the route; the place which your nation favors will be the territory; the wishes of your nation will be realized."

The soul of Gorkut Ata said:

"Write! The things that the nation favors, and the things that are written on the fate, mind, and heart of the nation are sacred."

The soul of Girogly said:

"The nation that travels a straight road is happy. The happiness of the nation is the basis of the brave preservation of the country and the territory. Today, the happiness of your nation is in your hands. Saparmyrat, show the way of the golden life to the Turkmen nation. This will be your task; this will be your way."

The soul of our father Magtymguly said:

Souls and hearts beat together,
The army marches, soil and stone dissolve.
If the food is prepared and served at one table,
The future of Turkmen is bright and prosperous.

My guiding souls, my father and my mother, said:

"Allah selected the four heroes of the Turkmens -Oguz Han, Gorkut Ata, Girogly and Magtymguly- as the inheritors of the prophets. Today, Allah the Great has designated you as their inheritor. Son, devote your life to maintaining the unity of the Turkmen nation and to sustaining the golden life for them."

Every human lives with hopes and desires.

Iwant Turkmens to live the golden life, in the golden spirit, with pride and unity.

Iwant you to live with the qualities of unity, cooperation, charity, and high moral values.

Ihave prepared Ruhnama for the Turkmen nation to be a light and a guide on its journey towards its goal.

All Turkmens, not wasting the breath bestowed by Allah, should devote their energy, effort, and capabilities to their nation and their country in order to provide our nation with a life of well-being. Then, there will be no target that cannot be reached, and no task that cannot be accomplished.

Sometimes, I wonder whether I feel too proud of my nation, or whether my eyes are dazzled by the light of the word "Turkmen," or whether I am enchanted by the magic of the word "Turkmen." However, so far human beings have never been damaged by affection. Nobody has ever been injured by his or her love of the nation. Be afraid of those who do not love their nation. If everybody likes their own nation, then the nations will like each other Those who do not like their own nations cannot like other nations. The word "Turkmen," lies in my bosom like a beloved baby warmed by the heat of my heart.

In this word can be seen the proper pride of a people who have been driving their horses on at full speed for five

hundred years, as well as their natural modesty and the warmth of their hearts.

This word, like an enchanted meal, gathered our people around itself and made us friends, united us and, thanks to this word, we became a whole.

Turkmen, the name of our nation.

Our fathers consecrated this word as a flag and they fought bravely against its greatest enemies. This word was an inseparable comrade to them even when they fell, a spear lodged in their breasts.

Feelings of duty and responsibility and action underlie the love of the nation.

Our nation prevented deviations from unity and collaboration even in severe conditions by the saying, "Do not leave your nation even if you are killed." One feels sorrow for the peoples of the world who have not yet achieved nationhood; and one feels twice that sorrow for those who leave the path of the nation and consider this great idea, the nation, to be merely the detritus of history.

Our nation is the greatest source of pride to us! We live to fulfill our due to this great word; even if we die, we desire to die as Turkmens.

If you live a wretched and dissolute life, whether near or far away, they do not say, "That man is like that," but they say, "That nation is like that."

If you live an honorable and excellent life, whether near or far away, they say, "That man is Turkmen! They are the nation that directed the course of history."

Turkmens! The mud thrown at you is also thrown at me; and my cleanness, my brightness is also yours.

Turkmens! All my love is for you; all the pain is for me.

Sometimes I become extremely downcast, thinking, "If the savage army of Genghis Han had not annihilated the Oguz inhabiting the regions of Kineirgenq Maruyahujahan (Merw), yihrislam, Abywerd, Amul, Zem, Dehistan, and their prosperous towns with great populations; if the libraries with thousands of books, the "homes of science" had not been destroyed and bumt, then now, Turkmenistan would be one of the most prominent and strongest states in the world in its politics, its economy, its civilization and science.

The Turkmen nation has been able to survive the ruthless cruelties and destruction of Alexander the Great, Genghis Han, Tey'mir Agsak (Tamurlane) and other invaders and managed to transmit its sacred values, name, honor, traditions and civilization, the legacies of Oguz Han, to the glorious days of the contemporary era.

Our great Turkmen nation overcame those terrible disasters and troubles by the guidance of the word "Turkmen." Being Turkmen has saved the nation from the fire.

Thus, how can I not be proud of my beloved nation?

My Beloved Turkmen Nation!

Your origin lies in Oguz Han. Twenty-four tribes, forty families constitute the essence of the Turkmen nation. In the course of history, some of these tribes have dispersed across the world and preserved their national self-awareness by means of forming new groups. However, today, when Turkmenistan has become an independent state, tribal relations are detrimental to the unity of the Turkmen nation. My

beloved Turkmen nation, it is on this issue that I am addressing you now.

The Turkmen nation has been reborn as a whole. To have an independent and impartial state is only possible by the unity and indivisibility of the nation.

The idea of tribe is temporary; it constitutes a lower stage in the progress towards national integrity. In the modem era, this idea causes the integrity of the nation to degenerate. Let us give up the idea of tribe from now on. Debates on tribes should be things of the past; each Turkmen should make an effort not to turn to tribal debates. All the Turkmens are brothers.

Beloved people, the one who will carry the Turkmen to the future is the Turkmen himself. Today, there are more than 22 million Turkmens in the world, and there are 5,500,000 Turkmens living in our independent and impartial country. I especially want to make clear here that there are people living in our territory from more than forty different nations; they are living in peace, happiness and unity with the Turkmens. They cooperate with the Turkmens and work in different fields of production. Uzbeks constitute two percent of our population and Russians constitute one percent. Five percent of our population is comprised of various other nations.

The Turkmen sees other nations as his own brothers, his own friends. Racism cannot find a place among Turkmens. Turkmens respect the languages, the religions and the traditions of other nations. The rights and responsibilities of all citizens living in Turkmenistan are equal before the law of the Turkmen state.

152

There are sacred values and wonders which have been wrought by the Turkmen nation in the course of our long history.

The dining table is assumed to be holy by the Turkmen nation. The dining table is the sign of unity and it gathers the Turkmens around itself. The dining table is the pledge of the Turkmen. When the Turkmens are asked, "Who is Han?" they answer, "The dining table."

Turkmens gather with their brothers, friends and relatives around a dining table. When a Turkmen wants to marry a girl, he takes a bundle with a loaf of bread to the girl's family. If her family accepts the boy as a son-in-law, then they take the bread from the bundle and send it back with a new loaf.

There is a belief among the Turkmens that when they go on a short or long journey they should take a piece of bread with them; that bread becomes a comrade to them and brings them safely home again.

Today, we have attained the understanding, the comprehension, and the unity that Gorkut Ata desired.

Today, we have reached the state and statehood that Girogly Beg desired.

Today, we have reached the unity, the integrity and the collaboration that our Father Magtymguly desired.

Today, Tirkmens have gathered around a dining table within the independent state. We Turkmens have reached the desires of our ancestors.

Turkmens, know the value of this destiny. Turkmens, trust in Allah and preserve these days.

153

I have borne many difficulties throughout my life. I grew up feeling the absence of my father, who struggled and died for the sake of the homeland; I have always felt honored by the name of my father. A sudden and terrible earthquake destroyed our home and separated me from my brothers, who were like my eyes, and my mother, who was my guide in life. Just as Girogly came into the light of this world from the grave, I also came to this world from the ruins.

When I see my father's contemporaries, I remember my father and live the feeling of captivity; when I see the contemporaries of my mother, I remember my mother and live the feeling of orphanhood. I have lived the meaning of the saying, "Captive without father and orphan without mother," and known Allah, the Supreme, as my sole protector.

When I learnt to read and write, I realized that my homeland was a captive and an orphan like me. I have lived in the bright world of the Creator along with my sorrows stemming from this reality throughout my life. Eventually, I began to search for the souls of my ancestors through the pages of books as a captive searches for the homeland or as an orphan searches for his close relatives.

Thus, when I was just a small child, 1 leamt who the Turkmen is and what the homeland is. I have consoled myself with the epigram, which is firstly recorded in my heart and then in my diary, "The one who bears the sufferings of the world earlier can understand the realities of the world earlier." In the course of time, I have realized that those injuries which were done to my heart have been removed.

i In the Turkmen version of the epic of Karolin, it is explained that Gi5rogly came from the grave where his mother had been buried. Gir means grave and the name of Gbrogly derives from this root.

I understood the nature of human beings earlier. On the one side, there was the man who was pleasant and cheerful. I considered this man good and was pleased with his words. On the other side, there was the man who was bad-tempered and angry. The words of this man were like poisoned arrows to me. When I attempted to beat them, my hands refused to do it; when I attempted to swear at them, my tongue refused to do it. So the only thing that I could do was to digest those words which were like poisoned arrows.

Girogly has opened new horizons in my life; there was justice in his world. I have understood that there can be nothing greater than justice.

Iwas separated from my homeland, which I love very much, when I began to study in

Leningrad. By going to the libraries there, I immersed myself in the depths of history so that I felt as if I was at the heart of my homeland. During my education in Leningrad, I learnt the five thousand year history of my people by reading every single line about it.

When you go for a long journey, your mother prepares your food. 1, however, have no mother, so I took the word "Turkmen" in place of food.

When you go for a long journey, your father sends you with his blessings; 1, however, have no father, so I have taken the blessings of my homeland on my journey.

When I considered my situation, I understood that I was not an orphan! How can someone be an orphan if he has a father like Oguz Han, a teacher like Gorkut Ata, an elder brother like Girogly, an adviser like Magtymguly?

The rise of the Turkmen commanders Togrul and qagry Begs annoyed the Soltan of the Turkmens, Gaznaly Mahmyt,

156

who had conquered huge territories in the East and West, including India. He called one of the Hans of the Seljuk Turkmens in order to learn about them. Ysra'yl Han started out towards the headquarters of the Soltan with ten thousand riders. The Soltan immediately sent a message to the Han and indicated that he had not summoned support but was only calling the Han to meet. Then Ysrayyl came to the meeting with three hundred of his riders. The Soltan cheerfully welcomed him and then asked:

"If we needed military support, how many soldiers would you send us?"

Ysrayyl took an arrow from his quiver and said:

"If you send this arrow, then an army consisting of thirty thousand soldiers will come from the Balkans."

"If we needed more than that?"

"Then, if you send this arrow, ten thousand more riders will also come."

"If we needed many more than that?"

"If you send this arrow towards the Balkan Mountains, then an army of a hundred thousand soldiers will come."

"Yes, but if we needed a greater force than that?"

Then Ysrayyl gave another arrow and said:

"If you send this to Turkmenistan, then an army of five hundred thousand soldiers will come."

Only a commander of a Turkmen tribe was capable of forming an army of five hundred thousand soldiers. This was a great army. Think how great was a nation which could form such a huge army.

157

The Gijrogly Era, the third era in Turkmen history, was the era when the world heard the reputation of the Turkmen nation.

By means of preserving its national characteristics, after many years the Turkmen nation has succeeded to great spiritual power. By building upon this historical foundation and the experiences of the past, we have managed to establish stability and well-being in our country in the transition period. Within a short period of time, the regulations and constitution of the organization of the national state have been prepared and implemented; the required background for our foreign relations has been achieved.

Our state structure is harmonious with our national characteristics, the traditions of the Turkmen people, and the "Universal Declaration of Human Rights" of the United Nations. In all of our policies we consider the national interests of Turkmenistan on the one hand and the stability of the region and the strengthening of international security on the other. We always see that all of these are indivisible realities.

We have huge resources. We want to draw maximum benefit and maximum utility from them. Thus, we are ready for relations which rest upon reciprocity, equality and cooperation. Destiny has bestowed on Turkmenistan the opportunity to be at the center of international relations between Europe and Asia. Our underground and surface resources are evidence of the possibility of a golden life for the Turkmens in the golden century.

In the past our ancestors presented themselves to the world by the strength of their swords; now, we should present ourselves with our rationality and with our immense spiritual values. Turkmenistan is known for its unique Ahalteke

158

horses, for its carpets that are examples of the wonders of the world's art, and for its limitless wonders of nature. Today, in its peaceful policies, the Turkmen nation displays endeavors worthy of recognition by the world. As our great thinker Magtymguly Pyragy once said, "Look at your future, do not forget your past, utter polite speech, restrain your anger. If you are able to speak, please say pleasant things; the public has suffered much from bad things." I can see happy days in the future. I believe that nothing is able to damage our happiness today and in the future and I am always proud of our statute of impartiality.

Independence has changed the fate of the Turkmen nation completely and has brought it to the point of perfection because the nation state is the clear evidence that idea of the existence of the nation is not only an imagining or a sweet desire. A nation is constructed only by the existence of a nation state. Thus, being a nation is different from being a people. A people is a community whose future is uncertain because it is deprived of the state which implements the values of the people in real life by means of a political movement. Since the future of that community is uncertain, this means that it is possible for that people either to survive or to disappear. There is only one way to sustain the existence of a people and that is to become a nation. To be a nation means to have a nation state.

Looking at history we can see that nation-building among Turkmens is not just a recent process. The historical fate of this nation is very complex; it does not only include progress and development, but also includes decline and underdevelopment. Marxism defines history as linear and only records forward progress. According to its understanding, firstly tribes emerge, then these tribes transform into peoples and these peoples

transform into nations. However, history shows us that fall and rise are different sides of reality. The life and the national history of the Turkmens display many such two-sided developments. There have been different periods when the various Turkmen tribes transformed into a unified nation and others when a unified Turkmen nation divided into tribes again. Thus, today it is necessary for us to embrace the idea of the new Turkmen nation, and this is appropriate to the objectives of our nation.

We are right to be extremely proud of our new Turkmen nation and our national state.

As we are proud of the beautiful buildings and infrastructure being constructed in our homeland, we should succeed in seeing the "beautiful buildings" being built in the inner world and hearts of our people. The most beautiful buildings should be established in our hearts and souls, rather than in our cities and villages. A certain amount of understanding is needed to see them. As our Father Magtymguly said, it is necessary to acquire wisdom to see them.

Ruhnama is a new worldview in the sense that it is a spirit that stimulates nature, society, and people to work. Without a spirit, it is impossible to speak of life; spirit is the source of life.

Nation is the transformation of human groups in the context of certain spiritual foundations. A nation is shaped materially according to these spiritual foundations. The reason for my frequent repetition that Oguz Han is the father of our nation is that Oguz Han has provided a political and national identity to the Turkmens. By means of his efforts,

160

the foundations of the Turkmens, who are one of the first nations of the world, were built upon. This gives us the following lesson: nation begins with the spirit and its material form, civilization; thus, spiritual integrity is needed for a people to transfonn into a nation.

Spirit is like the 'bismillah', the starting point of life. The starting point of everything is spirit. Life gradually disappears when the spiritual order weakens. If it is assumed that the world is the body, then the spirit is the life of that body.

As is understood from the Oghuznamas, the personality of Oguz Han matured very early. After maturing, he crossed his father. The area of conflict between them was the new attitudes that would shape their society. The basic difference between them stemmed from Oguz Han's conversion away from his father's religion. He believed in a monotheistic religion while his father believed in a polytheistic one. We feel the echoes of historical changes in these events.

Isay that the ancestor of the Turkmen nation is Oguz Han because, when Oguz Han is spoken of, the first things that come to mind are belief in one God, spirit and moral values. Furthermore, I want to emphasize an important point here: the main underlying reasons for the successes, campaigns, and developments of the five thousand year history of the Turkmen nation, founded by Oguz Han, are belief, spirit and moral values. Belief in only one God provided the Turkmen nation with the power to explain all the forces of mind, reason, and heart inherent in its very nature.

The greatest rivers rise from the accumulation of the smaller water sources flowing from the slopes of the mountains.

161

Even the largest forests are formed by the cracking of very small seeds.

However, rivers do not drink their own water.

Gardens do not eat their own fruits.

So, the main reason for the creation of the spirit is to constitute the source of life and to be perfected.

Among the first things that Oguz Han implemented were the use of the national Oguz alphabet and the wagon for during military campaigns. These were fundamental to other inventions which would contribute to various developments at a world level.

The ox-cart with two wooden wheels, which was invented by the leader of the tribe of Ka'nly, was the second important contribution of Turkmens to world civilization.

The Fourth Section
THE STATE OF Turkmen

THE ANCIENT OGUZ STATE

My beloved Turkmen!

In the course of the development of humanity, many nations and countries have made momentous contributions to the world community. China and India achieved enormous advances. These advances also happened among the Oguzs or Turkmens. World History, however, offers insufficient information about the progress made by Turkmens. Great efforts are being made to retrieve what has faded of Great Turkmen history. There is not infrequent distortion of the history of the Oguz who, ever since the period of Oguz Han, have left significant historical traces in the destiny, politics, economics and culture of Asia and Europe by founding many great states in the world. Sooner or later, however, time will put all things in their proper place.

The achievements of the Oguzs between the lslt and the

13th centuries cannot be denied. It is an undeniable truth that the Parfi'a State, the Gaznalys, the Seljuks, and the Kinetirgenqs affected the historical and political development of the world and reached a high level of accomplishment in the cultural and economic realms. But because some historians were Arab and Iranian in origin, they tried to connect all of these historical advances with Iran, or with the Arabs and later generalized them as Turkish... Our historians, brought up in the Soviet era, did not perceive the evil intentions of those historians writing without proper scrutiny

209

of their work, and simply repeated their views. They did not realize that these ideas form part of an invading country's imperialist purpose.

When I read and examined the history books, I realized that the word 'Turkmen' has been replaced by the word 'Tirk'for more than 50 years. In Ruhnama, however, I make the word 'Turkmen' regain its real meaning in order that today's Turkmens come to know their ancestors and became vigorous with their spirit. May God help us!

On the day I declared our independence, I stated that Turkmenistan and Tirkiye (Turkey) are two states, and one nation. For Oguz means Turkmen in one sense. The Oguz language is the Turkmen language. The language of the Seljuks and the Ottoman language is also the Turkmen language. Contemporary Anatolian Turkish differs little from Turkmen. Our religion, culture and lineage are identical. We Turkmens are proud of this and expect the same from our Turkish brothers.

5000 years have passed since the foundation of the first Turkmen state. This is proved by the arrowheads, arches and other remnants excavated in Bagabat, Altyndepe, Tdkgala, the Ary Region, Margiyana and Kineirgenq, which have yielded significant information about the Oguz civilization and state of that period. These lands under the rule of Oguz Han were known as the Oguz Homeland. We have accurate

16

information about this in the book Hududul-Alem, which was written in the

Medieval Period. Ancient sources tell us that the Oguz Homeland stretched from Altyntepe through ,&new, knew, Nusay', Tdkgala, the entire Merw, Kineirgenq

16 It means 'the boundaries of the Universe'.

and Caspian-Belh region, including Se'hun-Je'hun from y east to west up to the Idil Sea in the north. Belief in Gbk

17

Tairy was dominant amongst Oguzs. The word Gik refers to a feature of God: 'the Exalted'. This shows that Oguzs believed in one God. Their language was Oguzca, the ancient Turkmen language.

Oguz Han's lineage goes back in a chain to Hz. Nuh. The ancestors of the Tirkmens are the Kara Han. We have a noble lineage.

My Beloved Turkmen People! I have given vast amounts of information about the lineage of Oguz in 'The Turkmen Way'. Beloved Turkmen, I did this in order that you and your posterity should never forget your history again. Here, then, I want to quote some of the advice of Oguz Han for your good.

Oguz Han's advice about the land and homeland:

Whoever cultivates the land finds comfort.

The life of one who plants a tree becomes eternal.

He who does not love the soil does not love the homeland.

One who harms the land in the slightest degree is not a Tirk !man (Turkmen).

When you pluck a leaf, your life is curtailed by one year. If you crack a bough, you also break your arm or leg. If you uproot a sapling, you also destroy your life. By cutting down a tree you cut down the tree of your life.

17 The faith of ancient Turks, called the Sky God Belief.

18 The prophet Noah.

Do not buy gold; buy land.

Water is father; ground is mother

The soil is your body; the sky is your soul.

Even if your head touches the sky, respect the earth.

Oguz Han's advice about language:

The tongue tells what exists in the heart.

(If there is) no language, (there can be) no country.

A word is effectual if said by the heart.

Wisdom adorns the word.

The wealth of the language is the wealth of the country.

A wise man learns language.

One who knows more language, knows more.

The word of the generous is also wise.

When you set out, hold your tongue.

The language is the state.

A wise statement is eternal.

Teach your children the language with its meaning.

I have a language, so I have a world.

When the Oguzs are united, these signs are seen in them:

Their state becomes invincible, and they are blessed.

Wherever they go, they are victorious. They live on the

plateau in summer, and in winter quarters in winter. They

19 Nomads summer camping ground.

212

rule vast lands. They are ready to face dangers. They conquer and rule over the nations. They become very agile, active and eager to hunt. They are strong and powerful. They respect prohibitions. They are highly esteemed like old people. Their food is plentiful. They work honestly and are persevering. They are esteemed and their fame is widespread. Wherever they face the enemy, they go to war with them. They are both humanitarian and generous. Their livestock is well-fed. They set up good businesses. They are brave and lofty. Their advice is appropriate. They serve their elders. They are of high esteem.

When the 'golden arch'is found this happens: It illuminates your standard, shows the signs of the Seven Climates of the Earth. You become closer both to the Earth and Heaven. However, you will find your way by the 'Seven

2'

Stars. , Though you walk on earth, your way is to Heaven. Ease and tranquility is in your fortune, as you own the key. There are many differences between you and those who came before. Wherever you go, your way is open. All this is so because you have conquered the heart of the World.

The golden arch unites the top of three silver arrows and changes into abundance. You find the ancient waterfall and drink to repletion from the Oguz fountain. In order that you obtain the golden arch, the golden soul of the antecedent generations unifies in you. All the powers of the nation are united, and states are founded.

20 Great Polar bear star group, Big Dipper, Ursa major

213

OGUZ TORKMEN'S GREAT HUN STATE

2500 years after Oguz Han's state, there was another state founded with the same spirit and structure. One of the most omnipotent Hans of the Great Hun State was no doubt Mete Han. His name in Chinese sources is Mao-Tun. His origin was Oguz. Mete Han was also called Oguz Han because of his resemblance to his ancestor. In his reign, he ruled the country in a way very similar to that of Oguz Han. For this reason, there have emerged contradictory views about Mete Han and Oguz Han, some claiming they were the same person. Mete Han, however, was the Hakan who recognized the necessity of unifying the Oguz, Hun and all the Turkmen tribes and ensuring this unity by following the example of his ancestor Oguz, when he felt the state was threatened with complete collapse and ruin.

Mete Han's father was Duman Beg. In Chinese sources he is recorded as Teoman. About 220 B.C., Teoman expanded the borders of the state up to the edge of Chinese territory. After Teoman, Mete Han succeeded to the throne in 209 B.C.

Mete Han had whistling arrows manufactured and special factories built for the production of bows and arrows. Great Hun Han Mete brought 26 states under his rule and divided the administration into 84 provinces. He ruled over 18 million km2, land stretching from the Caspian Sea to the Indian Ocean on one side and from the Himalayas to Siberia on the other side. After Mete Han his son, Gik Han, took his place. Some of the letters written by Mete Han to the king of

China, Hiao-Wen, are preserved in the archives of China. Mete Han's ideas concerning peace, ease and security, mentioned in one of his letters sent to the Chinese king, are very interesting. In this letter he states the following:

214

"Great Hun Han enthroned by God sends his compliments and greetings to the Chinese ruler. Recently a letter concerning peace and our good relations was received from your exalted Person. This is the desire of both parties and the conditions mentioned in the letter have been fulfilled as is due.

In recent times, your frontier guards have disregarded Bati Han, Toki. On the other hand, provoked by Hu-Heu Nanchu and others, Toki has fought with Chinese guards without obtaining my consent. Thus the provisions of the treaty signed between two rulers have been violated and this has harmed our friendly relations. The Han made his country the enemy of the neighboring state. I received two letters full of rage from you. Our envoy, who was conveying our reply, has not yet returned. However, the Chinese envoy also might not return. This situation has caused an unintended eventuality between two neighboring countries.

It was the actions of some guards which violated the treaty. I gave an order to Toki Beg for the punishment of these men.

As our brave men are agile, our horses are strong and hardy, by the help of God, they won a victory in the battle against the instigators. Owing to the sharpness of our swords, we defeated the instigators and they surrendered. Recently we have taken under our rule a total of 26 tribes and countries in Central Asia, such as L6an, Usun, Hukut... The people of these countries have become subject to us and all their lands or countries have become our provinces.

After I secure peace and security in the northern countries, my intention is to rest the army and graze the horses. Leaving the things which have occurred between us behind,

215

I want to renew the old agreement. As in the earlier period, the people of the frontier tribes may live comfortably in peace. May the children grow up and elders live at their ease till the end of their lives. May peace and ease prevail for generations.

Since I have not received any information from the Chinese ruler for a long time, I am sending this letter with the vizier of the Palace, He-u-Tsiye. I am sending a camel, two saddle and eight carriage horses as a gift. If the Han doesn't want the Huns to violate the Chinese borders, he must order the people living along the frontier line and the frontier guards to stay at a distance from the border."

Because this letter exemplifies the policy of the Oguz State, when it had secured its unity for the first time, I give the text in its entirety.

GiK TURKMEN STATE

As a continuation of the Oguzs and the Great Hun State, the Gik Turkmen State was established by Bumyn Han in 552. It was demolished by the Uygurs and Garlyks in 745. The reign of Bilge Han was the most brilliant period of the state. Bilge Han was born in 683. His father was Ilteriy Gutlug Han. At the age of 33 he became the great ruler of the Gbk Turkmen State. Gik Ta'nry belief was prevalent in the country and the state took its name from this faith. The meaning of Gbk Turkmen is the Turkmen belief in the exalted God. Bilge Han declared his Oguz descent with a statement in the inscription on his tombstone: "The Oguz land is my own homeland."

The state had a vast territory neighboring the Sasanid, Roman and Chinese States.

As a consequence of internal turmoil, battles for the throne and declining power, the Gik Turkmen State collapsed in 630.

One of the well-known statements of Bilge Han was as follows: "O! Oguz Begs! Shudder and listen! Who can break down your country and traditions unless the blue sky above us tumbles down, the dark land below us cracks."

The power of the state lies in the unity and solidarity of the people who consecrate and protect their country and national values. Gik Turkmens had their own alphabet and they made notable advances in art.

GARAHANLY Turkmen STATE

The Garahanly state was founded in Turkmenistan and Maveraunnehir by Bilge Kil Kadyr Han in 840.

The state derives its name from the title of Kil Kadyr Han: the 'Garahan'. Garlyk, Jyky, and yagma tribes were dominant among the Garahanlys. The role of Islam was no doubt great in their growth.

After Kadyr Han, his sons Bazar Arslan and Ogulgak Han ruled the state. Saltuk Bugra, the son of Bazar Han was brought up by Ogulcak Han after the death of his father. When Saltuk Bugra became Muslim, Islam spread rapidly in Central Asia, especially in Turkmenistan.

When Saltuk Bugra Han died in 966, his son Baydai Arslan Han took his place and restored the state which was about to collapse. In 1006, Garahanlys took control of

Maveraunnehir, destroying the Samanly (Samanid) State. Subsequently, their struggle with the Gaznalys started. In 1042 the state was divided into two parts, East and West Garahanly, as they could not resist the power of the Gaznaly Soltan Mahmyt.

The Garahanly State has the distinction of being the first Turkmen state that accepted the religion of Islam.

GREAT OGUZ Turkmen STATE

This was the state founded by the Oguz tribes. In ancient Arab and Chinese sources, one comes across the word 'Yabgu'. yabgu (or yagby) is a title meaning 'Great'. Those tribes which founded the Oguz Yabgu State later established 'Nine Oguz Khanates alongside the Don River after the collapse of the Gaznaly State.

The most significant activity of the Oguzs was in Maveraunnehir at the beginning of the 10 h century. They called the state they founded on the territories they had inherited from their ancestors Oguz yabgu.

Retreating from Khorasan, the Chinese frontiers and the banks of the Idil river, they were squeezed into the land between the Seyhun

I

Garajyk, Sayran and Jent and Jeyhun Rivers. The yanykent, regions remained to them as a homeland.

The turmoil within the state in the middle of the 10th century and the rapid spread of Islam caused the collapse of the oguz yabgu State. Dukak, who was famous under the name Demir-yayly (the man with the iron-arch), fought with gUL YabSu. Later on his son, Seljuk, converted to Islam and broke away from oguz Yabgu.

218

219

The essential feature of the Oguz Yabgu State is that it strove to keep up the Oguz tradition. However, the rapid expansion of Islam caused the destruction of the state. Another important feature was that this state raised a shrewd and intelligent commander, Seljuk Beg.

The Seljuks were from the Kynyk tribe of the Oguzs and the lineage of Ayhan. They founded their mighty state in Jent.

Seljuk Dukak was a shrewd subasi[21]. Historians translated his name as 'the Man with the iron-arch' in different sources.

Expanding within the Maveraunnehir and Buhara regions, they lived near related clans and tribes who were living a settled life. They established good relations with the Kbneirgenqs and became friends of the Garahanlys.

The Seljuks were a brave and dauntless people who liked horses and rode them well. Otherwise, Gaznaly Mahmyt would not have invited them to Khorasan! Contrary to what many historians have claimed, Soltan Mahmyt's intention was not to do favors to Turkmens. Soltan Mahmyt was himself a Turkmen, as were the majority of his soldiers. Turkmens lived in the villages and cities in Khorasan. They dwelled especially in the Merw, Abywerd, Nusay, Sarahs, Amul, Balkan, Zem, Maveraunnehir, Mingyilak and Was regions.

Soltan Mahmyt had organized 18 military campaigns to India, and filled the treasury of the state with gold and silver. However, there now emerged a challenge to him and a threat to his state from his relatives, the Seljuks. Soltan Mahmyt's response was the wise strategy of having the Seljuks cross

21 The name of a rank in the military staff.

220

over the Jeyhun Sea and settle in Khorasan. This was a part of a policy known and implemented by many for thousands of years, 'Divide, Disintegrate and Rule'. The Seljuks migrated, but no-one would give them land or pasture. So, the Seljuks had to struggle for survival. Their struggle was against the settled Turkmens of Merw, Sarahs, Abywerd and Nusa'. In fact it was the Soltan himself who had invited the Seljuks but it was basically because the Seljuks were stronger and more vigorous than the settled Turkmens. The Soltan left the choice of land to the will of the Seljuks. These domestic conflicts were the harbingers of war. Thus Soltan Mahmyt would more easily organize his military campaigns to India because, he had sown the seeds of war among the Turkmens. On one occasion, to demonstrate his power in comparison with the Seljuks, Soltan Mahmyt called Arslan Han for a meeting and had him arrested and imprisoned in Kelejar fortress. Incidentally, the Seljuks did not fight amongst themselves over territorial claims. They challenged only the Turkmens in Khorasan and there existed no other option for the Seljuks at that time. Through all this, the Seljuks did not war with their relatives, the Turkmens, and chose to request a homeland officially from the Soltan himself. Soltan Mahmyt gave them a place. However the descendant of Soltan Mahmyt, his son Soltan Mesut, changed this policy. Relations between Seljuks and Soltan Mesut worsened continuously until Soltan Mesut sent a great army under the command of his pre-eminent commander Begdogdy. However, this talented commander was defeated by the Seljuks. In the battle, the Seljuks made use of the tactic called ' Strike and Retreat'.

After their victory in the Da'ndanakan War, the Seljuks

called a council. In the council they proclaimed the new Turkmen state and sent envoys to the Caliph and neighboring begs and Hans.

Seljuks increased their power still more by promising unity with the indigenous Turkmens. Consequently, they attained their ideal of ' World Domination'.

Because of ulterior motives, some historians accuse the Turkmens of barbarism, claiming that the Seljuks destroyed the Gaznaly state and the Kinetirgenq ended the Seljuk State. In fact, the Turkmens were peaceful, tolerant and conciliatory in character. Turkmens are highly tolerant. But they have never run away from war when faced with the injustices of surrounding Hans or Soltans. A Turkmen never swerves from his decision. He shows patience until the last moment, but he straps on his sword unhesitatingly in case the conditions become unbearable. Nothing can stop him after that point.

Soltan Mesut followed an unjust policy towards the Turkmens and attacked them three or four times. The Turkmens tried to bear this situation, but there was a limit to their patience.

The Seljuk Sultanate fell in Soltan Sanjar's period in the same way because of the implementation of an unjust policy like Soltan Mesut's. Relations between the Great Seljuks and the Turkmens around Belkh broke down. Soltan Sanj'ar refrained from warring with the Turkmens who were his relatives, though.

One may claim that Nizamylmilk ascended to the vizierate through trickery and shrewdness. He succeeded in sowing discord between Soltan Alp Arslan and the elderly vizier. The young Soltan ordered the old vizier's execution.

Before his death the old vizier said: You have taught the Turkmen Soltans to shed blood." In fact, the Turkmen Soltans believed that anyone who shed blood unjustly, distanced himself from Allah.

The last words of the old vizier were the best proof of this general attitude of Turkmen Soltans. In Turkmen Soltanates, and Khanates, the mothers and wives of the princes were shown great respect. They were called Tarhan (Terken, Tirkan) Hatyn... The wife and mother of the Soltan was respected as the mother of the entire Sultanate, though the Turkmen Soltans tried to restrain the interference of their mothers and wives in state affairs. Tijrkmens say: "Both the throne and fortune of the woman is her fireplace." Tirkan Hatyn, the widowed mother of Kineirgenq Soltan Alaeddin Muhammet, violated this sound principle. Tirkan Hatyn gained an equal say with her son in ruling the country. The begs and religious savants did not endorse her behavior. In the end, this great state could not resist the invasion of Jengiz Han and collapsed.

GAZNALY TCJRKMEN STATE

The founder of the Gaznaly State was the Khorasan governor, Alp Tegin, from the Gay (Kayi) tribe of Oguzs, who had earlier served the Samanids. He came to the city of Gazna in 962 and took it under his rule. The state took its name from this city. Although the territories of the state were extended by Sebik Tegin, the most splendid period of the state had been during the rule of Soltan Mahmyt.

In a short period, Gaznaly Soltan Mahmyt, having gained the support of the Oguz tribes, became a great power and endeavored to spread Islam in the neighboring coun-

tries. His main target was to expand his state and disseminate Islam. The borders of the state expanded to Khorasan, Harezm, Iraq, Belkh, South Iran and north India in a very short time.

For a certain period, he maintained friendly relations with Garahanly State. During that period, he could not come to an agreement with the sons of Seljuk. Furthermore he had Arslan Beg arrested and put into jail. However, he later authorized the migration and settlement of the Seljuks in Khorasan. Though he had disputes with Togrul and Cagry Begs, the grandsons of Seljuk Beg, he prevented fraternal quarrels amongst the Garahanlys. On this issue he said: "Stop your enmity towards each other. Put your swords in their sheaths. Everyone must concern himself with the province under his rule," and settled the disputes between

them. However, by his death, they had started struggling for the throne again. After Soltan Mesut ascended to the throne, the Seljuks settled in Khorasan became his main target. These two Oguz tribes could not share the land and fought first in 1038 near Tdkgala and later in 1040 near Sarahs on the Da'ndanakan Plain. This resulted in Soltan Mesut withdrawing with great losses and Khorasan, Iran, Kineijrgeng and Maveraunnehir passing to the control of the Seljuks. After this, the Gaznaly State faced great turmoil and finally became subject to the Seljuk State.

THE GREAT SELJUK Turkmen STATE

This State was founded in 1040 by Togrul and Qagry Begs after their victory in the Daildanakan War against the Gaznalys. The Seljuks are from the Kynyk tribe of Oguz.

The Seljuks underwent a very troubled period after arriving in Khorasan. When Seljuk Beg died, he was over 100 years old. In his old-age, leaving all else aside, he brought up his grandsons, Togrul and Qagry Begs. The son of Seljuk Beg, Arslan Han, settled on the Nur Plateau near Buhara, taking Togrul and Qagry Begs with himself. The sole aim of the two brothers trained by Seljuk Beg was to make Khorasan their homeland.

To attain their goal, Cagry Beg together with his brave men crossed over Khorasan to reach the Roman Land (Anatolia). The two brothers intention to conquer Khorasan intensified after the arrest and imprisonment of Arslan Beg by Gaznaly Mahmyt. After crossing the Jeyhun River in 1035, they settled near Tdkgala. They informed Soltan Mesut of their intentions in a letter. In it they demanded that Soltan Mesut grant them for settlement the Nusay and Paraw provinces, where they would put their animals out to pasture. They stated that they could suppress the insurrections likely to happen in the corridor from the Balkan Dagi, Dehistan, and Crgenq frontiers to the banks of the Je'hun River.

y

Soltan Mesut, who did not accept their offer, fought with the Seljuks near Tdkgala in 1038. Soon after, in 1040, there was another battle near Sarahs on the Da'ndanakan Plain. By way of war the Seljuks gained the things they had not been able to attain peacefully, and laid the foundations of the Great Seljuks State.

This victory made the fatherland their property forever. After the war, they summoned a council and declared their independence. Togrul Beg received the title of 'Soltan'. They made the city of Rey their capital (1040-1063). Cagry Beg
225
stayed in Merw (1040-1060). The two brothers ruled the state in unity and cooperation.

In 1063 Alp Arslan, the son of qagry Beg, ascended to the throne. Alp Arslan was the great Soltan who unlocked the gates of Anatolia. His son Mdlik yah expanded the borders of the Seljuks and his son Soltan Sanjar promoted improvements in science and civilization.

The Great Seljuk State promoted Islam along with the Oguz culture, and in this way they enlarged their frontiers from Istanbul to China. Furthen-nore, being a great state, the Seljuks were honored as being the guard of the entire Islamic World. In addition, intending to dominate the world, they treated the people under their rule equally and justly and made great progress in the realms of culture and civilization. They improved the whole country, building roads, bridges, caravanserai, small mosques, madrassas (schools, universities) and hospitals.

My beloved citizens! It is an important fact that great Turkmen heroes, Muhammet Togrul Beg, qagry Beg, Alp Arslan, Mdlik yah and Soltan Sanjar, succeeded in becoming the Soltans of the Islamic World with the states they established, their heroism, prudence, and policies. As the Turkmen Nation, we must study these great personalities. Oh Turkmens, be proud of your lineage!

KONEFJRGENC, Turkmen STATE

The Kineirgenq State was founded by Kutbeddin Muhammed of the Beydili tribe of Oguz in 1093. Kutbetddin Muhammet was the son of Anui Tegin, who was the governor of Kineirgenq in the Seljuks State. When the Seljuks
226
weakened, the Koneyrgeny State achieved full independence under the leadership of Atsyz. After Atsyz, his son 11 Arslan became the Soltan.

After the death of 11 Arslan, first his youngest son Soltan yah took his place in 1172, and then in 1174 Alaaddin Tekei ascended to the throne. In their era, the Kineirgenq made great advances. The Kinetirgenq State collapsed as a consequence of the Mongol invasion, which began in 1219. At that time, Jelaleddin Mefibumu'n (1220-123 1) was ruler of the country. He is known as a brave, valiant Soltan. The Kineirgenq State collapsed totally in 123 1.

KERMAN Turkmen SELJUK STATE

After the Da-ndanakan triumph of the Seljuks, the Kerman region was given to the Oguzs under the grandson of qagry Beg, Gara Arstan Gurda Beg. After taking power in

Ken-nan, Gurda Beg reigned for many years (1040-1073). ame fully independent in The Kerman Seljuks bec

Milikiah's period and their rule continued till 1187.

ANATOLIAN SELJUK Turkmen STATE

This state was established by Gutylmyiogly Sileyman iah in 1075 and endured till 1308.

One of the fundamental causes of the establishment of olian Seljuk State was the victory of Alp Arslan at the Anat ns who rushed in
Malazgi,7t in 1071. The Seljuk Ti-rkme GutylmYiOgly

through the gates of Anatolia gathered under ered Konya
Sileyman iah. Guty1myyogly Silleyman conqu
and, moving ahead, captured Iznik. 14e made Iznik his Capital. Later, Sileyman yah
conquered Tarsus, Adana, Mersin and Malatya and, by
1085, Antakya.
Gylyq Arslan became the second Soltan of the Anatolian Seljuk State. He is famous
for his great contribution to the settlement of Turkmens in Anatolia, the expansion
of Islam and the unification and strengthening of the Turkmen begs.

SYRIAN SELJUK TIORKMEN STATE

Tutus, the son of Soltan Alp Arslan was appointed to Damascus as Melik. The semi
autonomous Syrian Seljuks were dependent on the Great Seljuk State. After the death
of Mdlikyah, the brother of Tutui, they became fully independent. On Tutui's death
in 1095, his two sons became Melik (ruler), Ridvan of Halep and Dukak of Sham.
However, their reigns did not last long. While Artygyogullari took Ilgazi, B6riogulari
(Sham Atabegs) captured Sham. The Syrian Seljuks ended de facto by 1117.
Sham became developed greatly as a centre and, with the settlement of Turkmens,
contributed to the progress of civilization.

ARTYKOGULLARI TURKMEN STATE

The most famous ruler of Artykogullari was the Seljuk Emir, Artyk Beg. A-rtyk Beg
went on the Caucasus Campaign with Soltan Alp Arslan, and later was assigned to the
conquest of Anatolia. After the
death of A-rtyk Beg in 1091, his sons S6kmen and Ilgazi took his place.
Artykogullari rule lasted from 1101 to 1409. Later, however it disintegrated into
different branches.
This principality played an important role in the Turkmenification of Anatolia. The
madrassas they built, the scholars they supported and their works of art show the
great contribution of the Artykogullari to the progress of civilization. Moreover, the
first mechanical robots were invented by A-rtyki's scholars.

IRAQI SELJUK SELJUK STATE

From the first days of Islamic expansion in Khorasan, the number of Turkmens in
Iraq rose steadily. Turkmens played an important role in the establishment of the
city of Baghdad. However, struggles for the throne between Iraqi Turkmens were
always a great problem. Soltan Sanjar aimed to end these quarrels. Taking the
opportunity to capture authority and strengthen political power, he appointed his
brother Muhammet Tapar's son Mahmyt as Melik. With the death of Mahmyt,
ferocious crisis and turmoil resumed.

MOSUL Turkmen ATABEGS

The Mosul Atabegs was founded in 1127 by Imameddin Zei'ni who had been the
Mosul Emir of the Iraqi Seljuk Ruler, Mahmyt. Later, they became famous as
'Ze'n'nis.'They annexed Jizra, Nusaybin, Harran and Halep to their territory.
The 'Ze'n'nis separated into two branches, the Mosul and the Halep Atabegs. They
reigned till 1259.

230

EiiUBY TURKMEN STATE,

The Eyuby State was one that maintained the Oguz tradition. They were kin to the
Mosul Atabegs or 'Ze'n'nis . Sending troops under the command of Salahattin Eyuby,
Nurettin Mahmyt Zei'ni conquered Egypt. After Nurettin Ze'nii, Salahattin Eyuby
became the Soltan of the state. Salahattin Eyy'uby overthrew the Fatimid State in

Egypt. Later, the state became an entirely Turkmen state with its language, military and culture.

The Eyuby's lived their most sparkling period during the reigns of Kdmil Muhammed and Salih Nejmeddin. Between 1222 and 1239 the majority of the Gypjaks migrated to Eyuby land because of the Mongolian invasion.

The Eyuby State started to weaken on the death of Nejmeddin Eyuby in 1224. The Turkmen language and culture reached the lands of Egypt during the E' uby reign.

SALYRLULAR Turkmen STATE

The Seljuks were the Turkmen tribe which settled Shiraz after conquering Iran in 1147. This principality was founded by Sungur Ata Beg from the lineage of Satyr Han. It was dissolved in 1284, and passed under the rule of Ilhanlys.

ILDENIZLILER Turkmen STATE

Ilde'nizliler state was founded by Ata Beg iemsettin Ilde'niz in 1146. Its capital was Tebriz. Nahcivan and Gence were its most important cities. It kept Iraq and southern Iran under its rule for a period. It was demolished by Jelaleddin Kineirgenq in 1225.

231

DELHI Turkmen HANATE

It was founded by Gur Soltan Muiziddin Muhammed yah at the end of the 12 Ih century. Aybeg became more influential than the Gurlys and taking the title Kutbeddin ascended to the throne in Lahore in 1206. Turkmens also seized power and started to reign in Delhi. Being originally Turkmen, Aybeg was brought up by Kadi of Nisabur Fahreddin Abdulaziz. Punjab, Buhara, Kashmir and the Middle India Plateau were within the borders of his state. The reign of the Delhi Turkmen Khanate lasted till 1526. The Memluks, Halaqs, Togalaks, Seyits, and Ludis constituted the main elements of the state.

MEMLUKLAR Turkmen STATE

The Memluk state was founded in Egypt in 1250 by Soltan Aybeg. Soltan Aybeg ruled till 1257. After that Gutuz took his place. He is famous for his victory over the Mongolians in 1260. As a result of this victory, the Mongolians could not set foot in Egypt. The Memluks ruled the country according to the Turkmen-Islamic tradition till 1527.

RESULOGULLARY Turkmen STATE

Resulogullary was a Turkmen who settled in Yemen. The son of Muhammed, Karun, known as Resul, was one of the Turkmen begs from among the E'yubys who went to Egypt. Selahaddin yah sent his brother Turan yah to Yemen. Resulogullary went with him. Nureddin Beg of the Resulogullary held an important position in the state. He took power in Yemen on the death of the E ' ' uby ruler Melik yy

232

Mesud in 1228. In Yemen Nureddin Beg and his sons reigned till 1455. Resulogullary played an important role in the construction of Yemen.

OTTOMAN Turkmen STATE

The Ottoman state was founded in S6git in 1299 by Osman Gazi, the son of krtogrul Gazi from the Kayi tribe of the Oguzs, who had come to Anatolia from Merw.

Alp Arslan had opened the gates of Anatolia with his Malazgirt victory over the Byzantines. The Turkmens rapidly began a great movement for the conquest and Islamization of Anatolia and established the Antolian Seljuk State in 107 1. This state endured until 1308. As a consequence of the weakening and collapse of the Anatolian Seljuk state by the end of the 13th century, many beyliks emerged in Anatolia. The Ottoman state was one of these beyliks. krtogrul Gazi was a frontier beg who lived in S6git, with a cavalry of 400 at his command. krtogrul Gazi and his brother, Dindar Beg, had settled in Anatolia, but his other two brothers Gindogdy and Sungur Alp had returned to Horosan. After moving from place to place in Anatolia, krtogrul and Dindar Begs had finally taken Sbgit from the Byzantines. Later, the Anatolian Seljuk Soltan Alaaddin Keykubat granted Sbgit to them and S69tit became their property. The Domaniq and Enneni Mountains were given as pasture. krtogrul Gazi made S6git his home and died at the age of 93 in 1281.

After krtogrul Gazi, his son Osman Gazi replaced him. Gathering many Turkmen Begs around him, Osman Gazi established the state.

233

Osman Gazi was one of the three sons of &rtogrul Gazi. He was distinguished from his brothers by his foresight and vigorous personality. After the death of his father, he succeeded in unifying the Turkmen Begs under his leadership. He was 23 years old when he came to power. He was a very handsome young Turkmen, tall, deepchested,

with heavy black brows over hazel-colored eyes and a Roman nose. He was broad-shouldered and the upper part of his body was longer than the lower part. When &rtogrul was on his deathbed, he announced his last testament: " O! My Son! Every man will die. By the will of Allah, death has come at last to me. This state is entrusted to you. And I am entrusting you to Allah. Be just in all your affairs."

The state krtogrul and Osman Gazis had founded dominated one third of the world for more than 600 years under the title 'Devlet-i Aliye.'

GARAGOYUNLY TURKMEN STATE

Garagoyunly state was founded in 1380 around Erzurum. Ercis and Mosul. Garagoyunlys were Turkmens of the yuwa, -kazir, Diger and owiar tribes of the oguzs. They were divided into different clans, the Varanli, Duharli, Sadli, Karamanli, Hacili and Bozdogan. An Akinci beg called Bayram Hoja had been at the head of these Turkmens till 1380. After Bayram Hoja, Gara Mimmet expanded the borders of the state. After the conquest of Tebriz, he made this city the capital of his state. It means The Eminent, Great, state.

234

Kara Yusuf's era was the most marvelous period of the Garagoyunlys. By the death of Teymir, Garagoyunlys had became the most powerful state in the region. Kara Yusuf captured Mardin in 1409 and ended the A-rtykly dynasty. The Garagoyunly state became a great state after the conquests of Erzincan in 1410 and Soltaniye in Azerbaijan in 1415.

Jihaniah ascended to the throne in 1436 and became the sovereign of Kirman with the conquest of Baghdad, Soltaniye, Kazwin and Isfahan. The state became very powerful. The collapse of the Garago'unly State was caused by the Akgoyunlys. The ruler of the Akgoyunly State, Uzyn Hasan, fought against the Garagoyunly State several times. The Garagoyunly ruler, Jihan yah, was captured and killed in 1467 after his defeat in the war against Uzyn Hasan. After this incident the Garagoyunly State collapsed.

The Garagoyunly State played an important role in the dissemination of the Turkmen language and culture in and around South Anatolia and Azerbaijan.

KUTUBSAH Turkmen STATE

This was the state founded by Garagoyunlys in India. Its foundations were laid by Soltanguly in 1517. Soltanguly was from Bay'ram Hoja's lineage.

After Jihan iah, the Garagoyunly state was unsuccessful in resettling its power back again and under the leadership of Abdullah a great number of people withdrew to Khorasan and India. Soltanguly and his sons took refuge in India, Dakka and the State of Bahmani. The Soltanguly had been brought up under the tutelage of the Bahmani State ruler Mahmyt yah. After the collapse of the Bahmani State, the Turkmens founded a new

state under the leadership of Soltanguly. In a very short time, this state became the most powerful state in the region.

The Kutubyah State lasted till 1687. In time they were assimilated into India. This state produced Bayram Han, who was both a great statesman and a poet.

AKGOYUNLY Turkmen STATE

This state was founded after the collapse of the Ilhanly State in 1350. The Akgoyunlys lived in and around Diyarbakir, in Anatolia. It was founded by Turkmens gathered under the leadership of Tur Aly, who was one of the begs of Akgoyunly. The Akgoyunly people were of the Ba' ndyr tribe of the Oguz. Later, by uniting with the Dtiker, Ba'at and Cepni tribes, they increased their power. During the period of Tur Aly Beg's leadership, a military campaign was organized

against the Trabzon Rum Pontus State. The king of Trabzon Rum Pontus State gave his daughter in marriage to Kutlu Beg, son of Akgoy'unly Beg in order to prevent these attacks.

Under Gutly Beg's son, Ahmet Beg, the Akgoyunly people fought with the Garagoy'unly several times. In one of these battles, Ahmet Beg escaped from the hands of the Garagoyunly with the assistance of Sivas Emir Kadi Burhaneddin. The prestige of

the Akgo'unly State increased during the reign of Ahmet Beg's brother, Gara Osman Beg. Emir means the governor. It is Gara Osman who is seen as the real founder of the Akgo'unly State. In 1389, Gara

Osman captured the city of y

Sivas from Kadi Burhaneddin. In order to acquire full independence, the Akgoyunlys had to leave the Ottoman patronage. The Akgo'unly people therefore made an alliance with y

Berkuyarik, Memluk Soltan of Egypt against the Ottoman Empire. After that they sought the protection of Tamerlane. In this way, they took authority over Diyarbakir, Malatya and the surrounding areas.

The most famous of the Akgoyunly Rulers was Gara Osman's son, Uzyn Hasan. Uzyn Hasan recaptured Diyarbakir in 1453. In 1457, he defeated Jihan yah, who was the ruler of the Garagoyunly people. Later the Akgoyunlys added Khorasan, Bagdat, yiraz and Isfahan to the territory under their rule.

Uzyn Hasan was defeated by the famous Padiiah of the Ottoman Empire, Soltan Fatih Soltan Mehmet in the Otlukbeli War in 1473. yah Ismail, who succeeded in uniting the Turkmens living in Eastern Anatolia, Azerbaijan and the surrounding areas, founded the Safavid State, thus putting an end to the Akgoyunly State.

The Akgoyunlys were the people who maintained the traditions of the old Turkmens. Uzyn Hasan chose for the flag of the Akgoy'unly State the symbol that had been used before by the Bayindir tribe.

SAFAVID Turkmen STATE

Ih

At the beginning of the 16 century after the Akgoyunly State,' a new Turkmen dynasty came to power in

237

Iran. The Safavid people were the Turkmens who had migrated to Iran from Anatolia. There were several reasons for the migration of Turkmens. The Akgoyunly people who lived in Erdebil belonged to the higher religious elite of the Safavids; the Garagoyunly people returned back to Iran because they could not stand for this. The Turkmens migrated group by group because of the effects of the Safavids religious beliefs. The founders of the Safavid State, like the founders of the Ottoman Empire were Turkmens by origin. The mother of yah Ismail, the founder of the State established in 1502, was the daughter of the Akgoyunly ruler.

Iran, Eastern Khorasan, Iraq, Georgia, Azerbaijan, Daghestan, Turkmenistan, the Eastern coasts of the Arab Peninsula and Eastern Anatolia all lay inside the borders of the S afavid State. The period of y ah Abbas governance was the most splendid era of the Safavid State. This period lasted till his death in 1628.

This state is remembered as the Iran-Turkmen or IranTurk state. Despite the great influence of Persian culture on the Safavid people, they preserved their Turkmen identity.

OWSAR TURKMEN DYNASTY

Nedir yah, who had been a commander in Safavid state, came to power in Iran in 1736. Nedir yah was descended from the Owiar tribe of the Oguz. He defeated the Uveysi people, rulers of Iran for a short period, and expelled them from Iran. Using his military might, Nedir yah captured the throne. On Nedir yah's ascent to the throne, Iran gained many things. First of all, it regained the land which had been taken by the Ottoman Empire earlier. In addition, Nedir yah

238

defeated Babir yah and took over Delhi.

After Nedir yah's death in 1747, his descendant Adyl yah was not able to prolong the reign of the Owiar tribe. In 1750, the Owiar dynasty reached its end.

GAJAR Turkmen DYNASTY

The Gajars were the last Turkmen dynasty in Iran. The Gajars were also originally Turkmen. From historical sources, it is clear that the Gajars were one of the seven Oguz tribes sent by the Safavids from Anatolia to Iran as a ransom to yyh Ala. These tribes were as follows: Ustaqli, yamli, Tekeli, Baharly, Dulkadyr, Owiar and Gajar. The Gajars had control of Azerbaijan, Astrabat, Merw, Khorasan and even the lands up to Kazwin and Isfahan.

In 1779 Aga Muhammed Han from Gajar ascended the throne and declared his authority. The Gajar reign in Iran, which began with the reign of Aga Muhammed Han, lasted till 1925.

INDEPENDENT AND PERMANENTLY
NEUTRAL TurkmenISTAN

As the nation that founded all the many states mentioned above, we, the Turkmens, have established our own national, independent state in our own land again. The power of the state we have established lies here. Finally we have our independent and permanently neutral Turkmenistan, which will be the greatest of all the Turkmen states in history and a source of pride. We note and recall all these preceding states as a sign of our

respect for them. We have revived the soul of our forefather, Oguz. All these states in our history are related to the state we have now established. In addition this state has three distinctive features that previous states could only wish for: National Independence, Permanent Neutrality and the Ruhnama of Turkmen.

I want to touch on these three sound foundations. First, National Independence.

The Turkmens who believe in their people, their fatherland and their leader founded the Republic of Turkmenistan on the 27th October 1991. Independence ensured our confidence in our people, our fatherland and justice, and the unity and cooperation of the 24 tribes of our ancestor Oguz. By uniting sovereignty and nationhood we became independent in our fatherland. We took our flag and marks of the state from the essential meaning derived from our profound roots.

There exist many traces of our history in countries such as Saudi Arabia, Caucasus, Uzbekistan, Kyrgyzstan, Tajikistan, Afghanistan, China, Russia, India and Pakistan. In this region, there have been periods in which Turkmens established direct relations with everybody. However, this was not possible in recent times. Now after re-inspecting all our historical relations we have succeeded in establishing good relations with all of them. When I declared our status of permanent neutrality to the whole world on the occasion of the celebration of the 50th Anniversary of the United Nations, I mentioned our legacy to the civilizations which have developed in that terrain which was occupied by the

240

Oguzs, Turkmens and Seljuks. Today, our conciliatory nature constitutes a good example. Our peace-loving and conciliatory character is not peculiar only to today, however, and those countries, which had many relations with us in the past know this best. Therefore, our neighbors and other states in our region were first to support our status of neutrality. Later, all states showed their support for this policy.

Constant Neutrality was the second foundation we achieved on independence. It was Oguz Han's wish and prayer uttered five thousand years ago that our land may be at peace forever. Our ancestors belief was always that our blue sky should be dominated by peace and tranquility. We became confident that we could survive on earth by adopting and enacting this faith of our ancestors as the fundamental principle of our state. Since the very first day, we have known that peace and trust are the secrets of life on earth. Developing our good-will further, we started the Open Door Policy in the economic realm and we accepted neutral status in our foreign policy. Believing that integration with the world depends on our being committed to it and loving everybody and that this is possible first of all by ensuring peace in our own country, we regarded the foundation of the Turkmen State as one of our primary duties. All the countries of the world, starting with the neighboring countries in the region accepted the rightness of our path and started to support us. By a unanimous vote of 185 states, on 12 December 1995 the Central Assembly of the United Nations gave our state the status of Permanent Neutrality. Thus, for the first time in history, the neutrality of a state was legalized and we became officially the only neutral state in the world. We put the olive bough, which is the symbol of peace in the United

241

Nations flag, on our green flag.

To recognize the humanitarian ideas and particular qualities that make us a nation, and to bring these values to light as an example for us and our descendants is very important. I have thought a lot on this subject and I have always shared my ideas with my people. Finally, I have reached this conclusion: there must be a book that integrates the most valuable characteristics, the spirit of the Turkmens on earth. That is to say, the Turkmens shall have a Ruhnama. By the way, this book can take the place of our lost books and be, after the Qur'an, the book of the Turkmens. Besides, until now Turkmens have not been able to found a state on their own land based on such moral unity, though they have established numerous states elsewhere. We can now confidently say that we have established a state in a spirit of unity. Our Ruhnama has the nature of a bridge that leads us to this. Ruhnama is a book which advises so that Turkmens may not repeat in the future mistakes from their past, and so that they may always and everywhere be an example and show the way. I believe that Ruhnama will be one of the first guides of the Turkmens.

I want to remind you once again that our way gets its power from history. It is a fact that our ancestors migrated all around the world. Our economic route is also well-defined, as is our way of peace that leads to the hearts of the states and nations of the world. Our aim is to scatter intimacy and radiance into the hearts of the states of the world, that is, to heat and light the homes of other peoples with the natural gas from Turkmenistan.

Our independence and neutrality illuminate our Golden century and are illuminated by our national values. Reviving

242

with Ruhnama, God willing, we can alter our future in the Golden Age. In the Golden century, in the 21st century, our main aim is to build a Turkmen nation which can be a model for the entire world. With our independence, which lets us now cut our own cloth to fit, and our neutrality which spreads the sign of peace in the world, our nation will also prove itself a model in human relations by displaying its affluent spirit.

May our people and state live in security under our tranquil sky.

State is the unity of ideas and values; homeland is the unity of feeling and values of the heart. When I look at the map of Turkmenistan, the shape resembling a strong bull goring the Caspian Sea comes to life before my eyes...from the Caspian to the mountains of Serhatabat, from the fertile lands of Hojambaz to the vast plains and mountains of Daioguz Ayb6wri. On my office table there stands a five or six-thousand-year-old statue of a golden bull which was found in Altyndepe. There is a golden statue of a bull bearing the World on its homs to the right of Palace of the State Presidency...

In every comer of our land the golden pages of human development lie hidden. Indeed these lands are a treasury of humanity waiting to be discovered.

This land is the land that has granted many civilizations to the world.

This land is full of oil, natural gas and underground resources. Turkmenistan is one of the richest states of the

243

world in terms of underground resources. 30% of the world's oil and natural gas reserves lie in Turkmenistan.

Our peasants know that every handful of this land is more precious than gold or jewels. Agriculture began in these lands and this land is the fatherland of white wheat. There is no country which can compete with the quality, goodness and flavor of fruits, vegetables and cereals grown in this land.

Beloved Turkmens! This land is the Turkmens; these gardens, plains, deserts, mountains and plateaus are lands that we call our homeland. When we say homeland our ancestors come to mind and when we say our ancestors our homeland comes to our mind. Turkmens who never bowed before sword, spear or mace, shall bow to this land and our ancestors and kneel to show reverence for them.

In these sacred lands we have established our independent and permanently neutral Republic of Turkmenistan.

Independent and Neutral Turkmenistan! You are beloved because we found you in this sacred land.

Independent and Neutral Turkmenistan! As the world endures, you will live, because we are dedicating our lives to molding you with love and affection, to adorning you with sincerity.

Independent and Neutral Turkmenistan! You are blessed because you are the state which our ancestors, though it was their hearty wish, could not achieve in eight centuries. We have built you on the wishes of our ancestors.

Independent and Neutral Turkmenistan! The Turkmen miracle and consecration starts with you. Only Allah is over you.

244

There is an interesting tale narrated about Orgenq, the world-famous capital of Kineirgenq. In ancient times, the son of Kbneirgenq, yehzade Genq, fell in love with a fairy like girl. Since the father of the girl was also a Soltaıı, he bestowed on his son-in-law a caravan-load of gold. The gold he granted was so much that the treasury of Kineirgenq could not contain it. Therefore, the remainder of the gold was allotted to the people. For the share of posterity, the yah also scattered much of this gold over the land of Orgenq, and ploughed it in several times.

Turkmen land is the land on which gold was scattered. If you serve such a land, it will give back its gold abundantly to you.

Love your land so that its golden red becomes a crop, you become cheerful and the scents of the clumps of flowers permeate everywhere with their sweet fragrance.

Love your land so that your love fills your granary like the crops which wave like a sea. Your love endows with its blessed favor the plane tree, the pomegranate, the apricot, the plum, and the apple.

Reason and mind shall serve to strengthen our moral independence and sovereignty. The doors of our neutral state are always open to the external world. However, there must by intellectual laborers at the,5c, doors. Accepting idcab and

thoughts haphazardly does moral damage. We must adapt these values to our own moral, intellectual and cultural structure.

Our ancestors left us examples of the love and respect that must be shown to the fatherland.

245

Here is an example of the Turkmen's love for his fatherland.

At the period when Oguz Han's state was not yet very powerful, taking advantage of this situation, a powerful state tried to capture Oguz land by war. The enemy sent a messenger and demanded the best horse in the Oguz country. Oguz Han's commanders put forward their ideas:

"The enemy is ill-meaning. Let us make war, but let us not give the pedigree horse."

Oguz Han said to them:

"It is wrong to prefer the worst, when what is only worse is still possible. One never knows, we may lose all our horses if we are defeated. Give him the horse and let him

go. 15y The messenger that took the pedigree horse came back with more depressing news. This time the demand of the enemy was the most beautiful girl in the country. The commanders said:

"We can't accept this shameful demand. This time they want us to surrender our honor. There is no way out except

war. 5y

However, the prudent and far-sighted Oguz Han said: "In case of a war, many a brave man may die. One never

knows what may happen! If the enemy defeats us all at once, all our sisters, daughters, brides and wives may become slaves. It is frivolous to prefer the worst, when what is worse is still possible."

The messenger took the most beautiful girl and came 246

back with a more oppressive proposal, demanding land this time. Oguz Han who had realized war was approaching and had prepared his army cried:

"We shall give our heads, but we will not give land," and immediately he declared war.

He taught the enemy a lesson.

No historian can be sure of the number of wars which took place on Oguz land, but everybody agrees on one point. Every part of this land has been mixed with the blood of our brave forefathers and tears of our mothers. You can feel the warmth of the hearts and hands of our ancestors in each handful of this terrain. The love and affection, the efforts and pains of our ancestors permeate every inch of this country. Thousands of poets have described this land.

In this case, how blessed is this land!

As the first man and prophet Adam was created in his prime (28) by Allah, the Most Exalted, so the Turkmen State was already based on substantial principles at its foundation. There is a proliferation of examples of state-building and administration in world history. Some states have progressed well in terms of their administrative structure. Some of the types of state are: democratic, monarchic, theocratic, republic, and socialist.

247

Each of these state systems has unique characteristics. We are deriving essential and valid methods from each and adapting them to our state administrative structure. We also make use of some of the numerous experiences of our ancestors which are appropriate for the contemporary world.

Today, we have founded a state based on golden principles originating from Turkmen society's political, economic and cultural structure. We call this style of governance 'The Turkmen Way. This is to the benefit of the Turkmen state and people.

The making of our state is still in process. I hope that the Golden Century will be the most splendid and developed era of our state administration.

We are newly-embarked on a natural process. We have changed to a wholly different economic system. Initiating new economic relations, we put forward new ideas and ways that can inspire many developed countries of the world.

We do not hide the fact that we will only follow our own way without imitating any state or nation. No person repeats the life of another, nor can a state or nation follow the way of another state or nation. The ways may only resemble each other. However, in the development and regression of societies, it is possible and generally the case that many events occur which are beyond the control and will of mankind.

We feel at every moment the great love of Allah, the Most High, for his own creature, humankind. There are 380 thousand kinds of plant in the world. Each of them tries to show its beauty to humanity in its own language. For this reason, each of them is different in color, scent and beauty.

248

All of these are signs of Allah s love of humankind. Allah, the All-Mighty created the universe for humans. Nature, plants, animals, in short, all beings are created for humans. Being is the manifestation of Allah's compassion.

0, my dear countryman!

Look around you at once at the beauties around you, the manifestations of the compassion and mercy of Allah. Conceive that you yourself are the creature of Allah's compassion and try to merit that love!

You must love humanity!

The meaning of life is mutual love and affection.

The golden principle of your happiness is hidden in your affection for the world and life.

Man is the most excellent of all creatures. However, this perfection is possible only by living in accord with our creation. Man is human insofar as he knows himself (his own World) and lives accordingly. This is a completely different World. You cannot reach there by technological progress, science or technique. Zarathustra, who set out on his camel from Merw 2500 years ago reached these worlds and preached: "O, Men! Avoid the Fire and repent, because the sins are cleaned with fire in the other world."

Gorkut Ata also called the Oguzs, who had distanced themselves from being human, on a journey toward humanity

1500 years ago.

Man must know his status and capacity, and respect human beings.

249

Independent and Permanently Neutral Republic of Turkmenistan!

With my whole heart, I desire your development and progress and devote all my life to you. You must be exalted, the great Turkmen State.

For we founded you on this sacred Turkmen land.

Our ancestor, Magtymguly, keeping you in his dreams, wrote:

Know that what I built,

Is the peg of this world.

Forever it will stay independent, This is the edifice of the Turkmen.

It is we who have realized his dreams.

Independent and Neutral Republic of Turkmenistan! You shall be powerful because we established you following our ancestor's way.

Your national anthem is the anthem of justice, your emblem is the sign of justice. Your green flag is the herald of spring.

As it was narrated that the Prophet Ibrahim had built the Ka'bah, the last Messenger of God, Muhammed, first built a mosque when he migrated from

Mekka to Medina, before building himself a house.

Beginning in the name of Allah, we constructed a magnificent mosque, first in Gypjak and then in the middle of Aigabat. Later on, we built a beautiful mosque in Gikdepe

250

in the memory of the martyrs who sacrificed their lives for this country.

0, my beloved citizens, my dear people! May your heads be held high, and your spirits raised! Walk with pride, and be honorable, because you have this good state.

My brother, my beloved sister, my dear mothers! Never scowl, live happily because you have this good state.

Let's live, work, produce, reach our target, and so leave our future generations a stable, independent and neutral Turkmenistan as a legacy.

Let the state be our legacy to the generations.

As Gorkut Ata said, we are leaving a developed, powerful, rich and stable state to our children. There can be no happiness greater than this.

251

MY OPINIONS CONCERNING THE FOUNDATION OF INDEPENDENT AND PERMANENTLY NEUTRAL TURKMENISTAN

Beloved Turkmen people!

There can be no tree without a root, no building without a foundation. Our people have lived in tough conditions for the last 3-4 centuries; our dreams of unity did not come true. We lived as scattered masses. Our body broke into pieces, as if our head was somewhere and our legs and arms were somewhere else. So, the tree of life did not flourish, the state building could not stand on a firm basis and good fortune did not smile on my nation.

I did not rest by day or night until your head could be held high, and your heart had faith and hope, and your hearth was blessed. Thanks to Allah, and by His Grace and Mercy, in the blessed country of our ancestors we established a new independent state after many centuries. We prepared everything needed for each of our citizens and introduced our state to the other nations of the world and developed countries, and had it recognized. From now on, may our state be stable and eternal. I thank Allah, the Most Merciful, a thousand times for allowing me to gain for my country the neutral status which is a special privilege in the world.

My beloved nation!

252

Our ancestors, Soltans, Hans and begs clothed the naked and fed the hungry. They did not do this for reputation, glory and fame, but for the pleasure of Allah, the Truth.

I started building the state from the hearth of our people. Essential necessities, such as flour, natural gas, electric, salt and water, we made free. We expect no return for this policy. Our real intention is that our people live in comfort, be the owners and masters of our own natural resources, and be always proud and dignified beside others.

After the appropriate utilization of the economic resources of the country, we turn to the greatest and most significant issue, the moral and spiritual health of the people.

The State: The Independent Turkmen state was founded after 600 years. The significance of today's Turkmen State can be understood better when examined from a historical perspective. When the period in which Turkmens lived without a state is compared with today, it is seen that the state is the only principle that unites the people.

The People: It is the group of people which emerged as a result of free and nonobligatory
relations between different strata of society. There is no political aim or illegal sanction in the relations between people.

The Nation: It is the unity that owns the state organization.

The Language: The Turkmen language is the one with a wealth of words, expressions and meanings.

The People is a group of people, but the nation is the unity. The group refers to quantity, where unity is related to quality. Also unity refers to organization and the formation of

253

institutions. The People transforms into a nation when it makes use of its capacity to be organized internally according to differing political, economic and social norms. Institutionalization concludes with the state.

The nation is the unity of language, religion, customs and tradition, ideals and state. When this unity is composed, the fortune of the people is enhanced. The meaning of the state for a nation is the same as the meaning of the house and other necessities for a couple who will build a new family.

The state is like a grand family. Certain duties and places are attributed to each member in this family in order to establish order. If these duties are performed properly, the state lives long.

The fundamental feature of our state is its being a nation-state. This trait can be understood better when compared with the Soviets who ruled us for 70 years. Soviet domination worked to keep the Turkmens, who are the real owners of this land, backward rather than to make the country develop and progress. The Soviets did not only exploit the natural resources of Turkmen for their sake and the sake of others but also tried to annihilate completely the national and moral values of the Turkmens.

The Turkmen nation-state is the only owner of this country. 'Nation-state' means a state that uses the material resources and natural wealth of the country for its nation, and protects the moral values of its people and respects them. That is to say, the state is born and survives as the system that organizes the historical life of a nation.

254

Rule: As a form of administration, the state is composed of these three systems:
1) Laws
2) State Institutions
3) Local Administrations

The state's legislative organ is sovereign. The People's Council (Halk Maslahaty) is the Legislative organ of the Turkmenistan state. Government is the executive organ and is regulated by laws made by the sovereign state.

Turkmenistan is a democratic, law-based and secular state, in which the rule of the state is implemented in the form of a presidential republic.

Turkmenistan has ultimate and complete control of its territory and independently conducts its domestic and foreign policy. The state of

Turkmenistan is unitary and indivisible.

To defend the independence and territorial integrity of Turkmenistan and to ensure independent functioning of the legislative, executive and judiciary branches are the fundamental duties of the state.

The People are the sole source of power in Turkmenistan. Sovereignty belongs unconditionally to the nation. The People of Turkmenistan exercise their sovereignty directly or through representative bodies.

No part of the People nor any organization, institution or individual has the right to appropriate power in the state.

Human beings are the highest value of the society and state in Turkmenistan.

255

The state is responsible to each citizen and ensures the creation of conditions for the free development of each personality. The life, honor, dignity and freedom, personal inviolability, and the natural and inalienable rights of the citizen are protected.

Each citizen is responsible for the fulfillment of duties placed upon him by the Constitution and laws.

The state is based on the principle of separation of powers - the legislative, the executive and the judiciary- which shall exercise their authority independently and interactively.

The duties and responsibilities of the state and all its bodies and officials are determined according to the Law.

The Turkmenistan Constitution is the supreme Law of the state. The norms and provisions stipulated therein have direct effect. Laws and other legal acts that contradict the Constitution do not have legal force.

All the Legal information concerning the state bodies is published for general dissemination or made public in other ways, with the exception of that containing state secrets or private information guaranteed by law. Legal acts affecting the rights and freedoms of citizens that are not generally disseminated become invalid from the moment of their adoption.

Turkmenistan recognizes the priority of the generally accepted standards of international law. Turkmenistan is a full member of United Nations and adheres in its foreign policy to the principles of peaceful coexistence, rejection of the use of force, and non-interference in the internal affairs of other states.

256

Turkmenistan has its own Citizenship Law. Citizenship can be acquired, retained and fortified in accordance with the law.

Acitizen of Turkmenistan may not be turned over to another state or deported from Turkmenistan and deprived of his right to turn his motherland.

Citizens of Turkmenistan are guaranteed the protection and patronage of the state, both in the territory of Turkmenistan and beyond its borders.

Foreign citizens and/or stateless persons enjoy the rights and freedoms of citizens of Turkmenistan unless otherwise prescribed by law.

The Turkmenistan state grants the right of asylum to foreign citizens persecuted in their countries for political, national or religious convictions.

Property is inviolable in Turkmenistan. Turkmenistan confirms the right of private ownership of the means of production, land and other material and intellectual assets. These may likewise belong to individuals, corporate bodies and the state. The state guarantees equal protection and equal conditions for the development of all types and forms of property.

The state guarantees the freedom of belief and worship for all religions and their equality before the law. Religious organizations are separate from the state and are not permitted to interfere in state affairs. The state educational system is separated from religious organizations and is of a secular nature.

Everybody has the right to define his attitude towards religion, to profess any religion or not to profess any, either

257

individually or jointly with others, to disseminate and publicize his beliefs concerning religion and to participate in the practice of religious cults, rituals and rites.

In order to protect its territory, Turkmenistan state has its own army.

Turkmenistan guarantees equal rights and freedoms to its citizens, as well as the equality of citizens before the law irrespective of nationality, origin, property, status or official position, place of residence, language, attitude towards religion, or membership of any party, association or institution.

Men and women have equal civil rights in Turkmenistan. The violation of equality entails liability under the law.

The exercise of rights and freedoms cannot violate the rights and freedoms of other persons or the requirements of morality or public order or cause a threat to national security.

Every person has the right to life. No one may be deprived of life. The People supported

my speech on the abolition of capital punishment. The World Community welcomed this

significant initiative.

Acitizen may not have his rights restricted or be denied the rights belonging to him, or

condemned, or subjected to punishment, other than in clear accordance with the law and

upon the decision of a court.

Every citizen has the right to the support of the state in receiving well-appointed living

space and in construction of individual housing. There exists the inviolability of private

property. For the Turkmen, the house is sacred. For this reason I abolished unlawful encroachment.

258

259

Everyone has the right of free movement and the right to choose his place of residence

within Turkmenistan.

Women and men, upon attaining the age of marriage, have the right to marry and to create a family by mutual consent. Spouses have equal rights in family relations.

Parents or legal guardians have the right and obligation to raise their children, care for their health, development and education, prepare them for life, and to instill respect for

laws and historical and national traditions in them. Adult children are obliged to render their parents assistance.

Each citizen has the right to participate in managing the affairs of society and the state,

directly and through his or her freely elected representatives.

Citizens have the right to elect and to be elected to bodies of state government.

The citizens of Turkmenistan in accordance with their capabilities and professional training have equal right of access to the civil service.

All citizens have the right to work, to select at their own discretion a profession, type of

employment, and place of work, and to healthy and safe working conditions. Forced labor shall be forbidden, except in cases established by law.

Persons who work for hire have the right to payment corresponding to the amount and quality of their work. This compensation shall not be less than the established minimum

wage.

Workers have the right to rest and leisure. For persons who work for hire, this right shall

be reflected in the establishment of work hours of limited duration, provision of paid

260

annual vacation, and weekly days off.

The state has the responsibility to create conditions that are conducive to relaxation at the place of residence and rational use of free time.

Citizens have the right to health protection, including free use of a network of state healthcare institutions. Paid medical services shall be permitted on the basis and in the

manner established by law.

Citizens have the right to social security in their old age, and in the case of illness, disability, loss of work capacity, loss of the breadwinner, and unemployment.

Families with many children, children who have lost their parents, war veterans, and other persons who have lost their health while defending state or public interests shall be

provided additional support and privileges from public resources.

The procedures and conditions for benefiting from these rights are arranged by law.

Each citizen has the right to education. General secondary education is obligatory, and

everyone shall have the right to obtain this for free at state educational institutions. Organizations and citizens shall have the right to establish paid educational institutions

in accordance with the law.

All citizens of Turkmenistan may practice any kind of art. The legal rights of citizens in

the areas of scientific, technical, artistic and cultural activity are protected by law.

261

The state facilitates the development of science, art, popular creativity and physical training.

Exercise of rights and freedoms are inseparable from the performance by a citizen and a

person of his or her obligations to the society and the state.

The defence of Turkmenistan is the sacred duty of every person. For male citizens of

Turkmenistan, there is universal compulsory military service

Citizens of Turkmenistan are obliged to pay taxes and other payments in the manner and

amounts established by law.

No one shall be forced to give evidence against himself or close relatives

The highest representative body of popular power is the People's Council (Halk Maslahaty) of Turkmenistan.

Turkmenistan's administrative system consists of great provinces (welayats), provinces

(etrap), districts (shakhers), boroughs and villages in which central and local administrative bodies are formed.

The People's Council includes: - the President;

- the deputies of the Parliament (Mejlis);

-People's Representatives who are elected from provinces and districts for a period of five years and for the services they make they are not paid.

The President, the Parliament, the Cabinet, or not less than one quarter of the established

number of members of the People's Council have the right to submit bills for the consideration of the People's Council.

262

The work of the People's Council is chaired by the President or any member elected by

the People's Council.

The state is the essence of the national spirit. That is why the nation state is the realization of the moral and spiritual values that belong to the nation and a symbol of the

combination of unity with political will.

Our ancestors had the custom of all coming together and building a house for one of their number. Similarly, in the establishment of the foundations of the state, we came together and established the structure of our state following the same custom. It is the essential duty of every citizen of ours now to consolidate this structure, which will disseminate its light to the whole world, and to exert all their efforts for it to reach its goal - to enter the Golden Age.

To give priority to, show respect for, and refer to the opinions, intelligence, wisdom and

experience of the elderly has been one of the ethical values of the Tirkmen state since ancient times. This value is one of the main principles of the modem Turkmen state we

have established. The most essential element in establishing the state is to take into account national values, history, worldview and so on. That is why the Halk Maslahaty,

the People's Council, is the principal organ of the state administration, and it should remain so in the future. In this way, we will have retained the experience of state which

belongs to our national history.

The high spiritual dynamics which belong to the nation have become whole in the state.

The natural catastrophes which hit the Turkmens in the last few centuries occurred because such high and spiritual values had not come together. To serve the state is to strengthen the internal dynamics

263

that belong to the nation. Serving the state guarantees the present and future of the whole
nation.

The nation-state is the historical method of realizing the essence of the national outlook.

By means of a nation-state the values belonging to a nation are integrated. Such integration regulates national life historically and gives it direction. Establishing a nation-state is the expression of a nation's respect for its history and its trust in the future.

A nation state cannot be like a tree which has been brought from a different country and
climate and re-planted and which does not flourish but dies because it is unable to adapt
to the new climate. On the contrary, it must be born and bred in the soil of this land, rooted deeply in it, and stretching up into its sky. It is certain that imitation does not yield positive results in any field, and the dangers of imitation for the interests, benefit
and the future of the people and nation are of an enormous scale and dimension.

The establishment of a state is the action of a nation gaining existence for itself. New values, which did not exist before, in the social, economic, political and spiritual fields
are gained.

To be respectful to other nations and to respect and revere the faiths and principles of the
adherents of other religions lies in the Turkmen's blood. The Turkmens are of a nation which is generous, humanitarian, just, open-hearted, patient, contented and sincere. Showing the utmost respect to other nations has always been a characteristic of the Turkmens. There have not been any national disputes and conflicts among the Turkmens, and let there never be in the future either.

The internal disturbances, which have happened in the

264

last eight centuries, taught the Turkmens well what separatist movements mean. For eight centuries, states near and far have pursued the policy of 'divide, destroy and rule',
instigated unrest, stirred up disagreements, and caused either small- or large-scale conflicts among the Turkmens.

That is why it is no coincidence that we find so many mentions of unity, togetherness and solidarity in the works of hundreds of our poets. On the declaration of the Independence of Turkmenistan State, all our people acknowledged this as the nationstate
awaited for eight centuries.

All the Turkmens and the rest, the Russians, Uzbeks, Ukrainians, Azeris, Belujs and Armenians, united, bind all their hopes to Turkmenistan.

Independent and Impartial Turkmenistan is a rich state, and as long as unity and solidarity are maintained and preserved, people will prosper. Every Tirkmen understands this very well.

In no part of Turkmenistan today, is there any disagreement with or belittling of one another. There is political stability in Turkmenistan. All the ethnic groups live with a single view or understanding, that is, in friendship and brotherhood.

There are no political prisoners or restrictions in Turkmenistan.

We, in our independent and impartial Turkmenistan, have established our own national

military forces to maintain national security, to protect and patrol our borders.

On some occasions people consider that their personal

265

rights are being violated even when they are legally questioned and prosecuted. On some

occasions, individual rights are violated for the sake of another person without any legal

grounds. This can happen to anyone and this should be properly investigated and remedied by the state.

In short, the issues, which need to be investigated and dealt with are numerous. What is

important in all these is that every citizen should know fully his or her rights, duties and

liabilities, and retain his or her trust in the law, and belief that the law is just and trustworthy.

We, the Turkmen, became accustomed to ill and unjust treatment. During the 74 years of Soviet domination, we were oppressed and we were not allowed to express our own

opinions. But we bore all this. In all the administrative meetings of the central Committee of the Communist party, and in the General Assembly and Congress, in the

Parliament, and in Moscow, we, the Turkmens, were criticized in a profound sense. This

became a custom then. They always accused and belittled the Turkmens for not having

been able to rid themselves of the so-called harmful remnants and effects of the past, of

having an undeveloped social thinking, and of being backward economically, all of which accusations were beyond any comprehension. However, as some of us started to

take all these seriously and to appropriate them to ourselves, we started to undermine one

another, which, moreover, became normal for us. In that sense, some of our own writers

went further and started conceitedly to criticize harshly and unjustly our shared traditions

and customs and the moral values belonging to our nation. That in turn brought about mutual recriminations among people, and thus national pride and the honor and self esteem

of our people

266

and history were lost. Unfortunately, the Turkmens perpetrated such acts against each other.

I have learned all the details of the 74 years of Turkmen history under the Soviet era

inside out. In all those only the conflicts and clashes of the Turkmens among themselves
were mentioned, whereas not a single word was mentioned concerning the rich historical
past and works of the Turkmens, as if such a history had never been lived and as if anything matters as long as it concerns the present. The destiny of our nation and people
was taken into consideration and valued through that only. It was indeed very difficult to
produce alternative solutions to those too. All the issues on whatever related to Russia and the general problems of the USSR were shown and imposed as issues and problems
belonging to the Turkmens.
The basic reason for these events was the struggle between the Bolsheviks and Mensheviks (i.e. the socialists and anti-socialists) during the 20s and 30s. During the 30s
and 40s the nationalists were labeled as fascist and "the unity groups" of atheists were against them. In truth, during this period there was an ongoing conflict within which there were show trials, prosecutions and massacres. This struggle was carried out under
different names. Like all the other nations of the USSR, The Turkmens were not permitted to do any research into their history and destiny.
Were the Turkmens guilty in these events? If so, to what extent? This question is of importance to us. We know it is impossible to erase the reality that the USSR was founded in 1922. During those years in all the Soviets, the internal conflicts continued ceaselessly. However we must admit that the Turkmens damaged themselves mercilessly. The conflicts in

the names of new and old, religion and atheism were weakening the Turkmens and the
same struggles brought them to vanishing point. The worst such struggles were tolerated.
During the war years, the 40s and 50s, a new purge within the party was begun. The struggle against nationalism was continued by a different method. This struggle continued during the 50s and 60s. Some intellectuals were blamed and were exiled to deprived regions of the USSR.
Thanks to the achievements of the 60s and 70s, fulsome praise became a fashion: many
persons and institutions were praised. Exaggeration and delusion became common. This
was a social disease and it demonstrated the heartbreaking condition of society. To tell the truth it is impossible to show a single healthy period during those 74 years. Political
thought became dominant and people forgot how to think freely. They became accustomed to toadying and to delivering speeches praising the party. The individual had
no significance, and in the social context the status of the individual was completely destroyed. Social ideas were praised but individual responsibility was ignored; the administrative system was established according to this principle. In this way these

principles were presented to people as the successes of Soviet democracy. However all

the things cited were nothing but worthless developments. These slogans became part of

our society's character and they became a social disease.

Today it is so difficult to recover from those diseases. This is the most important and immediate duty in our Golden Century.

Dear Citizens!

I have repeated many times in my speeches that the

Turkmens in history were not defeated by external forces but were defeated by internal

forces. My aim was to draw your attention to the reality that as a nation we should learn

a lesson from history and we should re-organize our life according to this. Gorkut Ata advised that there are three reasons for any possible calamity and misfortune, and these

are: disagreement, egoism and taking something which is unlawful according to religion.

We should heed Gorkut Ata's advice.

My Beloved Turkmen nation!

Each citizen should work hard for the progress of our independent and neutral state, and

should strive for its eternal endurance, and should try to remove any obstacle that might

prevent our state's steady progress.

Many things are the direct responsibility of officials. 1, as President, have to be very careful when appointing new governors that they are sensitive to the nation's and the country's interests, that they are trustworthy, and that they are sincere in the performance

of their duties. For the selection of new civil servants we have to ratify a national act in

our National Congress. This act shall set out the following: what are the prerequisites of

being a civil servant, the rules governing appointments, civil servant posts in official bureaus and new cadres, and the boundaries of delegated power. Each citizen's right to

enter the civil service should be protected. In the selection of civil servants nationality,

citizenship, economic and official status, domicile and region, and faith should not be taken into consideration. Only their abilities and capabilities in a merit system should be

considered. Officials should appoint those who are capable and competent in their work

and should check the work carried out by them. If a manager is successful, there will be

progress and responsibility in his unit or department.

The appointment of those who are loyal to the nation according to their capabilities to the proper duties and posts is very important. An administrator, rather than for his own

personal interests, should care for the interests of his nation, people and state.

Iwant to emphasize seven elements which can damage the progress of the state:

First element: unqualified officials

Second element: the spread of tribal and sectarian consciousness

Third element: disagreements between people and tribes

Fourth element: religious and sectarian conflicts

Fifth element: disagreements with neighboring countries

Sixth element: domestic turmoil

Seventh element: the effects of natural catastrophes.

1, as the first President of Independent and Permanently Neutral Turkmenistan, accept as one of my basic duties the responsibility for preventing the development of the seven

elements cited above. I advise the presidents who will succeed me to be sensitive to them, always take them into consideration, and work hard in order to prevent the development of such calamities which might harm our state.

270

They Said

The snow-capped Kipetdag has a lovely tune, they said,

Roars from time to time like a young man burned inside, they said,

Has rains coming with thunder and lightning, they said,

Wandering the Turkmen land, there is a lot worth looting, they said,

There is the wisdom of Gorkut-Ata on her mountains, they said.

Her valleys and mountain ranges are like paradise The shadows of the clouds roam over

her ravines,

The Kipetdag is no ordinary mountain, this is the spring of a fortune,

The Ki'ten, Hasar and Balkan mountains and the whole Turkmen world,

There is the majesty of Oguz Han on their mountains, they said.

Tigers roar in her canyons and her summits are cloudy,

Her mountains where the eagles nest on their heights remain always young,

The great land, on her outskirts mountain cities are built, is safe,

There are bowers in Candybil and the future is the time of magnificence,

271

There are the messages of Girogly on her mountains, they said.

One of my sides is Garagum, which is a caravan migrating,

Kills those who come as enemies and gives the Turkmen freedom,

When angered, rises in fury like a tornado and flood, Like a witness who saw the creation of the world,

The desert with Hydyr, which Magtymguly certifies so, they said.

272

You are Turkmen

Let's, 0 my heart, walk my heart. Let's look around our land.

With lions in its fields, the beautiful land of Turkmen,

Now the day has come for the poor, sad, brave, men,

You are the Turkmen, with such heroes like Jelaleddin.

Let's select a thousand-winged horse

And travel praying over her plains and mountains

And seek for the ancestors who became part of them,
And You are the Turkmen which hosts 360 saints
The old people are as wise as Gorkut
The mothers are as merciful as yunus
If you feel lonely and sigh, you see compassion
You are the Turkmen with beautiful houri-like girls like Agayunus
You are braver than the brave, just find an opponent as you are
You are a lion more than a lion, just find a battle field for you Let your cream boil
over
always, never feel the lack of it,
You are the Turkmen, with Garagum, so many minerals in its core
273
History is your ancestors and grand children
And grandfathers, father, children and nation.
Entering the most fortified palaces with your horse,
You are the Turkmen with strong and agile arms.
The rich and noble are godly like saints
Your horsetail-standard is always hoisted brightly,
You words are fine, pleasing, and heart is illuminated
You are the Turkmen, with his face and heart smiling
Oguz is your forefather, and Gorkut is your master,
Your memory is the history of the sixty ages.
Your Garagum is your table and treasure,
Your provision is blessed, you are the prosperous Turkmen.
274

In My Motherland

Oh my crazy soul! Conceiving wishes and peace I find in my motherland,
Determination, learning, diligence, fame, glory, I find in my motherland,
The winter over the raging spring I find in my motherland,
Mourning my death and rejoicing over my birth-relations I find in my motherland,
Absurdity of living abroad and the cherished birth place I find in my motherland,
Through its deserts I roamed and its mountains I took for my protection
And the breeze that blew from the valleys I took for Allah's blessings
Its deserts, rivers, and mountains, I took for the edifice the True One Built,
The dutar became the source of my wisdom, while the great jangling of the gyjak was
the pain of my soul
The goal I pursue hard and endless riches and wealth, I find in my motherland,
275
Grazed our cattle and tended it by nights, roaming over all the Ahal plains without
naps,
Heard the voices of my ancestors in its thunder claps,
And my dear mother's groan in the melodies sung by winds,
Lone I was left, in this world orphan, between Arsh and Kursi,
Alas I lament my soul set on fire, but the place I worship in I find in my motherland,
For I am AKi'ly's son, my head I hold high,
Going through fire and Water never did I complain
Farewell to the bad lot, let me this life enjoy
Time and again the True One and my Lord I pray
My past, my future, amass great wealth I find in my motherland.

Every nation in the world, every reasonable and conscious member of a nation, every community... is busy finding the way to the best development and finding and establishing their own position in the course of history in our age.

No one can separate himself from this historical progress because the past does not guarantee that things will be all right if he disregards the future. The past is a kind of fulcrum on which our future decisions and jobs turn. Our decisions and plans for the future will be successful as long as they are in accord with the demands and developments of the future. This is most probably a feature of the new age.

Today, time passes so fast; this is just a point between the eternity of the past and the future. However time offers the opportunity to determine the future if it is recognized in and appropriate manner. This age shapes the a conscious worldview of the nation and guarantees the future of the nation. At the beginning of the third millennium, there are several important issues waiting for the Turkmen people to resolve immediately. These are issues of our people's political, economic, scientific, civic, health and social life.

If our government solves these problems in time, our unity and cooperation will survive in our country. The basic principle of independent Turkmen state is to believe in Allah, the Most Exalted, in our religion. This is trust in ourselves and humanity. This is confidence in man's power to affect the progress of human history and in the victory of productive and peaceful qualities. This is also our major philosophy of international relations and shapes our approach to foreign policy and our philosophy of development.

One of the most important problems of our age is to establish a healthy, just and mutually agreed and beneficial,

functioning relationship between the countries whose level of social, economic and industrial developments are not equal. Countries or continents cannot be blamed for problems which have become apparent recently in all their aspects but which in fact have accumulated over the past decades or centuries.

Never before has the world witnessed such a high level of injustice and disequilibrium among the nations in terms of sharing and benefiting from the wealth and resources of the world. Such danger, which shakes all the trust and stability of the whole world, has never been felt so clearly. Many hot conflicts and ethnic problems now ongoing arise from this inequality among nations in terms of social and economic interests. Bringing clashes between faiths and civilizations to the world agenda and defining them as "crusades" under present circumstances does nothing but distort the facts and add fuel to the flames. The real problem is not the conflict between the Eastern and Western ideas, worldviews or clashes between the different religions. On the contrary, it is the irreconcilability of the present forms of international economic relations, which have been concealed up until now, with the current social and political configuration of the world. This is one of the characteristics of the 21st century. Turkmenistan accepts mutual respect, conciliation, reconciliation and humanism as the basis of international relations, and employs the same principles in its domestic politics as well. Turkmenistan maintains and works for domestic, regional and international peace, welfare and social cooperation, and it sustains the same principles within its own society and state.

The day Turkmenistan became independent humans became the most important asset of the state. The State holds very highly its citizens lives, health, security, prosperity, education and excellence in physical and spiritual development. Social security in society is given its due top priority, and the necessary decisions, policies and infrastructure related to these have been completed. These developments contributed to social and political stability, and social trust in the new implementations grew. Thanks to new policies accepted and carried out in Turkmenistan, during the days following independence the rate of infant mortality fell, the average age and longevity increased, and the crime rate decreased. Also, the state took the protection of the health of infants and mothers, and the rights of children, youth and women under its own guarantee and protection.

The social policy of the Turkmenistan state is declared in the program of "The Basic Targets of Social and Economic Development Policy, The Main Targets Until 201 0. " The aim of the economic development policies since independence is to improve the social and economic conditions of the people. Today Turkmenistan is among the countries that produce all the grain it needs. Our country has accomplished the main parts of its program for economic stability. It is pleasing to see that the Turkmen people's endeavors and industriousness is praised among the nations of the world.

The main development plan in Turkmenistan entails setting the value of 18% as a minimum limit of progress in every different economic domain. Another important aim is to increase our production by 2010. As always, the fuel and energy sectors are very important in this domain. We plan to invest in different areas, which entails huge investment costs.

Considering current potential, the futures of several sectors are promising, for example, agriculture, food industry, tourism, house construction and infrastructure services. The main target in agriculture until 2010 is to increase the production of grain and cotton. In 2005 the projection for production of cotton is 2.5 million tons and for wheat 2.5 million tons. This year 2 million tons of wheat was produced. Let's make a comparison. During the early years of Turkmenistan, 70 000 tons of wheat were produced. These numbers are the fruits of independence reflecting our endeavors to contribute to the production of the basic needs of our people and humanity. In order to enhance our national economy existing opportunities and resources are being considered and reconsidered for possible new developments. This also entails investing in fertile and productive areas. It is planned to increase fiscal sources fixed for investments 2.7 times in 2010 as compared with 2000.

Economic development is not enough to improve the conditions of our people. This only sustains the essential conditions. For this reason our law must pay attention to and resolve the social problems of our nation in a pre-planned and targeted way.

The basis of Turkmenistan's social policy until 201 0 will be the improvement of people's standard of living. As in the past, the important parts of the budget are fixed for this aim. With respect to people's standard of living, the construction of new social facilities and the improvement of current infrastructure facilities are among our most important targets. It is especially emphasized that natural gas, water, electricity and salt are supplied to the people free of charge. Those who live below the level of average income should be supported and protected.

281

The growth in the private sector is of importance in our development strategies. The number of private business enterprises in this realm will increase remarkably. Development strategies will progress speedily with the improvement of private, public and mixed enterprises, the organization of agricultural cooperatives, and the legal arrangement of the related subjects in this context. In the context of the development plan three thousand state-owned corporations will be privatized.

Our aim is to make Turkmenistan a developed country and make it a valued and sacred home for every citizen. All the state programs of independent Turkmenistan have as their aim the improvement of people's standard of living and protection of its citizens rights without any exception.

In the related session of the Halk Maslahaty (the National Council) in 1999, capital punishment was abolished in law. With the intention of improving the social life a general pardon was enacted by the congress in Turkmenistan on the sacred occasion of Kadyr night.

These policies help people to find the true path, listen to their conscience and thus reform and find a new, proper direction for their lives. They also display our determination to establish a democratic, humanitarian, and just social welfare state, respecting the principles of human rights and freedom. We are also proud of the fact that we are the first of the states which gained their independence recently to realize the developments laid out above.

It is well-known by all that all events are interrelated and interdependent today. The line of development of events is as follows: citizen-state-region-continent-world-humanity.

282

Thus, no matter its size and importance each nation and state with respect to its capacity should accept its responsibility to contribute to humanity within the context of this chain. This reflects Turkmenistan's way of resolving issues in her domestic and foreign policies. Within this context, economic and political immorality and arbitrariness should never be given a chance. That some international organizations, states or financial centers provide financial assistance for a country should not mean by any means that the law of the sovereignty of that receiver state or its independence can be taken lightly. Real power is the respect for truth itself, which is a feature of our new century. Such a manner, policy and application has been the basic approach of Turkmenistan in the past and at present. This principle is in accord with the Turkmen nation's ethical character and its political understanding, which forms the basis of the state's neutrality.

The National Council of Turkmenistan that convened on 27 December 1999 accepted the document, "A Declaration on Turkmenistan's Foreign Policy of 21 s Century that Depends on Neutrality, Peace-loving, Good Neighborhood Relations, and Democratic Principles". In this historic document it is declared that Turkmenistan as a neutral state has and employs a foreign policy related to love and respect for human life, full respect for democracy, and protection of human rights and freedom. These principles are the basis of Turkmen foreign. policy and diplomacy.

Turkmenistan accepts international human rights standards accepted by other members of the international community. It was also stated in the document that Turkmenistan

283

now and in the future is willing to cooperate with the United Nations.

My dear nation!

We are all the people of the 21st century. Since we have difficult and important duties to face in the future, we should unite all our efforts and strengths. At the same time we should take care of our individual or private responsibilities. This is the politico-ideal structure of Turkmenistan. It is defined by its own development process within this age and millennium. When all the Turkmens unite all their strengths

and are united, Turkmens will transform the 21st century into

a more secure, just, prosperous and happier age than the 20th century, and make this new age the Golden century of the Turkmens.

284

May the Turkmen Country be Safe and Secure

0 God, bless and save our great people!

Make my Turkmen country safe and secure

I revere my land

May my Turkmen country be safe and secure

May the route we take be safe and secure.

The heart is a bird, let it fly to the sky

May each citizen embrace his fortune

Our generations are stable,

May my Turkmen country be safe and secure

May happiness be your companion.

May my green flag wave

May our people and country become prosperous

May our name be renowned

May my Turkmen country be safe and secure

May it always be the Golden Era,

285

My ancestor's sincere wish,

Which Pyragy passed away without having seen

We made it the Independent State

May my Turkmen country be safe and secure

May all our routes be proper and lawful

May all the Turkmens rise from the hearth

Lion is the Turkmen, valiant is the Turkmen

God is your Companion, 0 Turkmen

May my Turkmen country be safe and secure

May the future be the Golden Era.

286

THE FIFTH SECTION
THE SPIRITUAL WORLD OF THE Turkmen

My dear people!
My beloved countrymen!
I feel we are one and the same. I am no different from you. I hide nothing from you. Your joy
and happiness are mine too. I am pleased to serve you and to fulfill my responsibilities for
the purpose of making your lives easier. To achieve this end we have prepared the essential
conditions to grant you free access to the lands that you need to cover your daily expenses
including gas, electricity, food and agricultural products. We have also arranged that those
accommodated in public housing will not be liable to pay any fees. And those in need will
be able to have access to essential foodstuffs. We have worked to provide you with peace
and tranquility. We have done all these in line with the law.
I have thought since my youth that whenever a people has access to these facilities, the nation
that forms the basis of the state will elevate spiritually. Our present success is the fruition of
our Independence and eternal Impartiality.
May your spiritual power be raised! Let our spiritual strength be an example to the world at
large!
When I talk of the spiritual world of the Turkmen, I speak of his morally high mode, his
awareness of the fact that mankind always lives on hope, his confidence in his country,
nation and justice, and of his certainty that his needs and desires will be met.
When man loses hope, his spirit is drowned and he
287
becomes disappointed. A man should have feelings of mercy, honesty, justice, spiritual
loftiness, an ideal to maintain integrity, a love of his nation, neighbors, fellow citizens and
his country in his heart.
Allah bestowed upon man a body and spirit when He created him. The individual spiritual
strength of men contributes to the moral elevation of a society. If a man is strong spiritually,
the society he belongs to will have the same strength.
When one thinks of the concept of time in its peculiar conditions, one can see life shrink into

a single entity or being. That being neither speaks nor hears. However it expresses itself

through the winds whirling over the endless Garagum desert, and the winds surfing through

the peaks of the waves of the Caspian Sea, and the gentle breezes that flow down from

Mount Kbpet. And this has a bearing on the Turkmen spirit.

The silence that arises from the tongue of centuries rings in my ears; my ancestors whose

voices became the sound of the Garagum wind, whose vision turned into the horizon of the

Turkmen desert, whose high spirits changed into the clouds in the sky, whose honorable

love became springs under the ground, whose painstaking efforts turned into the Turkmen

Sun, whose shadows formed the shadow of Mount Kipet, whose bones turned into Turkmen soil, for five thousand years have been making my soul exuberant and adding to

my spiritual strength.

Just as the ear of wheat sown into good land comes back to life and gains vitality again, so

too are the souls of our ancestors regenerating in my soul. Spiritual ideals transfer from one

soul to another. These ideals regenerate in the souls

288

of future generations.

The spiritual life has three essential components. These are the mind, wisdom and memory.

The first two we inherit from our forefathers. I always see the making of human life and

maturity in two periods.

The first period is the one in which the person does not know about or recognize himself.

The second is the one when man starts to know and recognize himself. The period which

starts after man gets to know himself is called the period of memory. In this period the

human memory grows to completion and he remembers the events and happenings that take

place in this period. In other words, this period is the individual and personal life. The man

lives off the experiences of the lives of his ancestors before this period. It is wisdom that

presides over this earlier period. This wisdom includes properties inherited from our forefathers, such as body, blood, creativity, renewal, productivity and mobility.

The noble spirit of his ancestors makes the Turkmen very active and joyous in his spiritual

world. This spirit is the source of his love for the Turkmen nation, language, religion, nature, music, of his love for his family and life, in sum, for all proper traditions.

The Turkmen nation had a national character from its birth. This character adopted different
qualities at different times but it has not lost its core values and has progressed continuously
over five periods.

The first age of the Turkmen Spirit is the period from BC 5000 to AD 650. The spiritual
leader of the nation in this age was Oguz Han. He worked as a simple and honest Turkmen.

The sacred symbol of the era is the ox. The ox shapes nature through its own effort. The ox
causes Mother

289

Nature to yield crops. The ox moves the world and society.

The route led by Oguz Han is one of justice, lawfulness and propriety, and its features are
enthusiasm, courage, forbearance and endurance.

Only those who persist will reach their objectives.

Oguz Han is also symbolized by the bull. It represents the skill, cleverness, maturity and
strength of the Turkmen.

If Oguz Han leads us to unity, oneness and integrity, then such qualities as resistance to
problems, having willpower, strength and ability to remain hardworking are essential. Oguz Han said:

"The living need mobility" And the dead tranquillity."

This idiom shows how hard-working were the Turkmens who were the contemporaries of
Oguz Han.

The second age of the Turkmen spirit begins around AD
650. This was an era when the Turkmens spread throughout
the world.

This age caused the spiritual strength displayed in difficult
conditions by Turkmens during migrations, and campaigns. The Turkmens were
inspired by Oguz Han's instruction telling them, "not to remain immobile."

The spiritual leader of the Turkmen in this second age was Gorkut Ata. The spirit of this era
found expression in the tones of the kopuz. Gorkut Ata converted to Islam of his own
volition and discovered the new comprehensive space unique to the Turkmen soul. Gorkut
Ata established new moral principles inspired by his personal faith and philosophy of the

290

afterlife. Life was divided into three, and not two parts. People believed that in the next
world they would have to account for what they did in this world.

Turkmens retained their moral values in this era. We know that a wolf figure was found in
Altyndepe in addition to the ox figure. And we know that Oguz Han was led by the

wolf.

Therefore, the ox was replaced by the wolf in this second era. This is because the days of
continuous peace and tranquility had come to an end. Islam opened up new ways for the
Turkmens. The power, bravery and speed of the wolf were essential for survival in these
new spaces. The Turkmen spirit exceeded its former borders and spread to the Islamic world.
This spirit became the wolf of the desert, traveled vast lands, and hunted prey. As such, it
adopted qualities of extra mobility and having access to an infinite amount of space. It also
became courageous and resistant. It took notice of the weak and the powerful. It did not
enrage the powerful, nor did it oppress the weak. It resided in the open spaces, gave birth to
offspring, and felt the love of its country. It did not allow strangers to trespass on its land. It
did not have a desire to acquire lands belonging to others. Its coat and mane bore the color
of infinite skies and eternity. It did not grow arrogant in happy days, nor did it fall victim to
the hopelessness of unhappy days. It inspired others to say, "The face of the wolf is sacred."
It did not let others trap it, nor did it enter the cage of the lion or do the circus tricks of the
tiger.

The third age of the Turkmen spirit is from the 10th to the 17th centuries. This period does
not only represent the era of the Turkmen sword. This is also the period when the Turkmen
spirit became known to the whole world. World history confirms that there were large-scale
Turkmen states

291

in this period. The Great Seljuk State, the Ottoman Empire, the Garagoyunlys and
Akgo'unlys States were signs of the eminence, and political and historical success of the
Turkmen spirit at that time.

The legendary hero Girogly did not play his dutar in vain. The spirit of this age was
symbolized by this particular instrument. The spirit of this age accumulated the strength that
broke stones and destroyed mountains. This strength had impacts not only on the ground but
in the sky as well.

The political and military pace at which Oguz Han traveled became a cultural and historical
pace. The spiritual leader of this era is Girogly.

The Oguz Turkmens gained a permanent place in history in this period. They gained a great
deal of political and administrative experience. There was an adage in the East, "If you want
to found a state, call the Turkmens." There were a number of Turkmen states established in
the Orient and the Occident, in Egypt, India and other locations. Many of the Turkmen
Soltans had names given to eagles. In fact, every grandchild of Oguz Han had the name of
an eagle, for example Gaya-iuikar, Begdili-bihri, Dodurga-garqgay, Owiarlagyn, Cepni-humay, Salir-birgit, Bikdiz-itelgi.
The founders of the Great Seljuk State, Dawud and Muhammed, were known by the names
Qagn and Togrul which were eagle names. The phoenix and humay birds served as a point of
reference for the Turkmens.
The Turkmen spirit hovered over the summit of the rocky mountains like an eagle. It
became morally elevated and strong. It hunted prey that flew in the sky and that fled along
the ground. It became very active and ebullient. It moved close to the sun, and absorbed its
heat. It settled on an
292
unreachable rock, one no voice could reach and no arrow could strike, and saw how
transitory and deceptive the world was, observed the greedy, mortal struggles of those
below. Thus, it acquired qualities of grandeur, comprehensiveness and depth.
The fourth age of the Turkmen spirit is between the 17th and 20 centuries. This period was
the weakest in terms of cleverness and skill. Action was replaced by idleness and waste,
resoluteness was replaced by spending time doing nothing. The Turkmen started praising
the achievements of the past and regretting his deficiencies. The historical creativity of the
nation's spirit ceased to exist. Having discarded the historical burden, the Turkmen made
efforts to maintain his national characteristics. Innumerable and complex historical events
divided the nation into various groups and tribes. The sincere leaders of these divided groups
made painstaking efforts to give unity to the nation's spirit. The Turkmens needed occasion
and a peaceful life to pass their historical experience through the sieve of the mind, and to
set future goals. So the Turkmen remained aloof from the foreign world and became
engaged with himself. Magtymguly Pyragy is the spiritual leader of this period.
When the Turkmen changes his traditions and his way, he is defeated. For example, the city

of Merw, which is also known as 'the Capital of the World', was a major city for the Turkmens of 4 thousand years ago. During the reign of Soltan Sanjar it had a population of
more than 2 million.
'h
Jingiz Han devastated this beautiful city in the 13 century, but the Turkmen people reestablished
Merw again. Then, in the 16th century Tamerlame sacked Merw. And the Turkmens restored Merw again. In 1787 the city was severely damaged

293

by the Han of Bukhara and was re-constructed by the Turkmens. Is there any other city in
the world that has been ruined so many times? The sublime spirit of the Turkmens protected
the city and it will do so forever.
Here is yet another example. There were bloody battles between the Sayyl Han of the Yomut
tribe and the supporters of the Akat yah of Iran. Battles took place in the villages of Astrabat
and many people were killed. Many Turkmens killed their wives themselves during these
battles since they did not want the enemy to capture their loved ones. Nevertheless, eight
thousand Turkmen women and children were captured and many of them committed suicide
to protect their chastity. 0 Allah Almighty! May You let them reside in Heaven, and May
You bestow upon all Turkmens of this day the beautiful Turkmen spirit inherent in them!
Internal conflicts shaped the essence of the Turkmen spirit in this age. The lack of state
caused dispersal and weakening of the historical memory. Relations between the nations in
Eastern countries diminished. Historical skills were seized by these nations.
Despite all difficulties, Magtymguly emerged as an outstanding figure. He inspired the
whole Turkmen nation. Magtymguly's nephews talked like him; Zelili talked about patriotism; Seydi about heroism; Mollanepes and Kemine about love and peace; and Mdtdji
about ideas on life. They all worked so that the Turkmen could be proud of his nation and
have moral strength.
The 20th century was one full of severe difficulties. The Turkmens who had never before
been subjugated to the rule of a foreign country were forced to endure foreign rule. The death toll of Turkmens who fought in the First World

294
295

War from 1914-1918 is around 80 thousand. More than 900 thousand Turkmens were deported between 1917 and 1930 because they were wealthy. Some 4 million Turkmens had

to leave the country in the same period. Countless numbers of people were killed and sent

into exile on the grounds that they were nationalists, enemies of the public and terrorists.

Their number cannot be known precisely because people were seized secretly from villages,

towns and cities. People were afraid to learn about what happened to those seized. The

Turkmen nation lived in a state of moral discontent.

We sometimes come across people today who say that they were better off in the Soviet era.

My dear Turkmen! Don't be mistaken! Don't you ever bring the greatness of the state and

independence down to your own level! Our values, such as independence, freedom, and

sovereignty, are priceless.

0Turkmen! You almost lost your native tongue during the Soviet era. You were not admitted to schools and you could not find employment if you did not know Russian. You

forgot about your religion, tradition and values. You lagged economically. Our nation lived

under terrible conditions in villages and towns. It is essential that our old tell the young

about all this.

Turkmenistan contributed revenue of US$10 to 18 billion from the production of oil, gas,

cotton and chemicals to the Soviet Treasury, and less than US$l million came back. Because

of this, moral values ceased to exist, and immorality, lack of trust, infidelity and fraud became widespread.

The 5th Golden Age of the National Turkmen spirit starts on 27 October 1991.

In fact Allah the Almighty decreed an interesting fate for our nation. The Turkmen spirit

rises at the beginning of each millennium. This was the same for the beginning of the third

millennium. Allah the Almighty granted the return of historical creative inspiration to the

Turkmen. This is the age of maturity for the Turkmen spirit.

This spirit now takes the form of a horse. The spirit of this age requires that not only the

traditional musical instruments of deprek, kopuz, dutar, gicak are played but that 72 instruments are played harmoniously. The horse took its place in the Turkmen flag and

brought Golden life, Golden spirit and contentment to the Turkmen soil. The horse became

an example and a symbol of the Turkmen nation's affluence and wealth, Golden spirit,

and
Golden life.

Our ancestors and forefathers maintained carefully and passed down through the generations
the ideas and thoughts that had an impact on the Turkmen spirit. Fellow Turkmens told
what they knew to their children and grandchildren. Thus, the invaluable advice of our
ancestors has reached this day.

MAY YOUR SOULS BE RAISED AS HIGH AS THE FLAG!

The Turkmen bears a great feeling of responsibility in his blood, soul and heart. No matter
whether you are a director or a servant, a farmer or a holy figure, a shepherd or an ordinary
soldier or a commander, you should try to be the best person in the age of Independence. If
you are not a good person, all that you do in this world is in vain.

The Turkmen nation has high morals. The Turkmen hopes that his neighbors have the same high morals as well. The Turkmen is very pleased to do favors and to support
297
humans morally. The Turkmen may sacrifice his own benefit for the sake of others. If you ask for a loan from someone, he will lend you money, even if the lender is a bad
person. But if the lender is a good person and does not have money, he says, "Come and
relax, and have a cup of tea," and then goes out secretly and borrows from his neighbor so
that he can lend money to the asker. Even the bad person will reply to all requests for help,
but the good one shares his bread too.

Only thanks to the will of Allah can we breathe. Our heart is a great and enchanting table
where love, peace and spiritual blessings abound. When the contents of this table are shared
they increase. If you act meanly, then they will cease to exist and fade away.

The more it is drunk, the sweeter and more abundant the
water in an artesian well becomes. if it remains idle, the
water supply decreases and smells stagnant.

Smile at your fellows when you greet them. When you
smile, so will your fellows, and their smiles will invoke blessed feelings in your heart.
When you meet a crowd of people, don't hurt anyone and pay compliments to everybody,
and you will win everyone's heart. This way you will see that they smile not only on the face
but in the heart and their hearts will blossom like roses. Both you and others will be pleased
to see this.

So you should be a good person, not for the sake of others, but for your own sake first of all.

Man lives on the earth but his spirit is both sky and heavens. If a man is morally degraded,
no order or decree can
change him.
States make efforts to educate people and make them
298
aware of being a member of a state, and to protect and provide people with happiness.
All religions, first and foremost, and then literature and art which aims at the good of
mankind put forth an exemplary model of man.
The main objective of our state is to educate excellent people who will be praised in world
literature's, who have good spirits, who are generous, brave and bold, and who set great
goals. Every member of our nation should be comfortable. But they should first be
knowledgeable, consistent and have a progressive view of the world.
The Indian dervishes, Muslim Sufis, and Tibetan monks make contact with Allah the
Almighty through their words of praise. They say repeatedly that this is the most pleasurable
thing to do in the world. We Turkmens set out into the world with our own slogan too. Our
slogan is to lead a life which is spiritually high. There is no substitute for the pleasure of a
high spiritual life.
There are so many awards and titles in the world that grant man reputation and raise him to
high ranks. Among
4 6 such titles are "hero Tabourer", "artist of the state", esteemed artist" etc. There are
medals awarded in return for services rendered to the nation and the country. But there are
no ranks, medals, titles or honorary designations that relate to the exemplary man. But such
titles are necessary. I hereby establish the medal of "Virtuousness." Let us award this medal
to people who bear the most humane qualities, who win the hearts of the majority and who
share their love and affection.
The Independent and Eternally Neutral Turkmen State
299
has displayed great respect for the Oguz Han traditions and remarkable philanthropic ideas,
and, as such, enhanced these traditions. An honorary title, "Outstanding Public Figure," was
established. We award honorary titles to professionals, to people with high ethical standards
and to philanthropists. We encourage others to show more respect to these people. The new
titles are appropriate for farmers, laborers, musicians, governors and shepherds, but there is
only one condition for receiving the "Outstanding Public Figure" title: that one has

good
ethics.

When people with good ethics increase in number, life itself becomes more beautiful. The world is moving towards perfection, love and concem for humanity and integrity. Man is moving towards Allah! All religions tell us that after a man dies his soul is purified and reaches a place before Allah.

Man should set out on this voyage when alive.

If we are to appear before Allah, we should be in proper condition for that appearance.

The Turkmen should recite the following poem when going out to the world at large:

Be grand and noble, set your sights at grand targets,
May your soul be as noble as the standard!
Wave goodbye to the old-age sorrows,
May your soul be as noble as the standard!
The hopeless look healthy but they're not,
The spiritually high have double the blessings

300

Don't drown in indecision,
May your soul be as noble as the standard!
An upright man will never be down even if his work does not go well,
He will have no grief in his high place,
His dreams ebullient, his mind joyous,
May your soul be as noble as the standard!
Be high in spirit, as your people always are,
Being a low Turkmen is a shame on you,
Allah loves generous souls,
May your soul be as noble as the standard!

Once, a number of people were talking about a thief in a village. During the conversation Divletmdmmet Azady spoke of the good manners of the thief. As if they had agreed in advance, all the sufis started saying good things about the thief. Other participants in the conversation thought that the thief was being treated like an angel, although he was clearly far from being one.

Days and months pass by, and the thief visits Azady in his home.

"Azady, Your Highness, I am enchanted by your power, look where you've placed me," he cries out. "I heard of your remarks in that conversation praising me. I felt elevated and immediately gave up stealing. Even when I engage in any minor deed that might be improper, I always question myself as to what Azady His Highness would say in such a case. You really won my heart." Azady says in reply:

301

"You have faith in your heart, so your conscience awoke."

In another exchange some people said to Azady, "Your Highness, you knew that so-and-so

was a thief, but you praised him. Why?"

"If you say good things about a man, and if I do the same and so do others, then the good

aspects of that person will come out. But if you say bad things about that man, and if I do

the same and so do others, then it will be as if that person were coated in black pitch. If

possible, talk about the good qualities of a man, and not the bad ones. This is what wisdom

tells you to do."

If a man blushes, his heart cannot be all bad.

If you don't have a brother, the blame is not yours. If you do not have a friend, the blame is

not Allah's.

Behave in such a way that even strangers become close to you.

Speak well of Allah's subject, so that he may correct his evils by himself.

As a member of this nation, you should live together with and attached to your fellow members of the nation.

If you improve your relations with other people, then people will have better relations with

you. If there are a great number of good men around you, you will be able to build a fortress. It is your fellow Turkmen who will maintain the essential qualities of the Turkmen identity. No outsider will come up, arrange and order our own society. We need

to correct our own people.

302

IT IS THE Turkmen

The real brave man, the gallant! Think, contemplate,

It is the Turkmen himself shall make this nation grand

Visit your past and take an excursion to the future

It is the Turkmen himself shall make this nation grand

The Turkmen boy is a lion, and a lion's son is a lion,

Unwillingness and avoiding duties are a shame

For those who run for the other, it is victory which accompanies them,

It is the Turkmen himself shall make this nation grand

Take lessons from the past and be an example for the future,

May all seven climates be proud when they see the Turkmen,

May the route the Turkmen take be the course the world follows,

It is the Turkmen himself shall make this nation grand

Try to be the equal of the learned Pyragy and Gorkut,

Try to be the equal of the valiant Alp Arslan, Qagry beg and Togrul,

For Oguz Han people lagging behind does not suit

It is the Turkmen themselves who can make this nation grand.

303

If we help each other on the way to perfection, Allah will help us more.

The existence of a united people in a place is a harbinger of progress.

May your spiritual power be great! If you are strong spiritually, Allah will love you and

bless you more and give you longer life!

When a miserable person approaches you and talks complainingly of the world and other

people, his lack of enthusiasm will affect you and you will grow indifferent to your tasks.

In contrast, if a man full of joy and happiness with high moral powers approaches you, then

your soul will be pleased, you will apply yourself to your tasks with a new enthusiasm.

Spiritual eminence gives you an infinite amount of courage. So you, Turkmen, should have

that never-ending moral power.

Life itself is a competition. If you are in competition with good people, then you become

good too. May goodness and good people be with you.

Allah loves men who are strong spiritually, He is proud of such men. And you too would

love the most joyous, the most attractive, the most life-loving among your children.

No one has ever conquered a fortress or reached his goals by being discontented. You do

not relieve yourself of grief and sorrow by merely complaining of grief and sorrow. That

only helps grief and sorrow to invade your soul.

May you be strong spiritually! The soul is a bird placed by Allah in the cage called the

body. His breath is a fresh and

304

noble one. Allah gave that to us in order that we could live peacefully and in joy and happiness.

Maintain your spirituality at high levels. Let your soul flutter in the skies like your noble

flag!

The ultimate direction of your soul is the way of Allah.

One should not arrive before Allah with a soul in grief. Love your life, living and your

children!

Love your beautiful country, Mother Nature and the generous land!

Once you do so, your soul will rise and your spirituality grow, and you will benefit from

your duties!

My dear citizens!

My beloved countrymen!

The soul is a part of Allah located in ourselves. We must maintain properly the soul granted

to us by Allah.

It is not difficult to drown in grief. One needn't be knowledgeable, skilful or privileged to

suffer from grief and sorrow. And it is very easy to complain. You can continue complaining even though you have everything on track and you are wealthy and a man of

rank. That's because there is no limit or border to wealth. The same also holds for ranks.

Wouldn't the wealthy man who thinks he's wealthy but who complains that his wealth is not

as great as that of Karun drown in misery? Certainly he would!

There was a sufi of Turkmen origin called Bayezit-i Bestami. He left us a myriad of words

of wisdom and stories. Here is one:

Ebu Musa asks Bayezit the Sheikh:

305

"O, Our Master, what do you plan to do tomorrow?"

The Sheikh says:

"I know nothing about tomorrow or tonight because Allah said to me:

'O Bayezit! There are various prayers and services rendered to my Treasury. If you wish to

arrive before me, bring me something that is not already with me.'

I asked then:

'O Allah, the Merciful! The Almighty! What is there that is not with you?'

Allah said:

'Hopelessness and weakness, poverty and neediness, being offended and miserable are not

with me or in my Treasury. Because these are not the things I need.' Allah is the

Undisturbed. Allah is Great. Allah is to be praised with good words only. Allah's will is an

obligation upon the Turkmen."

Bayezit is a leading Turkmen figure in Islam. His thought is:

We are simple and mortal human beings. We are human beings sent to the world to live.

We should live in line with high humanitarian principles and follow the way of the great

nation called the Turkmens; we should make use of worldly benefits, keep our head high,

make efforts and see the beauties of life according to the same principles.

Our great thinker, Magtymguly, is undoubtedly a great figure in the East. We should look

to Magtymguly as a proper example at every step we take. Would it be proper for us to

follow Magtymguly at this age in exactly the way he did,

306

in that he adopted the sufi way, waking at dawn and cry and pray with all the plants, trees

and creation? We are different from those people who adopted the sufi way.

Two types of power are granted to man for survival. A man spends all his efforts on worldly affairs in the first half of his life, or his youth. He establishes a family, receives

training to provide his daily needs; renders services to people. Thus, he shows himself to the world at large. But when he grows older, and he thinks more about life he starts understanding that he was not created for this world with its limitations of time and space.

He starts to grasp otherworldly realities. As Magtymguly says "There is a period of transition from one era to another." In this period, he perseveres and expresses regrets by

saying: two poems again.

You ploughed the earth, you did indeed,
And you reaped benefits thereafter.
You've reached forty years of age.
Mature, you've become a man of wisdom.
Mind grows to completion when one's forty
So holds it for the mankind
And the things done in youth seem strange to man
After he passes forty and becomes mature in mind.
Then repent for them and follow a spiritual guide.

All Turkmen poets express similar philosophies.

307

During the reign of the Seljuks when the Turkmens ruled, Soltan Sanjar read a poem by

Enweri and invite him to his palace:

The course of the world, the wicked world,
Caused severe pain and damage.
All evils on earth and in the sky ask,
"Where is Enweri's little home?"

Immediately after reading the quatrain, the Soltan says:

"O poet, if all evils strike your home alone, don't just complain, but think a while. And say,

'What if it is the result of my sins?'Nothing is groundless. Even the slightest motion does

not take place without a cause for it. There is a sign of wisdom in everything."

Enweri listens to the Soltan and understands what he means: "Even when he is living rough, the soul of man resides at the top of the legendary Kaf Mountain." He realized that

not every single one of his desires could be fulfillled, that he could not adapt to every condition and that he could not reside in a particular place for long.

It would not be right to remain idle and claim that this was our fate. Everyone should strive

to improve his future and be happy in his life. "Perseverance means success," as the saying

goes.

Remain upright, even if you encounter a difficulty. Don't just be upset. When you suffer

from grief and sorrow, just think that these are the salty ingredients in a sweet soup.

It is hard to live in a world colder than ice, if you don't have wary heart. Man's life after

the beautiful days of childhood is not full of peace, joy and comfort only. No matter

308

how wealthy, prosperous and affluent a society is, daily hardships and duties will continue

to exist. Man should not lose his human qualities when he encounters such difficulties. One

should not let oneself be morally disheartened or unable to solve problems. Man needs to

have spiritual strength so that he cannot be embarrassed and overcome by difficulties.

The Nobility of the Soul means not losing love and the desire to live.

The Nobility of the Soul means not losing your determination and perseverance to live.

The Nobility of the Soul means feeling the honor of being a human.

The Nobility of the Soul means not losing wholeheartedness and sincerity.

Men are active and high in spirit during their youth. But many forget these beautiful feelings when they grow older. This is because the body is strong when men are young and

they feel more the joy of life. The body is so programmed that it gradually grows older and

weaker. The real man is the one that remains strong throughout his entire spiritual life.

For his eminence in spirit does not depend on ambitions, lust and sexual desires, but on the

contrary, it depends on spiritual enthusiasm and values. A man grows all the more enthusiastic spiritually when he feels the same as his fellow countrymen do. The union of

hearts is the love that does not separate you from your fellow people and country. The life

and the heart of a man with spiritual eminence is his homeland. The concept of homeland is

a comprehensive one and it has many connotations. One's spouse, children, brothers, relatives, state, friends, place of birth, colleagues, history and today are all contained in

reference to the concept of home-

309

land. Values and ideas should be personified so that a people becomes united and integrated. The process of personification is a sophisticated one. The personification speaks

of the perfect degree of man and the national identity. When man reaches the right level of

maturity in his ideas and thoughts on soul and spirituality, he reaches His Creator, Allah,

the idea of His Oneness and Uniqueness. By the same token, the individual both generalizes and personifies the values that are important to him and refers to them through

the concept of homeland. The homeland is one and unique. Unique means unequalled and

invaluable.

Once he understands how sacred is the homeland, through his mental perception and feelings, the Turkmen can never yield to spiritual debasement. Since for him the concept

of homeland turns into a proof when he speaks, into love in his heart, an unbreakable belief

in ethics, perseverance in working, and into benefits in motion.

Spiritual debasement is a result of loneliness. If a man has faith in his heart, he will never

feel inferior to others even though he earns less and lives in a simpler house. Regression in

material things does not necessarily mean spiritual debasement. Material deficiencies might

harm one's body. But, only spiritual poverty, slackness of spiritual strength and faith can do

harm to the soul. Therefore, maintain a pure heart, and never, ever neglect your spirituality,

your spiritual well-being.

Man is a spiritual being. The most important problems and the most severe difficulties have

to do with the soul. Even though he has material needs, man can survive if he adapts to the

world at large in a modest way. But in the cases of spiritual hunger, needs of the soul, or

ethical weakness, it is harder for man to maintain his human qualities. Man can be subjugated only when spiritually debased. Therefore highness in spirit is essential for everyone who carries the name Turkmen. It is as essential as

the air we breathe, or the food we eat. Just as air is essential to the lungs and bread to the

stomach, so too is spiritual highness essential to the heart and soul for the Turkmens and

all others.

The Turkmen people have held various viewpoints in their rich and complex lives. These

are the springs that feed the Turkmen soul. So here is my real advice: always remain strong and sublime spiritually!

A FATHER HAS THE RIGHTS OF ALLAH

I wish to draw your attention specifically to three sayings by Gorkut Ata:

The Soltan's right is the same as Allah's right.

The father's right is the same as Allah's right.

The mother's right is the same as Allah's right.

The word haq, right, is synonymous with the word justice, huquk. They are indeed the same thing.

Thus, the Turkmen grants almost the same rights as Allah's to only three people in society:

the ruler, the father and the mother The ruler's rights imply each and every citizen's responsibilities before the law and the ruler. The rights of the father and mother also imply

one's responsibilities to one's parents.

If you are indebted to someone, it means you are to give something to them.

The indebtedness of children originates from the patronage provided for them by their parents. The children are dependent on their parents in various respects.

311

The children should be indebted to their parents because they were born.

The children are indebted to their parents because they raised them to be benevolent people.
The children should be indebted to their parents because they helped them become members of society.
Allah Almighty created man as follows:
Allah created the child so that he is dependent on his parents until he reaches maturity. Man
should thank Allah because he is born. And he should remain indebted to his parents and
pray for them as they provided for him with proper care and upbringing.
But the youth mistakenly think that they grew up on their own. They can only understand
the sufferings of their parents in raising them when they get married and have children.
Therefore our ancestors said the following:
"You will understand the value of those who helped you subsist only when you help others
subsist."
"You will understand the value of those who protect you only when you protect others."
Helping others subsist and protecting them does not merely mean providing them with
material needs. This is patronage and maintenance.
Every age has its peculiar properties. The child has different thoughts of his father at different ages:
5 years old: "My father knows everything."
10 years old: "My father knows quite a lot."
15 years old: "I know as much as my father does."

20 years old: "To tell the truth, my father does not know anything."
30 years old: "Nevertheless, my father knows something."
40 years old: "It would be fine if I consulted my father." 50 years old: "My father knows
everything."
60 years old: "If only my father were alive and I could consult him about this and that. I
should have appreciated him properly when he was alive."
One understands the value of one's parents when one grows older. We start thinking about
the value of things only after we lose them. But Turkmen girls and boys should recognize
the value of their parents beforehand. Fortunate is the child that pays respect to his parents.
Being born itself is a blessing. Transforming the Allah-given blessing of life into real
happiness depends only on man's ability to do so. Life is a blessing bestowed upon us by
Allah. Leading a meaningful life is not only a right but also a duty on us. Allah granted me

the chance to lead a life in this world. But Allah deprived me of maternal affection and

paternal patronage. Therefore I knew of the value of parents even before I had children. I

felt lacking and low in myself compared to my friends when their fathers expressed affection to them. I used to feel bad, in a way inferior, when their fathers would smile at

them.

Yet Allah provided me with the cure for my suffering. Although I was an orphan, I was

given by Allah the spiritual power to overcome inferiority, neediness and loneliness. Allah

Himself provided me with parental affection and patronage. Allah Almighty also gave me

the chance to con-

314

vey my experience full of pain to others and to tell them what the homeland meant.

My beloved child!

Allah is followed by your father in terms of your patronage.

Life is led in three castles. One castle lasts for a lifetime, and the other two follow the footsteps of time.

The lifelong castle is your homeland. You are in it from your birth till your last day in the

world.

The second castle is the home you are born and raised in. You are raised with parental affection in this castle. This is a sacred place for you because this place includes your mother and father who provide for you and protect you from evils. You start speaking in

this castle. You become mature in this castle. This castle provides you with the necessary

means to survive in the third castle.

The third castle is the home you establish with your beloved one. This is the life castle that

will blossom like a rose and gain meaning. You should always remain indebted to your

parents when you are in this castle, and you should express your indebtedness. You should

behave consistently and show that your parents raised a good child.

Your dignity, reputation, honor, your respect toward them and the services you render to

them add to their lives. The daily greeting you express and assistance you provide are signs

that express your indebtedness. In this way you obtain the approval of your parents and

behave in a way that shows their affection for you was not in vain.

Your mother gives shape to your intrinsic qualities, and your father protects you from external evils.

315

When a child is scared, he cries out "mother" for help. When he grows up, he seeks

the
support of his father.
The father is an example of wisdom, logic, patriotism, chastity and justice in the Turkmen
tradition. The father is not thought to be the one who raises the child because he never says
"Be like this, do this and that." He sets an example for his child through his actions, his
deeds, clothing and characteristics as to how one should be and live. A father can talk to his
child through his eves.
Once a father and his son were unjustly convicted of theft. They were brought before court
and the Soltan. The judge decreed 40 lashes for the alleged criminals. First forty lashes are
administered to the father. He suffers, his whole back becomes a pool of blood, but he does
not cry out a single
word that expresses pain.
Then they start to lash the son. Each time they hit the son, the father cries out, "Oh my son,
no." The Soltan calls
the old father to him:
"You were flogged with forty lashes but you did not utter a single word of pain. Why do
you cry now?"
"O Your Majesty, the lashes were touching my flesh only when they beat me, but when
they beat my son, I felt the
pain deep in my inside."
The Soltan was pleased with the answer and ordered that the two be released, saying that
such a father could not
be accused of theft.
0 sons of the Golden Age, the Awaited generation!
You have matured and become older. When you become older still, don't think that your
fathers are a burden upon

you. For your fathers carried you on their shoulders carefully as a burden on them, and they
raised you.
Listen to the advice of Gorkut Ata: "Gain your reputation while your father is alive, and get
ahead while you have your horse."
Your father is a base for you in society. People measure your value first by looking at your
father. Don't let your father be ashamed among others because of you.
You are the heir of your father. It is not merely wealth that you inherit. Your father's

reputation or dishonor is left to you, too. Your father's heritage is divided equally among

his children, but his authority transfers to you and your brothers undivided.

May you never forget who your father is. Let others say of you, "Better than his father,"

and be proud if they say so. Be ashamed if they say of you, "He is not up to his father."

Don't you ever forget that you were created out of one drop.

If it weren't for your father, you wouldn't exist. You would not have been born if not for

him. It is your father's existence that made your existence in the world of beings possible.

Your father is your previous self.

Disregarding your father means disregarding yourself. Being disrespectful to your father is

being disrespectful to yourself. The more favors you do your father, the more you do the

same for yourself.

Ispend much time thinking about the relations between fathers and their sons. A Turkmen

saying goes: "If your father is a dog, then feed yourself at a trough."

317

Once in the old times, a saint spoke ill of a certain man, saying:

"May you bark as a dog does." The very moment the saint uttered this, the man became a

dog, by Allah's will. That man's son fed his father at his doorway. After people went to bed,

he washed the dog, brushed it and ate at the trough with his dog-father. This lasted seven

years. When the saint saw how honest and sincere the son was, he prayed to Allah for the

man to become a human being again and afterwards he said to the man:

"Indeed you should have lived in this world as a dog because of your deeds, but I see that

you've raised a perfect son. It is for that Allah elevated you to your human status again."

Men are parts in a chain. Each individual is a part of the chain. You are a part only because

your father was a part. Never, ever seek benefits from your father in return for what you did

for him, and if he does that, then be patient.

Life means existence, and death is absence. Absence is one, existence is of three stages.

You yourself are the present existence, your child is tomorrow's existence and your father

is yesterday's existence. Death comes all of a sudden. If you are not one of three, you cannot win victory over death.

The fear of death settled on earth at the same time as the human being. That fear is removed when your first child is born because your child is a continuation of you.

Fathers don't die. They live in the souls of their children. I noticed a certain feeling after my

youth. I think all mature people have that feeling. I sometimes feel that I am not myself,

and I am my father instead. It is as if I touch through his hands and not mine. It is as if 1

move forward on his feet

318

and not mine. It is as if I speak through his tongue and not mine. This sounds strange and

interesting at first sight. It is indeed not the kind of feeling that you could talk about to

someone unless you had felt it. At those times, I feel that my father's movements, characteristics and behaviors are reviving in me. I understand that my father is reviving

in me.

This is the kind of feeling that shows one is mature. Try to have this kind of feeling. By

doing so, you will extend the life of your father and show respect toward him. Respect for

the father is respect for the homeland.

NONE WOULD CARE AS MUCH AS MY MOTHER WOULD

My dear Turkmen Nation!

The mother is a sacred being. Then talk of the mother is sacred too.

One can understand the value of sacred things only after one has lost them. The values of

certain things can only be perceived after they are lost. A man's real nature can be understood by looking at his respect toward his mother. A Turkmen saying expresses how

beautiful a mother is to her child:

"Fatherless, I am orphan; motherless, I am captive."

This saying clearly speaks to one with Turkmen feelings and consciousness of how sacred

the mother is.

Turkmen people compare the mother to the father to express the fact that the privileged

status of the sacred mother cannot be compensated for by anything.

For the Turkmen has a national understanding of the concept of "sacredness."

319

Afather s endless efforts, and a mother's heart feeds the child.

The heart is where feelings reside; and humanity is home to various comparisons.

The Turkmen combines the words mother and heart, and tells us that sacredness has nothing to do with material benefits or values.

Achild is a part of his father's body, but he is a part of his mother's heart.

The word orphan has connotations of material insufficiency or having material needs. But

the word captive refers to spiritual lack, insufficiency of spiritual patronage, and lack of

spiritual ground. Being a captive means falling away from one's homeland and suffering

from all kinds of difficulties. The captive suffers not from the lack of material support from his friends, but from the lack of spiritual aid and from their insensitivity.

The world itself seems ruthless and cruet to the captive.

The orphan is better off than the captive.

Fate decreed two pains for me. I was both an orphan and a captive. This double suffering

is recognized only by those who have faced it.

Ican say that the severest pain is the need for maternal love. The pain felt by the heart is

sharper than bodily suffering. Bodily pain abates, but the pain felt by the heart goes on,

bleeds all the time and remains with one, as long as one's heart remains beating.

If one's father passes away, then one is in need of material things.

If one's mother passes away, then one suffers

320

from lack of love.

Amother's love and compassion for her child is the source that binds the child and the mother, and that is home to invisible warm feelings between the two. This warmth transforms the mother and her child into a world that is composed only of the two.

One's blood comes from one's father, whereas one's body is from one's mother.

The mother is the first place where one resides. The first homeland where one lives for

nine months, becomes a human being and enters the world is the womb of one's mother.

The mother's lap is the second homeland where the child lives, is taught to speak, has his

mind and feelings developed from infancy toward adolescence. Compassion originates

from the warmth of the mother's lap.

The caring hands of the mother are a homeland that raises the child from infancy to adolescence, provides it with desirable qualities and brings it to perfection. People who

were cared for by their mothers grow up as individuals who are ready to love the homeland which is our ultimate place to reside.

Compassion results from the mother's womb, lap and hands. Sacredness finds a safe place

in the human body and becomes the essential factor that improves him. Therefore it is the

mother who renders the individual sacred.

Allah creates; He is the Creator. The mother is the reproducer, the deliverer.

Human beings other than Adam and Eve gain life in their mother's wombs and are prepared for worldly life there.

321

The creation of Eve shows that Allah reserved creation for Himself, but shared the power

to reproduce humans with mothers.

Thereafter, Allah did not create another human being without a mother, except in one instance. This instance was the creation of Jesus Christ. Magtymguly says the

following
on Allah's creation of Jesus Christ:
"He is the one that came into being without a father."
Allah Almighty is definitely powerful. He could have created Jesus Christ without a mother too. But that's not how He did it. I think this a sign of the special value placed upon the mother by the Creator. It is an obligation upon every Turkmen to praise and love
the mother, who is given a special value by Allah, the Creator of you and me and all, Who
creates everything out of nothing by His Will and Command, Who is the Creator of the
whole universe.
If any word at all has the quality of a miracle, if any word at all has superior qualities about it, that word is mother. Life has its origins in the mother.
Once upon a time the great Seljuk poet Enweri approached a saint with great enthusiasm.
The saint said:
"Allah has given me a special privilege; ask of me any wish you desire and it will come
true."
"I wish to see my mother who is the ultimate direction I turn to, and my father's face for
one last time. Let them see that their child lives in the world in a benevolent way, causing
no harrn. Let them be in peace in the other world knowing this," asked Enweri of the saint.
By Allah's will, the saint let Enweri see the faces of his mother and father. They met and
were happy.
322
The saint said:
"You could have been given wealth or a Sultanate if you had wished. But yours was the
most sacred of all desires. Go and you will be rewarded with the Sultanate of hearts!"
Under Soltan Sanjar's patronage, Enweri the Poet became the most famous poet of all Seljuk Turkmens, Arabs and Persians. He is deemed to be one of the three poets who followed the way of the Prophet.
There is a myriad of anecdotes and stories about mothers. Man can understand that the
most miraculous thing in the world is the mother, although he does not necessarily understand everything. He elevates the status of the mother with wise sayings.
Once there was a couple in love. The girl wished to learn how much her beloved loved
her:
"Tear apart your mother's chest and bring her heart to me, if you really love me," she said.
The girl's beloved was mad about the girl and he tore apart his mother's chest and took the
bloody heart, which was still beating, in his hands. He ran to the girl's house. A stone

on
the way tripped him and he fell down. At that moment his mother's heart in his hands
gained the power to speak and said:

"O my dear, you haven't hurt yourself, have you?"

This is a mother. No matter what happens, she feels and lives for her child with such
love,
compassion, attachment and dedication that it can never ever be given up. After a
long and
painful delivery, between life and death, every mother gives birth to her child in
difficulty.

Once, a mother was dying during delivery. The physi-

323

cians resuscitated the baby and the baby uttered a very loud cry. By Allah's will, the
mother who had just died, revived at the cry of the baby.

Idon't believe everything I am told. I am not very pious either. But I do feel like
believing
very much in the story told above.

Doctors who work in the maternity ward say:

"On some occasions, it is really hard to save the lives of some mothers. Realizing the
dangers, those mothers always say, 'Save my baby. Leave me but deal with my child
and
save it,' and so give life to their babies."

The following story is attributed to a poet who lived in historic times:

The poet's mother wishes to eat apples when she is with child. There are dark red
apples
hanging in the trees in the gardens that belong to their neighbors. She cannot ask for
apples from the neighbors since she is at odds with them. She cannot buy apples
because
she does not have the money. She goes back and forth to the gardens wishing for
some
apples and thinks she should not take them since the apples do not belong to her, so it
would be wrong to take those apples. Then the baby is born and grows to be the
famous
poet. The poet says:

"Our neighbor's garden is a fertile land for apples. I sometimes wish to fulfill my
mother's
wish and eat those apples. But I don't, because I do not want to hurt my mother's soul.
Therefore I control myself."

There is no limit to the respect to be displayed toward parents. A couple of years ago,
a
man was talking to a famous religious figure:

324

"We were raised under Soviet policies. I wish to believe in Allah, but I can't. I am so
old
now but I just can't live without a faith."

The religious figure said in reply: "If you do not believe in Allah, go bow to your
parents
graves." Faith has its origins in belief in the parents. Magtymguly also expressed
something in the same vein, "Forgive my sins, for the sake of my parents." Maintain

respect for your parents. Allah will forgive you for the sake of your parents, if not for your

own sakes.

The Turkmen nation does not know much about the great poet Enweri. I sometimes think:

"Enweri was so happy that he saw the faces of his mother and father once again, and I would also give all that I have to be able to see the faces of my parents."

The women who knew my mother say, 'How dear and affectionate a woman your mother

was!" Those who knew my father say, "Saparrnyrat, your father was a bold and fearless

man. He would help people, and if he couldn't help others himself, he would try to find

others who could. He had such light in his face, he spoke courteous and beautiful words,

and he was a man to be heard with joy."

Thus I saw that what my parents had left for me was more valuable than what the Soltans

left to their children. I raised myself to be the proper son that my parents would want me

to be.

Stay away from people who hurt their parents. Such people cannot be human. Do not believe in people who do not take care of their parents. Such people will not be of any use

to the public and their homeland.

It is not proper to pay the slightest respect to a person

who does not take care of his parents. Even Allah's angels would not pay any respect to

the person who does not take care of his parents.

We say the mother is the soil, the father is the homeland.

The mother teaches us to love the soil, and the father teaches us to love the homeland through their painstaking efforts and their lives.

No matter if her child is deaf, disobedient or stupid, a mother will always understand what

her child says.

The Turkmens say, "Only the deaf person's mother understands what the deaf person says."

"My son, when you were a baby, all you could do was to cry. You could not speak. You

could not say a word. I would understand what you meant, though. You are now grown

up, but I simply cannot understand you," complained a mother of her ungrateful son.

An ungrateful person who breaks the heart of his mother cannot achieve anything all through his life.

One who does harm to his mother could do harm to other people and the homeland, too!

Don't believe it, if they say of someone that he does not take care of his mother, but there are others he takes care of.

Ibelieve the mother carries with her powers and miracles. This I have witnessed many times in my life. If I am going to be happy or upset tomorrow, I see my mother in my dream.

My dear daughters and sons!

Don't think that you were not taken care of. Your mother's careful eyes over you watch out

for you day and night. Wherever you are, your mother's heart is with you.

326

The Turkmen have a beautiful saying: "Only my mother's tears are real, others are fake."

The mother always takes care of her children. Respect mothers! Love mothers! We wouldn't be paying them the respect they deserve, even if we carried them on top of our

very heads. People who are respectful of their parents are happy and productive in their

lives. Don't believe in the greatness and goodness of those who are disrespectful of their

parents. A man's real essence can be understood in the respect he displays toward his parents.

OUR CHILDREN ARE OUR CONTINUATION!

My dear citizens!

My fellow countrymen!

The child is the product of the love, sincerity and will of the mother and the father. For

parents, even a single hair of their children is worth the whole world. Because Turkmen

people are hardworking and determined, sons are given a special value. When a son is bom, the parents say, "We are wealthier, stately, now," and his relatives say, "We have become more fist (powerful) in the family now." When one asks the number of members

in a family, they don't tell you the number of mouths in the family, but they tell you the

number of heads. The Turkmen's love for his daughter requires special mentioning. That

is because daughters are more vulnerable and they will become parts of other families in

the future. A daughter should be very happy in her parent's home.

The love found in a child's heart has its origins in the child's mother.

The dignity, bravery, foresight, and fearlessness of the child stem from the father.

327

The father is like a high mountain with a grandeur of body and a snowy summit as high as

the clouds in the sky.

The mother's heart is an ocean full of love and peace.

When our father, the Prophet Adam, had a son and a daughter, he asked Angel Gabriel:

"I haven't felt the mercy of a mother, nor do I know of paternal love. Then why was I granted this fate?"

"Allah is your father and mother. Wouldn't He replace both?" Gabriel replied.

It is an obligation upon the child to please his parents. When are parents happy with what
their children do?

When a child surpasses his father in work, respect, wealth and affluence, then his parents
will be as pleased as their child makes them.

The child is the most precious belonging of the father.

The child is a continuation of the parents.

Achild can leave his parents upon obtaining proper consent and approval from them, as
required by a proper upbringing. And on the part of the child to gain consent is a debt to
his or her parents.

Turkmen people have various sayings, principles and ethical rules regarding children's
responsibilities to their parents. These are the accumulation of thousands of years of
experience. The Turkmen family lies at the root of these. Society is in fact based on the
family. So the ultimate aim is the reinforcement and strengthening of society. Therefore
personal values, familial values and social values are not separate entities in the
Turkmens but they stand as inseparable parts of a whole. It is this harmony that helped the
Turkmen

328

nation survive as a nation for thousands of years. It was only under the Soviet regime that
the relations between mothers and daughters, fathers and sons, and our national values
were grievously harmed. The aim was to destroy the Turkmen family. They understood
that this was the most appropriate method to decimate the Turkmen nation, and this policy
was implemented on purpose.

In our contemporary age, the Golden Age of the Turkmen, our main objective is the
revival of familial relations and revitalization of family values. In this framework, the
responsibilities of the child to his parents have a special role.

The well-behaved child does not grow on his own. The child needs guidance. An unguided
child is like an untrained horse.

Equipping the child with social values, and rendering him beneficial to society at large as
a skilled individual are the main aims of this guidance.

Man is born to live as part of a society in this world. Without a society, it is impossible for
a man to live. However, there are certain rules and principles to be honored when living
in a society. There are certain responsibilities that are to be fulfillled.

The first responsibility of the child is the fulfillment of the duties that are incumbent upon
him regarding his parents.
The main ethics to be pursued when fulfillling this responsibility are as follows:
The- child should definitely know that his parents always want the good of their child, and
they only wish happiness and peace for their child.
The parents hearts reside in their child.
329
But the child needs beautiful examples, not insincere
advice.
The best guidance is being a proper example. That is possible through being consistent in
word and deed. Only under these conditions can a child be expected to grow up as a proper person.
The provision of subsistence is a duty, finding means to live on is a task; but providing
proper guidance is the task that precedes both of these tasks.
If the father does not regret that he made certain mistakes, it is a fact that the child will
repeat these mistakes. Therefore if you love your child, stay away from improper and unlawful deeds and show regret for what you have done improperly!
If the child does not observe ethical conduct, then he cannot be expected to display such
conduct. The best way to conduct oneself ethically is by imposing certain restrictions upon
oneself. It would cause social disrespect against one if one did whatever one wanted and
tried to fulfill every improper desire, ambition and sexual desire. That would also result in
others being ignorant of your words. That would also make one ashamed. The disrespect
toward a person is a great shame for that person's child.
The best inheritance is ethics. A child who knows how to behave well is one who has learned how to do so from his fathel
Your child is a part of you. You are responsible for that part of yours. if it is harmed, then
that means your whole body will be harmed.
Dear mothers and fathers, I ask of you to do the following:
330
331
Show the difference between the proper and improper; permissible, lawful, and forbidden,
unlawful;
Show the difference between the truth and falsehood;
Show the difference between the good and the bad;
Show the difference between honorable labour and work driven by greed;
Show the difference between knowledge and ignorance;
Show the difference between benevolence and malevolence; good and evil;

Don't do this through words. If you have understood the difference for yourself, in this

case you will have provided proper guidance for your children. Benevolence means sacrificing your own interests, and malevolence is the disregarding of others interests. The

damage caused by malevolence and the benefit that benevolence generates are not immediately obvious.

The malevolent man blames time and society for his faults, without ever looking at himself. Teach your child to improve himself, he will do the rest himself.

Don't do favors for the sake of gaining title or reputation.

Faith in Allah is the greatest guarantee that you will serve the public.

Avoiding difficult tasks, turning to improper and forbidden deeds because they are easier

is a betrayal of your child. A person seeking worldly benefits by doing favors to others

could easily engage in improper and unlawful deeds too.

Protect your child so that he doesn't become like that!

332

Possession of wealth does not mean living apart from the ordinary people, but rather it is a

means to unite with them.

If you take on a good deed, have confidence in Allah, in your people and country.

If your child is malevolent, then blame yourself.

Don't engage in affairs unacceptable to the public. As long as you desist from such things,

the public and society will readily accept you.

Improper, unlawful and forbidden mean acting contrary to the good of society

Proper, permissible and lawful mean acting toward the good of society.

My dear fellow Turkmens!

Engaging in lies, gossip and slander lie at the source of all evils. For these are means that

set a veil over sins and improper deeds.

If proper deeds are replaced by improper ones in a society, then it means that society does

not value moral guidance. Moral guidance means protecting the society and bringing about

social unity.

Teach your child how to be pure.

Suspicion of others is a burden on the heart. Being suspicious of one's fellow, of society

and the state is in fact the first step toward committing a sin.

Improper, forbidden and unlawful deeds say, "We are the proper and lawful thing to do."

For that is the only way they can exist. Man must use the pen-nissible and lawful as a shield.

333

Proper deeds do not say, "We are the proper thing to

do," for that would be meaningless.

Purity, integrity and humanity are the protectors of the proper, permissible and lawful.

It is
when he has bodily cleanness combined with internal purity that the human being becomes
a proper man. If one has bodily cleanness but lacks internal purity, then that is the most
despicable condition.

The child is indebted to his parents to an enormous extent. The child cannot repay the value of even one single day's effort spent by his parents even if he serves them for a whole lifetime.

Parents are obliged to their children in the following ways and they should:
give the child a proper name; guide and bring up the child properly; provide training for
the child; provide the child with a profession; help the child maffy;
help the child establish his or her own home and family;
make the child available for service to the public, country and his or her fellows.

Although not great in number, these obligations are very important. These all add up to
mean that the parents have to raise their child as a proper man or woman and make him or
her available for service to the nation.

Parents should think about these even before their child is born because one can only do
useless things without planning. Good deeds require planning in advance. Therefore, if

334

you do something wrong, you will regret it; and if you do a good deed, you will receive
blessings.

Teach your child how to make efficient use of time.

The Devil keeps a close eye over your time and faith, both of which are your precious belongings. Time is your life in this world, and faith is your life in the other world.

Wasting time means losing one's life or oneself.

Teach your child how to save his time and life.

All that you can save of time will belong to you.

Time is a mace. Hit or be hit!

Be clever, skilful and hard-working! Laziness means 'being profligate and leaving oneself
to be blown about by the winds of fate.

Be hard-working and you will generate returns in cash; be lazy and you will get into debt.

The comfort that laziness provides is like the taste of a sour cucumber.

Out of mercy for yourself, work.

Joblessness, lack of wisdom and laziness will damage you more than your enemies ever
could. Time is a wild predator, but if you train it, you may use it to your benefit.

Do not be subject to time; let it be your subject.

Live so that you regret nothing when you die.

Living does not only mean passing time. It means reaching eternity after passing through time.

Teach the foregoing to your child.

If you do so, the child will be proud of his parents and fulfill his responsibilities sincerely.

335

The child is indebted in the following ways in the
Turkmen tradition:

Do whatever lawful thing your parents tell you to do. Don't engage in tasks unapproved

by them. Don't lead a way of life unacceptable to your parents. Maintain a smiling face

toward them.

Be their lifelong companion.

Be with them when they are in need. Do what they tell you to do on time.

Don't seek benefits for what you've done for them; don't remind them of what you did and

do for them reproachfully otherwise you will harm them.

Keep your voice low when speaking to them or in their presence.

Always help them if they have bodily pain or illness.

Don't offend them, nor be offended by them.

Address them with the polite form of "you."

Don't utter bad words to them.

Don't speak to them looking at them directly in the face and eyes.

Pay compliments and be courteous to them.

Avoid false or inappropriate words or behavior when in their presence.

Always remember that they are your closest friends.

Share their happiness and grief.

336

Don't warn them offensively if they boast or speak highly of themselves.

If they cause problems because they are old and unable, be patient.

Share their problems.

Try not to cause or give them harm.

Don't be suspicious of them.

Wish them a long life when they are alive.

Provide them with clothing better than yours.

Provide them with food better than yours.

Serve them in a serious and sincere way.

Help them reach their desires and make them happy.

Provide them with their needs.

Do not be mean toward them.

Adopt their friends as yours.

Remember them after they die, do favors and charities on their behalf, recite from the Qur'an and have its verses recited for their benefit. For the Turkmen holds that it is the

prayers of the children that reach the souls of the deceased parents first. After their demise, one means of doing good on their behalf in this world is their children's righteous

deeds.

My dear child!

Continue serving your parents even after they pass away. The services you render to the

homeland will be of use after death, as well. Don't forget about your homeland. The homeland can continue to exist only because it is always remembered.

337

It is a very sacred duty upon you to love and protect the father's and the mother's homeland and your independence in the way you would protect your most precious belongings.

Our fathers have spilled lots of blood on the way to independence. Oguz Han, Gorkut Ata, Alp Arslan ... the heroes in the Gikdepe Castle.. all made the Turkmen known to the whole world. You are their descendants. Only patriotism and bravery will suit you. Be

loyal to the country whose resources you make use of, and to your mother who feeds you

with her milk. For the resources granted by the homeland to you and your mother's milk

are sacred. Allah Almighty ordered that we should not waste his treasures. It is an obligation upon you to protect these sources of wealth because generations to come after

you have a share in them. You will always be fortunate if you share their grief and happiness, and act in harmony with your fellow countrymen. Your fellows are valuable to

you. Look for guidance from your homeland. Follow the path of justice. For those who

follow the path of justice will never be misled. This way is a source of light in the darkness. Be guided by the moral conduct we inherited from our forefathers. Be obedient

to them and you will become the most caring person in the world.

My dear son, my beloved daughter! Read! Learn! Produce! It is essential that you be knowledgeable and skilful so that the homeland can survive powerfully and independently, and so that our people remain prosperous and heroic as ever.

338

LET ME SEE WHAT I'VE WORKED FOR IN YOUR SMILING FACES!

My dear Turkmen people!

The rose blossoms from within, and may you blossom as a rose would. This way you will

win the hearts of other people. Speak of good things, do good and favors to all, be courteous and complimentary to them. The smile is a sign of love. Smiling faces bear a

sacred light in them. Allah says, "Those smiling high-spirited people are closer to Me, I

will grant them twice as much as I will grant to others." The smile is the reflection of the

human soul. People who smile are generous because they are successful in the jobs they

do. Through a smile, man pleases not only himself but those with whom he has contact.

People who smile become more beautiful.

"There will never be any wrinkles on a smiling face," as the saying goes. This means people who smile do not easily become olc.

Ioften remember my mother. Her smile still appears before my very eyes although she passed away more than fifty years ago. The smile is visible to me in the dark of the night,

even if I have my eyes shut.

My mother wove rugs all day.

The sound of the loom echoed in our home like the clatter of hoofs. I woke up early, as

usual, and I saw that my mother was awake working. She kept on working after putting

us to bed. I was rather worried, for my mother did not take a rest as other mothers did. She would not go out either. It was only after she passed away that I could understand that she worked day and night to provide a living for us. She

339

relieved herself of her pains through working. I remember saying to her:

"My dear mother, please have some rest. Look, your hands seem tired." Then she would

take me on her lap and would caress me as if she was hugging and caring for a baby. She

would look me in the face, watch me with her dark eyes and smile at me. That smile of

hers is still in my heart, mind and world. I always remember the smiles of my mother. How interesting! Neither years nor winds have been able remove that smile from my memory. When I encounter a difficulty, I remember my mother's smile. That smile spreads throughout my soul and takes away the pain I have. It is as if a hand stretches out

and takes the pain away. Like the hero in the tale, I get rid of all my pains then. With the

power of the smile, I turn into a little child instead of the old man I am, just like the old

man in the tale; my soul flies like a bird in the sky; and I even feel as if I understand the

language of all the birds, flowers and other creatures. The sacred light in my mother's eyes brightens my heart. Then my life becomes sweeter than my mother's smile. That smile gives me extraordinary powers.

That smile I inherited from my mother is my treasure, my wealth. I can't find anything

worth that smile even if I pay thousands in gold for it. I can't find it anywhere even if I

strive like a treasure hunter.

in fact, people can all have access to these smiles. Your mother who is as valuable as the

holy Ka'bah, and your father who is as precious as the Qibla to you have left lots of such

smiles to you. It is those smiles that make us live. But it is probable that we may not have

understood and appreciated fully the real value of such smiles.

340

Asmile can make a friend for you out of an enemy. When death stares you in the face, smile at it and it may leave you untouched, I believe.

Spring is the smile of the earth. Smile at each other. Do it honestly when you meet. Greet

one another through smiles. Talk to each other with smiles.

My dear Turkmens, you are much closer to one another than relatives are. You are the Turkmen nation that lives around the same hope, on the same ground and under the same

flag.

It is a blessing from Allah that He taught us to smile.

Asmile can open up your soul, gives you pleasure and relaxes you.

It is that smile which elevates your heart just like an unexpected sunny day in winter.

It is that smile which removes grief and hatred from your heart just like the ocean wind

that disperses fog.

Your smile can also serve as a remedy for your problems when you talk to others. That

very smile is to the benefit of yourself, the friends you talk to, and your homeland. If your

smile is an essential quality of our state, then isn't our country a beautiful and fine place?

The smile is a sign of peace and love. A person who can smile can love too. Your smiles

become love and spread through the world.

Love all beings. Through love you can understand the meaning and the expressive language of plants and animals and have some kind of wisdom and saintly perceptions.

341

Love your vast lands and plains where Hydyr I strolls...

I

Love your mountains and seas where Kowus and Kyyas travel.

Go see for yourself where Girogly and Togrul Beg fought, and love the mountains Magtymguly loved...

Love the human, the most miraculous being in the world! Love the nature that is endlessly at your service. Love the trees that call out to you with their flowers, leaves, branches and fruits.

Aman can be a saint through climbing the ladder of love.

Aman can incorporate himself into nature and become as pure and fine as nature. From

such a stance and understanding, Allah the Most Exalted is not far away.

If the oceans and seas did not rise and fall in the wind, then their waters would lose their

beauty and have a dull smell.

If soft winds did not blow over the seas, then what would touch man's face gently? Who

or what would clean up the air man breathes!

The waves of the lively seas, and the soft winds of the earth are indeed their smiles.

Smile, for the smile is the door to man's world.

May smiles start from your very eyes. For that smile is the door that opens to the world of the soul.

They asked Joseph the Prophet: "What makes you so incomparably beautiful?" He replied:

"Throughout my whole life I have engaged in deeds that would please and give benefits
to others. I smiled at them,
1 the immortal Helper that arrives unexpectedly and in time to help people when in trouble
342
and this made me beautiful in the eyes of those who believe in me."   ·

Isometimes get so tired. I take the first opportunity to visit the stables at that time. My white horse starts neighing and moving around when he hears my footsteps. He expresses
his love for me like that. He approaches. I caress his head. I comb his mane. I look into
his eyes that are like apples. Gbrogly's saying comes into my mind: "White horse, if you
can speak, then do so." Although he can't speak, he expresses his pleasure with his eyes. I
feel like I should give him a hug. Then I remember Girogly again. I understand better why he says, "I didn't wish I had a son, but I wished I had my horse."

Gorkut Ata says: "When words fall short to convey feelings, then the saz (musical instrument) will be in charge." And I've seen that when the saz does not have anything to
convey, the smile is in charge. The sacred and enchanting smile...

The smile is home to a sacred blessing and power.

The lover is ready to sacrifice his life for one single smile of his beloved.

The poets for centuries have not been able to do more than define the qualities of the smiles of those whom they love.

A single smile can touch you with sacred power.

Iremember I would spare no effort to obtain a single word of gratitude or a smile from my
mother. I would try to do more than she would ask of me and to please her.

Today, you are my relatives, friends, protectors my fellow Turkmens! I am sparing no effort to win your smiles and gratitude.
343
So happy would I be to see that I have a share in your pleasure and happiness! I would
not regret anything if I could see that. I am ready to sacrifice my sweet life for my nation.

For no honor in the world would place me higher than the honor of winning your smiles and seeing your happiness, my dear Turkmens!

Ican understand at a single glance whether you're truly smiling and if I see this I will understand that my sincerity was not useless.

KNOWLEDGE IS THE LIGHT OF HAPPINESS

The most beneficial knowledge is the one that works to the benefit of society.

One should doubt the authenticity of the kind of knowledge that has no social use. Every
single deed of man should yield a result. For this is what makes social life possible.

The scientist should work to help improve society in material and spiritual respects. If the
scientist forgets this task, then the knowledge he possesses is meaningless, useless and of
no value.
Knowledge is not the sum of pieces of information which serve no purpose for anyone.
False knowledge is the collection of such pieces of information that have no use for anyone, just like the wealth accumulated by a mean man.
The real scientist holds real knowledge. That knowledge should first of all be of use to
society. This also amounts to saying that it should serve the holder of it too.
The kind of knowledge disliked by society is vain.
The scientist elevates knowledge, and society elevates the scientist.
344
Asociety cannot live without proper knowledge, just as a man cannot survive without his
mind. The most vital means of survival granted by Allah to man is the mind. Therefore,
mind precedes all other material aspects of the man, such as the hands, legs, working tools and hand-power. Centurieslong accumulation leads to proper knowledge. That knowledge is a privilege for man.
It is of that proper knowledge that a man is made.
The mind is the source of proper knowledge, and wisdom is its seed.
The soul compensates for the bodily losses of man. It elevates him and proper knowledge
is a sign of spiritual completeness and activity.
Allah Almighty bestowed upon man the mind, which He did not in the case of other beings. The human mind becomes more mature with the aid of proper knowledge and gains access to more than it initially finds. Man has no wings, but he can fly above the
birds, thanks to his possession of proper knowledge. He can't move so fast, but proper knowledge allows him to reach the greatest of speeds. Man does not have a predator's claws, but he can accede to the greatest strength, thanks to proper knowledge.
The mind and proper knowledge bring man closer to Allah.
Possession of proper knowledge allows man to look into the far distance.
Proper knowledge is a means to save oneself from the flood of life that would otherwise
have a devastating impact.
Only proper knowledge can provide an answer to the question of how to live and what to
do to live. The kind of
345
knowledge that fails to provide answers to this question is in fact an illusory attempt, totally in vain.
Man should know himself-, this is what renders him superior.
Man is indebted in that he should know.
Knowing means thinking about the world, finding a proper place for oneself in the world

and proving oneself.

The time of the sword is over. But even the sword itself is a product of the mind and proper knowledge.

When I say the time of the sword is over, I mean that the mind and proper knowledge that

was once utilized to produce the sword should now be directed to producing and inventing new useful things.

There are three steps to knowing:

Education;

Science;

Proper Knowledge.

Science is a treasure created by mankind. Education is the key to that treasure. It is a door

that provides access to the world of science through literacy.

Science teaches man about the treasures and perceptions of those that came before him.

Man selects from among these and leaves aside the ones that are of no use to him. He takes those pieces he needs and internalizes them.

Dear fellow citizens!

Istarted implementing a "New Science Policy" after major reforms in the fields of science

and knowledge in the Independent and Eternally Impartial Turkmenistan. The schooling

of the Soviet era does not meet our contemporary

346

needs. The main objective of the science policy is to protect children from the evil guidance of the streets, and to provide assistance to parents in guiding their children. If the teacher teaches his classes at school and does nothing after that to guide his students, then the students will be open to the evils of the streets. There he will adopt useless habits.

If we wish to protect our children from the evils of the streets, then we should provide them with proper guidance in the family and at ,;chool. Our tomorrow lies in the hands of

our children. If we wish to see in the future an affluent Independent and Impartial Turkmenistan respecting science then we should do all that we can to provide proper guidance for our children.

I think it would be proper to quote a letter I received:

Dear Saparm.Yrat Atayevi(!

This letter I am writing to you is not an ordinary one. This is a part of my sincerest feelings, and an indication of my regret.

Iworked under your supervision. You appointed me to a post that required responsibility,

and you had confidence in me. You appointed me to the chairmanship of an enterprise,

though not a major one. But, but...but.

But Allah decreed an undesirable fate for me. I was brought up in very harsh and difficult

conditions, and in severe need. Ijust wanted my two sons not to sufferfrom the kind of hardships that affected my life. To that end, I stole money, accepted bribes, and accumulated so much wealth that it was enough to use till my death. I bought apartments,

cars.. such beautiful cars. But...

347

My younger son had an accident while he was drunk and driving. He almost died. It would have been better if he had died. His backbone is severely damaged; he will stay in

bedfor the rest of his life. My older son acted irresponsibly and wasted time during the

privileged days of his father, and became a drug-addict. One day we'refine, the next two

we fight. He squandered all that wealth in five or six years. He made my younger son a

drug-addict as well. His mother could not bear the sufferings of this world and died of heart disease. I suffered a lot when I was a child. I encountered many difficulties. I was

raised as an upright man, but the wealth I obtained was of no use to me.

Istole and fed my children on what is forbidden and unlawful. The improper deeds we engaged in have their effects now.

My two sons were my sharp eyes; they were my hands andfeet. I would not complain if I

was blinded at my discretion by a physician. It would be my fair share to live as a creature with feet and hands cut off. If only death couldfind me and take my soul away.

Unfortunately this is not so; I can neither live nor die in this world. This is how I ruined

my future and did the same to both of my sons too. I am the only one to be blamed. Ifed

my children on what is impermissible and unlawful. Magtymguly was right to say, "You

will give your account of your proper deeds, but you will definitely be punished for the

improper, impermissible and unlawful." Now I have received the punishmentfor such...

348

Either a devout saint or a criminal can be made out of a child.

Happy is the man who raises the child as affectionate toward mankind, as a knowledgeable person that has the ability to foresee trouble.

An Atabeg educated the son of a Soltan for 18 years. Upon completion of the education

the Atabeg awarded him a certificate showing that he had received proper training. The

Soltan's son was raised as a brave man, a perfect horseman, and as sharp as an eagle. He

had the mental abilities that would allow him participate in discussions with scholars. The

Atabeg showed the skills he taught the Soltan's son. The Soltan was pleased and said: "Go swim through the sea, my son Oguz"

The Soltan's son replied, "Master Atabeg did not teach me how to do that."

The Soltan turned to Atabeg and said:

"My son's friends could have taught him what you taught. If he ever needs to swim, neither his friends, nor 1, nor you could help."

There are certain things in life with respect to which parents, friends and brothers and relatives cannot give any help. Man faces the realities of life many times. At those times,

one should be able to overcome difficulties without needing assistance from others. If one

cannot do so, then one is not properly and sufficiently raised. I lived under very difficult

conditions. It is a mistake to prevent a child from encountering difficulties. Indeed this is

a form of enmity toward one's own son. The child has to prove to himself certain things

by undertaking tasks proper to his age. The efforts

349

spent earlier by the child will yield positive results for him in the future.

Proper knowledge is the summit reached after following certain procedures. It is not the

mere reception of inforination from others; it also has to do with displaying what you know to others.

Proper knowledge prepares one for life, and helps one face the realities of life.

Proper knowledge means the ability to change and improve life. If one wishes to understand whether a form of knowledge is the proper one, one needs to look whether that particular form has the ability to change and improve life. If it does, then that is proper knowledge.

Education puts the hands, words and ears of the man into action. Science puts the mind

into action. Proper knowledge puts these into a coherent unity and moves them in directions related to life.

Science means taking information from others and using it for oneself.

Proper knowledge means giving information from oneself, and creating from within. The

greatest miracle is the mind given to man. Proper knowledge can release that power and

make it apparent.

Proper knowledge is the freedom of the mind.

It is never too late to learn science. The mind does not grow old as the body does. The longer one lives, the more sophisticated the mind becomes.

The teacher is superior to the student. For a student receives training for a couple of years

only, but the teacher is engaged in education for a lifetime.

350

The best teacher is the one that learns when teaching.

Reviewing your knowledge is the key to science. Adopt it as a habit. Each time you review you learn something new; this is the main principle of science.

Creativity is the essence of proper knowledge.

Wisdom is the guide that leads the mind to science.

Teaching without leaming is similar to spending money without ever earning money.

Proper knowledge takes worldly and religious forms. Proper religious knowledge is aimed at knowing Allah; proper material knowledge is meant to grasp the nature of realities. The first yields faith, the second affluence.

Everyone has a duty to society. The teacher has a duty to society in that he should provide the youth with proper knowledge and science.

Proper knowledge should increase our affluence and spiritual strength.

Science and proper knowledge decrease the likelihood of evil to the minimum.

If you fail to improve the wisdom given by Allah, you will lose your mental power.

The best way to learn is to read. And the best way is reading through reflection. If there

is no reflection, then there is no science at all.

The real man of proper knowledge has the following properties:

He doesn't seek to gain material benefits through his possession of proper knowledge;

351

He does not see proper knowledge as a form of skill, but thinks it is matter of progress;

He is calm and modest;

He has good moral conduct;

He confirms his words through his actions;

The type of knowledge of no use to society is meaningless to him.

Engaging in the type of knowledge that has no social use is similar to trying to sew cloth

with a needle with no thread.

No day is possible without a night, and no society can exist without proper knowledge.

The real man of proper knowledge is a friend of realities and serves his society.

My blessed Turkmen nation! The Golden Age must be one where the Turkmen way of knowledge must spread to and enlighten the whole world. The doors of proper knowledge are always open here. We desire that all Turkmen citizens may have access

to proper knowledge. Proper knowledge should attract public attention in our country. For the 21st century is one of proper knowledge. The door to the Golden lifestyle of the

Golden Age of the Turkmen passes through proper knowledge.

MAY BROTHERS BE FRIENDS, AND FRIENDS BE BROTHERS

Our forefather Gin Han's son, Diyp yabgy Han, was a wise Soltan, so wise that he would himself examine potential employees or others whom he would appoint to posts.

There were two friends among Di' Yabgy Han's commanders. yp

Those friends were both very brave, virtuous, handsome and

352

353

polite men. Diyp Yabgy Han kept a close eye on the two friends for a long time. He once wanted to appoint one of them as the chief commander of armies responsible for the protection of the whole nation and its lands together with the provision of security for the Soltan himself.

Diyp yabgy Han issued an order. The guards of the Soltan would go and seize the potential chief commander, tie his hands and beat him almost to death, and jail him. And later the judges of the country would accuse him of attempting to assassinate the Soltan

and sentence him to death.

The commander whom the Soltan was planning to appoint to the post of chief commander was thus awaiting death.

The Soltan subjects the jailed commander's friend to the same plot. He is accused of the

same crime and jailed. Before the execution of the penalty, the Soltan calls the first commander before him and says:

"I loved you as I did my son. I was planning to appoint you to the office of the chief commander, and I now see what you were after."

The commander replied:

"Soltan of the world, I don't know how I betrayed my country. How could you decide that I had done so?"

The Soltan said:

"Before I take decisions of any type, I spend much time thinking. This friend of yours told me that you were planning an assassination. Here's his letter telling me that." In all

seriousness, the Soltan told the commander that he had been betrayed by his friend. Knowing that the Soltan was a man of integrity, the commander said in a shocked manner:

354

"If it is my friend who told you that I was planning that, then do punish me. My friend

would never lie. I trust him as much as I do myself. The death penalty is right for me."

The Soltan said nothing in reply. He went to the jail where the commander's friend was

detained. He told him the same as he had said to his fellow commander. That commander said in reply:

"If it is my friend who did what you said, then carry out the punishment. For my friend

would prefer death to lying."

The next day the Soltan called the two friends before him.

,,Now that I have such upright and honest men like you, there is no castle I can't conquer," said the Soltan, tears in his eyes. And he told them about the scheme he had planned. The Soltan then appointed one of these fellow commanders to the office of the

chief commander, and the other to the office of the vizier.

In fact, it was a tough test. But it is also tough to keep the country afloat in difficult times. A friend is a mirror that reflects one's heart. The Turkmen is ready to sacrifice his

life for his friend. There are many cases in history that exemplify this. No one is to sacrifice his life today. But a friend in need is a friend indeed. It is necessary to have friends, but this need is much greater at difficult times. One should pay compliments to

others, say words that express friendliness, know how to appease people and encourage

people toward life.

My dear Turkmen Nation!

May friendship and brotherhood always accompany the Turkmen. Let us set it as an essential principle of our age of independence to pay compliments not only to our friends but

to everyone else, to utter friendly words, to know how to appease people, to encourage

people toward life and happiness, and to wish a long life and joy for others.

We should visit the ill and give them moral support.

"A sweet word can even break up a bone," as the Turkmens say. They say this for they believe sincerely in the power and strength of sweet words.

The Turkmen reached his desired day of independence. Let us adopt friendship and brotherhood as our main principle in our independent society. The Turkmen should live

in unity and be one and the same with fellow Turkmens in our independent nation.

Friendship is a great power. Let our power of friendship be the main ground on which our lives rest. Let it activate our souls, and let it help us reach our desires and goals. May

it add to the meaning and taste of our lives.

Man is composed of a body and a soul. The relations between the two components have

come to change throughout the development of man.

There are certain activities that take place in man's life. They have a pure form. These are related to man's soul and his spiritual composition. The soul is, in essence, free and

independent. Among the said activities is friendship. Friendship means the harmonious

relations that result from the love and respect between people. Friendship is a spiritual and ethical issue. It is for this reason that friendship is peculiar to human beings, or it is a

concept related to man.

Friendship does not result from any spiritual need of the human being. One does not have the option of choosing one's brothers. It is not dependent upon one's wish that one

has a brothel But having friends is at one's own discretion

and will. That means friendship is a spiritual need and is an evident indication of human

personality and freedom.

It is the man's internal wishes and his inner "self' that motivate him to have a friend or friends. The human soul looks for a fellow that shares the same thoughts, same fate, same inclinations and character as him. As such, a friend is the inner "self' of the person

who seeks a friend. For as soon as one feels that he has matured as a person one starts seeking an individual close to him. Those who succeed in finding such people are happy.

Just as one rarely comes across real love, so does one rarely find real friendship. Making

friends, being friends to others is a rarely accomplished task.

There is a story full of examples that is about how the Turkmen values his brother: Once a family had to escape from the enemy. But there was one horse to ride in the attempt, it would be able to carry a limited number of people to a limited distance. Then the young man thought and took his brother first to the horse, and escaped the enemy, and saved all his family so, as the story goes.

Only brothers can understand their mutual values, and the one who gave birth to them.

If parents die, among the remaining children the oldest in age replaces the parents. He is

to raise all the other children, help them be educated, maffy and socialize. I remember reciting the following lines when I was a child:

0 my brother, o my brother

Whose head is high, upright brother,

Fights against the enemy together

357

,speaks like a castle in support of you!

You are the shield in my left hand

And the dagger in the right, my dear brother!

Even the younger of twin babies should pay due respect to and greet the older when they

grow up, no matter that they were born on the same day and at the same hour.

Two brothers make the two hands of the same body. One hand washes the other hand, but two hands together can wash the face.

Our father Oguz Han told his elder sons that they were the bow and told the younger ones that they were the affow, and they had to go where the bow sent them.

Abrother and his elder brother should pay respect to one another.

When the Turkmen wishes to speak well of someone, he says, "May your brother be your friend, and your friend your brother." The friend and the brother are the same in rank.

Afriend is one's second "self'. But it is not possible to say the same of every brother. The

Turkmen says, "Identify the brave man by looking at his friend." A man's friend is a measure against which that man is evaluated. A man becomes a friend only to people who are close to his heart and with whom he has a rapport.

If it is blood relations that fix brotherhood, then what measures friendship? In old Turkmen thought, every man had a jinn. The jinns were short in height, and their napes

were as bright as their faces. Every man's jinn always stood nearby. When walking, the

jinn would go a few steps in front.

358

Therefore, before men contacted one another, their jinns had contact and talked to each

other. If the two jinns that met before the men could have rapport with each other, then

the two men would also become friends. For this reason, we have certain idioms in the

Turkmen language such as, "His jinn could not get close," or, "His jinn did not like the othel"

Iam not talking about these national characteristics only because they are interesting by
nature. What I wish to say in particular is that in this old line of thought, one sees clearly
that friendship is a pure and spiritual thing. For the jinns are not after any material
benefits whatsoever. They don't have any special wishes either. They established
relations only on the basis of whether each one's "self' agreed to talk with the other. This
means that real friendship has nothing to do with material benefits. It is first of all the
harmony between souls, characteristics and ideas.

Therefore there are different kinds of friends:

True friends;

Friends of gluttony;

Friends of women;

Friends of material values;

Friends of professional posts.

Only the first one is your real friend. All the rest are false and after their own benefits
from you.

Friendship is a great concept. For it relieves one of spiritual loneliness. Since friendship
is an excellent matter of ethics, there are many beautiful literary works on friends and
friendship.

359

Friendship between the same genders, mentality or interests are usual.

The relations between two people take place in the private world where third parties are
not allowed to intervene.

The friendship between the brave man and his horse are dealt with in many beautiful
works. These works define friendship as sharing the same destiny and the relations
between the two in moments of difficulty. This is the sincerest form of friendship.

There is a friendship between man and his Creator. Allah the Almighty's friends are
called saints or holy people. These are people that devote all their lives, and bodily and
spiritual assets to Allah. Some of them even avoided marriage so that their hearts were
not divided.

"You told all your secrets to that friend of yours. What if he intends to speak ill of you
and discloses them to the public?" one man asked another. That man replied:

"If that friend of mine speaks ill of me and discloses my secrets to the public, then life
would be meaningless for me. It wouldn't be worth living then. For that friend of mine is
the meaning of life for me."

The friend is what gives meaning to life. When one talks sincerely to one's close friend,
one feels relaxed. Man wishes to talk about certain things that cannot remain inside him.

Such things man can share with his friend. Then he will become relaxed.

Friendship means devotion of one's heart to another person. This means friendship is an

ability that resides in the heart. The heart's main ability is to love.

Friendship is affection, compassion and mercy.

360

The wealthiest is he who is rich in love and mercy.

Turkmens should be rich in love, compassion and mercy. Independent and Eternally Impartial Turkmenistan should be a country of friendship and brotherhood.

WEALTH IS A MEASURE AGAINST YOUR WILLPOWER

Wealth is not an end in itself, it is a means. A means to become a proper man.

Wealth provides benevolence as long as it remains as a means. When it becomes an end

in itself, it works counter to the good of man and does severe harm to man, and in the end, destroys man ' totally. In that case, wealth acquires that man, and the man himself

becomes a tool.

Wealth should be at man's service, and not vice versa. Therefore one of the most important problems in life is this: What should one's view of wealth be? What matters is

that one should not surrender his heart to wealth. In that case you will always manage wealth. One should really be able to manage wealth because man has the following essence: Allah created man out of light and soul, whereas all types of wealth are material, so such material things must be at men's service. Therefore, excessive love of

worldly goods is attempting to be the ruled rather than the Ruler.

Your bodily appetites are the most dangerous threats to you. If you do not put an end to

them at the beginning, then they can devastate you completely.

Wealth is water and man is the seed. If you use water sparingly and use it efficiently, you will obtain great amounts of crop out of the seed. If there is insufficient water, the seed will die. And if there is more than necessary, then the seed

361

will rot. Find the golden ratio between drought and devastation, and this will make a man out of you.

If you do not satisfy your desires by saving, contentedness and spirituality, then you will

not be able to satisfy them through material things. Greed will debase man, and it will make enemies out of his relatives.

Bodily appetites are a problem; your modest self is the solution. Your modest self can teach you how to live happily on limited resources.

Wealth is a flood. You cannot a resist a flood. It is preferable to step aside and avoid the

flood. What can save you from that flood is your modest and contented heart.

Bodily appetites cause greediness.

Allah Almighty created everything in such a way that creatures can decompose in themselves. Your bodily appetites might ruin you from within at an unexpected moment.

Be concerned about your head, and not about your stomach.

The best thing in the world is holy light. The best kind of wealth is spiritual wealth.

If you have enough for your subsistence, then don't try to be rich.

Everything is transitory. So is wealth. Allah is the possessor of time. All wealth belongs
to Allah and he gives extra wealth to the wealthy. He bestows wealth in your account. It
is deposited in the names of people, So that wealth is in fact not yours but granted or
deposited to your account. Wealth cannot last forever. For it cannot stay at a certain
place. It transfers from one name to another by the order of Allah.

362

The man who is rich in his modest self and heart is indeed one who does not surrender
himself to wealth, and run after it greedily.

If the amount of labour spent equals the wealth acquired, then that wealth will be
acquired through halal or proper means.

Wealth acquired through improper (haram) means is the kind acquired through the abuse
of others.

Proper wealth comes after honest deeds, and improper wealth follows from deceit.

Allah made you wealthy so that you may use what you have for the benefit of humanity.

The best kind of wealth is the one utilized to the benefit of society.

Proper wealth is an equal of faith.

Generosity is the sign of propriety, and meanness is the sign of impropriety.

If a man cannot free himself, society cannot free that man, either. One can free oneself
through integrity. Integrity gives you the right to live as an upright man and to feel
relaxed. An honest man will never feel guilty.

Let your thoughts and plans be true in esse nce, let your words be right and let the jobs
you do be proper in nature. This is how real truth will come around.

Proper acquisition of wealth, and spreading the accumulation of this type of wealth
everywhere is directly proportional to concerns over the unity and oneness of society,
and social well-being and happiness. When wealth is acquired in improper ways, the
moral structure of society is harmed, and society is damaged gradually. Honest men are
a guarantee of faith and security in a society. They are the

363

means to purify the moral conduct of the society. The more honesty there is, the better
humanity will be.

Maintenance of wealth and utilizing it in proper ways are more difficult than acquiring
it. The first condition for utilizing wealth for proper ends is the acquisition of it through
proper means. I do get upset when I see that some people are spending money on
improper deeds. Learn more about how to spend when one is wealthy. When you earn,
spend so that your expenditure benefits your nation, relatives and family! Spend so that
your spirit becomes richer, your reputation grows, and your mind and knowledge
expands! Strive to be consistent in your spending or using your wealth. Do not let

additional spiritual benefits leave you by depending on one single such benefit. Work always, so that the spring of wealth continuously releases sources. Always focus on this

issue. Wealth should make you closer to the ordinary people, rather than separating you

from them. You need your mind to be rich. Buried money is of no use to you or society.

That will only add to your fears, hesitations and doubts. It will ultimately cause problems for you.

Wealth that does not benefit the public is not real wealth. That is not Golden wealth, but

an ordinary piece of iron. Wealth is not the pleasure of one's self, but it is the interest of

the public. If you utilize wealth for proper and righteous ends, it will grow. If you don't,

it will shrink. For the value of wealth will be evident after its proper use.

Avoid doing improper deeds with the wealth you have. That is the gravest of all sins. Investing money in the exchange of things that lead astray or corrupt people in fact does

harm to one's nation. For the gains you make out of such investment would only be a disaster that your own family would suffer from.

364

Wealth results from labour. But work not for extra gains first of all. In the beginning work to survive and be happy to a modest extent. The amount you need for survival will

be enough for you live on properly. The kind of wealth acquired improperly is the total

of gains unjustly seized from others.

Properly acquired wealth is a blessing. Get others to call you not merchant, but blessed,

noble. Let people see that your wealth is legitimate and blessed and not without legitimacy or blessing. Labour helps you survive. Proper labour relieves man of his illnesses, being upset, greedy and poor.

Laziness is the essence of one's bodily self.

Labour is the source of being blessed.

Labour is also the source of wealth.

Think about how you will make use of your wealth before attempting to acquire it. Don't

wait too long to think about it. If you don't know where and how you will spend it, then

unfortunate results await you.

The real Turkmen is the one whose heart moves away from the concept of wealthiness

as he gets wealthier He does not display arrogance on the grounds that he has accumulated lots of wealth. Nor does he become upset if his wealth decreases. The wealthier he becomes, the broader his horizons get since he can find proper ways to make use of his wealth for his own needs and to the benefit of society.

Wealth is the foundation and its construction on that ground is Allah's mercy.

Let your wealth be at the service of your spiritual world.

Wealth is not the possessor of man but man is the possessor of wealth. Now that you are

the master already, don't try to become the slave!

365

Once in ancient times a modest fanner had two sons. They told their father:

"Father, we wish to travel the whole world and look for the means of subsistence that will make us happy. We would like to give it a try. If we become very poor, we will come back and follow your path," and they left the village.

Allah's grace made them meet a saint on the way. The saint said:

"Boys, you are the sons of a generous farmer, ask of me whatever you wish to have. It is

my duty to fulfill it."

The more knowledgeable of the young boys, mounted on a farm horse said:

"May Allah thank you, I did not come to this world to call out prayers and wishes all day. I can work. I am mentally sound. If I am not worthy of what I have, may I find what

I'm worth."

The saint said in reply:

"May Allah be with you, my son, go find your fortune."

The other young boy, who was riding on a mare, said:

"My master, how lucky that I met you. I don't want to spend my whole life trying to earn

just one loaf of bread. Give me wealth."

"OK, pass through this river, and you'll find a cave in the mountains there. You will see

a grand gate to the cave. Open that gate and take the treasure inside," said the saint and

gave him the key. "My advice is that when you go to get the treasure, just don't forget the real thing."

Obviously the young boy did not listen to the advice of the saint, for he had learned exactly where the treasure was.

366

He took off his clothes, held the key in his teeth and jumped into the river. He swam to

the other side of the river. As the saint had told him, he reached the cave and opened its

door. He saw that there was a great treasure inside. But he had nothing with him to put

the treasure in; he had no bag or sack! Then the boy realized that he had forgotten to take

the real thing. Nevertheless, he tried to take as much as he could and left the cave. He wished to enter again, but the door was closed already. The saint appeared nearby at that

very moment:

"So, that's your share of the treasure, young boy! Because you forgot three essential things: First, you should have thought about how much you should take, second, how to

take it, and third you left the key to wealth inside for a fistful of gold!"

Once upon a time a saint was told to visit a mean man called so-and-so who lived in such-and-such street.

The saint arrived at that man's house in the evening. He knocked at the door. The mean
man asked:

"Who is that?" The saint replied: "I'm a visitor that Allah sent; I thought you would be able to help me."

"That's fine. If you are a visitor that Allah sent, then there is a little mosque over there.
Go there and stay as long as you wish. Obviously Allah will not expel you from that place," replied the mean man, without even opening the door.

Facing this unexpectedly, the saint turned back towards his home. But before he left he
saw that a poor man was warming himself close to an oven in the mean man's garden. The saint approached and the poor man, who did not know the saint who greeted him said: "Come, have a rest."

"What are you up to here?" the saint asked.

367

"The judge has called me before him tomorrow. I have no place to stay now, nor do I have anything to eat. I saw that the oven was very hot. I think loaves of bread have just
been baked in it. I took the smell of the bread, that fed my desire, and with the oven's heat I have warmed up my body."

The next day, the saint accompanied the man to the office of the judge. The judge assessed the case and gave the man the death penalty. The judge asked the poor man: "You will be executed in the afternoon. Tell us your last wish."

"I complain of nobody in this world, but they call Turan $ah a man of justice. If he is really so, may he let me dig my own grave in the ruins of a former estate of ours, and may he allow me to be buried there," the poor man said.

The Soltan was informed of the man's wish, and gave permission for what he wanted. The Soltan thought:

"There is an interesting side to this event. Let me see for myself how the man digs his grave. For this is the first time a criminal has requested something like this." The Soltan then went to the ruins where the man would be. He saw that the criminal was digging his grave in the comer of the field. Those who saw the Soltan all stood up and greeted him. The criminal dared to extend a hand to salute the Soltan. The Soltan did not feel offended since the man would soon be executed. The Soltan said:

"I read the decree ordered by the judge. There are three witnesses against you, but you
have none who will speak for
you.

my Soltan, I had two such witnesses. Didn't you just hear them speak a while ago?"

368

"I heard them indeed, but the judge wouldn't accept them as witnesses."

Thinking that the criminal was trying to avoid execution, the judge cried out: "He has no witnesses."

The man was still digging at that time. He unearthed a large jar at the bottom of the pit. He took the jar out of the pit. They opened it to see that it was full of golden coins.

The Soltan said:

"Here he has a third witness."
The saint added:
"No, my Soltan, the witnesses are four in number."
The judge grew angry and asked:
"How come? Where are the witnesses?"
The Soltan said in reply:
"Didn't you just notice the man's hands when you first came up to him? His palms have got callouses on them. A man whose hands are so because of the hard labour he has done cannot be engaged in theft. His two witnesses are his two hands!"
The saint continued:
"I heard a secret voice telling me to look for my share in the property of a mean man. But that mean man did not even take time to open his door to me. Therefore not the mean man, but this man who was warming himself up next to the mean man's oven found a fortune. Neither the judge nor you, my Soltan, is to be blamed. For if this man
had not been sentenced to death, and if Allah had not inspired in him
369
the feeling that made him wish to be buried in these ruins that once belonged to him, then this fortune would never have come out. By Allah's will, this man has found the fortune he had a right to have."
The Turkmen has a peculiar and interesting understanding of material wealth. The Turkmen does not like material wealth. But that kind of wealth is essential sometimes.
The Turkmen adopts a modest way as usual with respect to that mattel Man should not yield to material wealth, for this would make man greedy; but complete denial of it
would make him abstain from the world as a whole.
The proper thing to do is to find the medium way. But to do that requires the existence
of your own moral values and a philosophy. What does the Turkmen's philosophy say in this respect?
That philosophy aims at adding a s iritual aspect to wealth. The Turkmen has never praised wealth to an excessive extent. Money, wealth and material things have never occupied a significant place in the Turkmen's heart. But properly acquired wealth is welcomed by the Turkmen. He thinks that kind of wealth is a fortune and he respects such wealthy people.
How does wealthiness differ from proper wealthiness? At first sight, it seems as if there is no difference since they both refer to material things. But the matter concerns the thoughts behind them. Every idea is a measure against which the extent to which the citizens agree to the truth can be measured. Material things do not differ from one another but ideas are totally different.
Wealthiness refers to ordinary material things.
"Proper wealthiness" refers to the material benefits that
370
have a spiritual aspect. That kind of wealth is acquired through proper work. The benefits are the gifts granted by Allah to man in return for his honest deeds. This wealth and these gifts relate directly to the proper deeds. Properly acquired wealth does not lead one to excessive behavior or bad deeds. This is the essence of the whole mattel

Proper wealthiness is limited in amount. Allah grants to every being its proper share. That is, Allah loves those who are moderate. For sure, no one will be granted another's

share since man does not need a great amount of wealth to survive. But there is no spiritual limit to proper wealthiness. Therefore try to acquire proper wealth and not material wealth. Material wealth will lead you out of the way. Material wealth is the source and result of improper acts. Proper wealth is acquired proper deeds and it leads one to a pure soul and ethical conduct.

The Turkmen of the Golden Age should limit himself in material respects, and should try to gain all that he can spiritually.

Improperly acquired wealth will be the share of those who are impropel Therefore, those who acquire improper wealth develop uncontrollable inclinations toward improper deeds. His desires shackle the man, and he becomes their slave. The total of these desires is called the "evil self" by the Turkmens.

Properly acquired wealth and comfort purifies one's heart. The man with a pure heart feels that a giant force stands behind him. He has no sins to be ashamed of, he is clear before everyone else, before the nation and before Allah. This is spiritual freedom. Wealth enslaves the man, properly acquired wealth yields freedom.

371

Escape slavery, march toward freedom!

If you want to build a house you should first flatten the ground and lay a foundation. Wealth brings evils to the unskilled. You see many examples of this in your daily life. The Turkmens say, "Even the beggar needs to spend some effort." To be wealthy, you should first prepare yourself for the idea of being wealthy. Then you should learn how to maintain that wealth. Maintaining wealth is more difficult than acquiring it. This is the all the more difficult for the Turkmen. The Turkmen is generous in material and moral terms. The Turkmen is like the Hatam Tayam, who was a generous man.

Iam not arguing for meanness, stinginess or greediness. But I don't like profligacy either. The best way is the modest way. The modest way is the Golden guide!

The Turkmen nation has access to infinite wealth. Our citizens may become richer and richer if I distribute all we have to them. But are our people ready for such richness after 70 years of poverty?

"It is the sheep that likes comfort, especially the sheep darkest in color."

Man needs great willpower to be able to cope with wealth. Man needs to have a comprehensive grasp of things, be wise and thoughtful to be able to cope with wealth. Dignity is essential!

One of my main goals is to prepare the Turkmen nation for the acquisition of wealth. I

am making my nation adapt itself to wealth slowly. Your lives are improving day by day, year by year. Maybe you don't notice this. But this does not escape my eye even for a single moment.

372

The Turkmen nation must be one that can cope with wealth and that can utilize wealth to the benefit of society and its bright future.

Adopt it as your desire to acquire proper wealth. My main goal is to realize this desire of yours. When we join hands, we will definitely reach our targets.

THE WOMAN IS THE CORE OF THE FAMILY

Those who love deeply and who marry their beloveds in sincerity and deep affection are the fortunate ones whose ways are paved by life and Allah!

Men who respect their wives and who can get on well with them without harsh quarrels and without being attached to an excessive extent are those lucky people who have a great fortune. It is unity and integrity, fortune and mutual understanding that prevail in such a family. Such a family is a very fortunate one.

The woman is the Soltan of the home; she presides over the household!

Women should be given their proper value through affection, love, and mutual respect.

If newly-weds do not treat each other with respect from the first day of their marriage, but always do harm to one another and damage their reputation, then in-laws will not respect them for long. Then their relatives and neighbors will not respect them either. In this case, one or other of the pair starts struggling for survival day and night, and the

two of them fight with one another and the relatives and neighbors. Gorkut Ata wished that one might be protected by Allah against the evils of a bad spouse. Yet Allah will not

373

protect one from a bad spouse because, "even a monster would flee from such a spouse," as they say.

A sweet word opens all doors; a bitter one causes enmity toward you!

It is the husband's and his relatives duty to help the new bride to get used to the habits and behavior of the family.

The Turkmen have a beautiful tradition; a new bride bows her head to her father-in-law

and mother-in-law, then the daughters in the house take her to the neighbors and relatives houses. The bride greets them in the same way. She shows respect to her new

relatives by complying with this wise Turkmen tradition. This amounts to saying that if you have respect for your husband, then you should also show respect to his family. That is how relationships are grounded on the foundation of respect. May this respect and affection turn into a great love and friendship as time passes. May the new bride be the most beloved and beautiful bride of the family and the neighborhood. This depends on how the men act in this regard.

There is a principle in life: One should choose a profession and spouse for oneself in youth. However the young have their heads in the clouds. They wish they could maffy

the most beautiful and cleverest girls. But the wisest thing to do is to choose your equal.

I remember listening to a story when I was a child:

Once, a young boy jumped into the river to swim. He sees with surprise that a water fairy is swimming in the river unaware of what is happening around her. The young boy moves close to her without being seen and catches the fairy:

"I love you. Marry me!" he says.

374

The fairy replies:

"Brave boy, your lot is to be loved. But you cannot live under water, and I cannot live above it. This love would ruin us. The best we can do is for me to try to realize some wishes of yours. But be wise and choose your equal as your beloved! "

The fairy then tells the young boy to swim across the river and light a fire at the foot of the mountain. She gives a lock of her hair to the young boy before he leaves, and tells him to put the hair into the fire he will light. The moment the young boy does what she

says, the skirt of the mountain splits into two and a grand door opens. The young boy enters through the door and sees a magic mirror the fairy mentioned before he came to

the cave. The young boy looks at his image in the mirror for a long time and then walks through the curtain hanging there. He is startled. He sees a fairy living in a fine and beautiful mansion, and he starts trembling as soon as he looks her in the eye. To that fairy's right was another fairy. She was hardly visible as her clothes were so heavily embroidered in pearls, silvers and golden jewelery. On the left was another fairy displaying affection, love and merciful feelings.

The young boy looked at the fairy girls for a while and took away the one that was living in the highest place. As soon as they left the cave the beauty of the fairy surpassed the light of the sun. Proud, the young boy looked at the fairy and got a huge shock: the beautiful fairy whose hand he was holding was in fact a snake. Surprised, the young boy calls out to the water fairy:

"Who is this I am holding in my hand? Wasn't it a fairy?"

"She is not a snake. By the will of Allah, she will

375

become a monster after your wedding!"

"What harm did I cause to you? Why did you give me a monster?"

"Didn't I tell you to look in the mirror at the cave's entrance?"

"Yes, you did, and I did what you said."

"Although you did, it seems that you couldn't see yourself properly. Although you saw

yourself in the mirror, it seems you didn't recognize yourself properly. You were silver

yourself and you took away the golden fairy. It'll be a fairy one day, and a monster for the next two. Your share was the girl who was displaying affection and mercy. She was the proper one for you. You won't be a lover to the fairy you chose, you'll only be a slave to her." The water fairy then plunged deep into the sea and disappeared.

One who marries a wealthy girl without considering his own poverty will obviously have to suffer from many difficulties. He lives on earth, but falls in love with the one in the sky. He sticks to a branch where he shouldn't, and this becomes a lifetime's evil for him.

Know yourself, and know the girl you will love and choose for yourself!

If a man and a woman pass over the bridge of love, then they will always be happy!

If the man and the woman pass over the bridge of logic and wisdom, then they will have a long-lasting family!

If the man and the woman are not proper for each other, then this family will be an unhappy one!

It is the child that brings strength, friendship, love and happiness to the family. The existence of a child in a

376

household turns the love between the man and the woman into one between the father and the mother. That is the noblest among the various kinds of love. For the parents can dedicate their whole lives and happiness to their child, and this gives them happiness.

My advice to the young is to love and be loved but be fit for one another! You can tie a horse and an ox to the same carriage, but then that carriage is not a carriage proper, and you cannot go any further with it.

The woman is the ground on which the household stands. One wishing to have a longlasting
family should first respect the woman who works hard for the good of the household. The woman will then spare no effort for the household.

The husband and the wife constitute a new family, a new household and a new core. No matter how many children you have, if the ground is tom up, then the household becomes uncared for. When the woman is gone, then the comfort of the household is gone, When the man is gone, a major component of the household is gone. Allah created everything in pairs. The sky and the earth, the Moon and the Sun and even the mountains and the seas exist as counterparts of one another.

In Turkmen folklore, in the tale of Akpamik, the souls of the giants are kept secure in a glass jar under a rock. That is why no one can kill the giants. As the soul of the man is maintained in the heart of his beloved, they have the desire to live. The courtesy of the beloved elevates men and makes them persevering. If a man's wife is at odds with him at home, then he will not be spiritually strong at work or in other places. The man whose wife awaits him with deep love, who has no credit in his own home is easily recognized through facial expression, speech and clothing.

In another tale, once they asked the Moon:
"You sometimes become full and polish the world with your silver light; and sometimes you are very small and one can hardly see you in your crescent form. What
is the reason behind this?"
"When my husband the Sun smiles at me I will be the full Moon; I become very happy. And when he glares at me angrily, I become so small that I cannot be seen."
0Youth! Each of you is a Sun. If you smile at your wives they will fill the world with light just as the Moon does.

In fact, the Turkmen nation is one that knows how to be thankful to Allah, how to save, and how to maintain the traditions of their forefathers. It has no respect for digressions from the true path.

The great independence of our nation, the sovereignty and freedom of our nation, and the eager spirit of our "10Year Development" program and the national development movement requires us to maintain and add to the value of each and every acre of our land as if maintaining pieces of gold.

Small peoples that survive by depending on a greater state lose their own traditions and get intermingled with the people of the sovereign people. But we the Turkmens have not lost our identities and we are protecting our traditions. We have great plans and we want to become a great nation. This we must be proud of.

My beloved people! If this Ruhnama inspires your souls, then you will not need to worry about your powers to

sustain the development of Turkmenistan's independence and the peace and comfort of its citizens and to protect its land.

Our youth and the rest of our nation should be strong morally and be rich in spiritual wisdom.

From now on, we should make sure our entire Turkmen nation, our grandmothers, our grandfathers, our children in kindergarten, our young boys and girls, never loses its enthusiasm. We should always strive to make our people happy. Honesty should be their companion; they should be enthusiastic with pure desires and wishes.

A people living in its own land freely and independently and without fear is a happy people.

Nothing in history could degrade the humane qualities and hospitality of the Turkmen nation. Neither has anything reduced its spiritual power. Any Turkmen you can come up with would either be writing a poem or playing a musical instrument to express his or her happiness. Many of the lines that Magtymguly recited as the signs of the brilliant Turkmen spirit have already become proverbs in the daily lives of the Turkmen nation:

Pyragy asks from the Turkmen land / May the enemy keep away from its red rose / Before we pass away / May the enemy retreat immediately!.. 0 mankind, the Turkmen land is my land / No other farther land is preferable to me... Pyragy my eyes are so tired reflecting upon the homeland / It seems that I will remain apart from my homeland ... May vast lands Hydyr wonders about be the share of ours/ Let our homeland be settled and permanent / May we eat at the same

380

table ... A brave son comes from a brave father, a coward will never become brave, / Never will a land be unpleasing if those born in that land are honest! ... Rather than remaining homesick in lands far away, / I'd prefer my being in my homeland despite difficulties, or bad treatment ... Come my self, listen to my advice,/ May you not leave

your hometown ... Fighting against one another is not an affair for true men, / This is the devil's affair, or maybe they are blind against one another, / Conflicts will remove peace from our land / And this will give the enemy privilege in this world ... Pyragy I fell in love, / I jumped into the sea and was captured by the waves, / May my descendants not be held low, / I wish for a sustainable peace ... The great lands will disperse and slacken / If the brave men do not remain so ... A land in conflict, / Is as if it lost peace ... One would be ashamed / If the country was headless ... If I stole your valuables I did not mean to assault you / Since I am the poor, I have no place other than beside you..."

My dear Turkmen! Let me briefly express some of my advice to you. We've been living as a free and independent people for 10 years.

Our souls become one in various festivals and commemoration days attended by all the public in every comer of our nation to remember past sorrows and anniversaries. These events contribute to the spiritual strength of our people. They make people closer to one another. This is life, and it bears an infinite number of difficulties. The festivals help us erase these difficulties from our minds.

Each Turkmen should enthusiastically celebrate our festivals in the way our ancestors did. Life will seem to be a form of beauty, the bright

future in the vision of smiling faces, smiling eyes and tired souls who are celebrating one event here and another there.

Turkmen rugs, jewelery and handmade golden and silver products should always be exhibited in those events. Our historical silverware and goldware have come to be the favorites of women as beautiful as fairies. The Turkmen horse should be on view at every event. Our historical silver and goldware that somehow appear in the world market are priceless. Famous movie artists, theater stars, famous women of arts and letters would deem it a privilege to own Turkmen made silver- and goldware. Pay attention to the jewelery worn by Turkmen girls; the gupba-tuvulga, qekelikbukav protects the neck from attacks with swords, the gilyaka protects the chest. The bracelet covers the wrist, and various pieces attached on the front and back of dresses prevent injuries from arrows and spears. If the Turkmen girl wears all her jewelery, she becomes like a warrior shielded by her jewelery. Calculations tell us that a woman should be carrying a total of 36 kilograms of silver and gold if she wears all her jewelery. The Turkmen praises the woman highly.

Our forefathers said of the various kinds of saz (musical instruments) that add color to celebrations and festivals, "Music and celebrations provide guidance for man. The celebration relates to the bodily world, and the music relates to the spiritual world. When combined, the celebration and the music will guide man's material and spiritual world."

I wish to say, "If you want to understand the characteristics of the states and nations, listen to their music; if you wish to know of the level of happiness in the family listen

and see how songs and music find reflection in that household!" When setting out for warfare, our ancestors brought with them musical instruments, standards and flags to support the enthusiasm of the soldiers. The sound of the Kis, reminiscent of thunder, the sounds of the zuma that shake hearts, and the sacred tone of the gicak2 have all been sources of power, courage and inspiration for the Turkmens. Each musical group plays seven to twelve instruments. Now is the time to show the whole world the continuity of the rich Tirkmen music with its national qualities pleasing the ear and soul, inspired by our ancestors. And first we ourselves should own and reclaim it.

I have traveled in almost all the places in the Turkmen land consecrated by the Turkmen nation. I traveled recently to the highly esteemed Uzboy.

Uzboy means the place where the houses of Oguz stand in order next to one another. In the past, the villages and towns of the Turkmen people were arranged in order by the Jeyhun. Gardens, springs, trees, and flowers and all the facilities needed all stood in unity. This was called the Turkmen garden. And now? Nothing but ruins. Deserted villa es and towns. See the plain that lies below; all the graves are dug into the ground and lost. The graveyard is the memory of history! Why did Oguz leave Uzboy? Because the Oguz river dried up. If there is no water, then there is no life. The Oguz had to migrate because of drought.

Although it is centuries since the Jeyhun river changed its bed and left Uzboy, we still see little ponds here and there. There are wild grasses around them! Part of the water in those ponds came from the ground and part is still not salty.

2 a small stringed musical instrument made out of a gourd keeping its original shape and played with a fiddle on the knee

One still sees Turkmen villagers in Uzboy who are engaged in animal husbandry. The grass and dried shoots are in fact invaluable for livestock and wild animals as food during winter is also a haven for wild game and hunting animals!

Water is scarce in Turkmenistan. Were it possible, we would re-vitalize the

Uzboy for the sake of the memory of our ancestors who were not pleased with the situation of Uzboy in the past.

Wait, my Uzboy! One day I hope you will recover your former beauty. We have started building the Turkmen lake here. One day we will transfer its endless waters to you through refineries and provide you with an abundant amount of water. The Turkmen nation will follow the path left by their ancestors and hoist the green flag of life in Uzboy again!

If Allah helps us, the Turkmen's gardens will be watered and the waters will reflect their full dazzling colors, fragrance and splendor once again.

The whole of Turkmenistan will have many productive gardens!

This matter should be adopted as a state policy. My dear Turkmen! Make every effort to make a paradise out of Turkmenistan. I am calling out to every wealthy Turkmen family. Those wishing to pay their indebtedness to Allah and the public should plant a tree in the streets, gardens, neighborhoods and graveyards that are nearby!

My Dear Country!

Every people aspires to wealth. Such aspirations cannot be realized unless they are guided and led by the state. In order to render Ruhnama the Turkmen's essence, present,

384

and future, we need administrators who are wise, foreseeing and who have not engaged in any improper and unlawful deeds. If you want to be a proper headman, you will act as if you are mother or father to the whole village. You need to be a man that serves the village day and night. If you think that you are the owner of the village and hold your interests superior to those of the villagers then the way you lead people will diverge from our way.

If you are a district governor or governor, then you will have the whole district's or city's burden on your shoulders. If you cannot warm the people under your administration with justice in the way instructed in Magtymguly's lines, "If you are a judge, then warm your public equally in the way the Sun does," then you will not be a proper official.

In today's world where we are leading a peaceful and harmonious life, various Turkmen officials must be supportive of the chief leader of the Turkmen in the event of a catastrophe, or other disasters that might arise out of the bad will of domestic and external forces (May Allah protect us in such cases). Standing before threatening bullets and agreeing to die or hiding at times of difficulty are defined as cowardliness by the Turkmens. There is a Turkmen saying in this context which runs, "Cowardliness is far worse than death."

My Dear Turkmen!

Unite in days of happiness and sorrow as proper Turkmen! ... If you stand united, there is no difficulty that you cannot overcome.

Whenever the Turkmens got stronger, they yielded to internal conflicts and caused their powerful states to collapse. We should learn our lesson from history and reinforce our unity.

385

These words are valid for state officials, department administrators, factory managers, governors, and in sum for all Turkmen administrators. I will give you some information on three official decrees out of a total of 36 issued in the year 1150 by Soltan Sanjar's imperial office. These are found in the official archives called, "Steps to improve clerks."

Appointment to the governor's office in Girgen and vicinities

Allah (Praise be to Him) granted us the Sultanate with all His All-encompassing Compassion and infinite Mercy. He gave us keys to conduct official responsibilities and the means to reinforce the basis of the living conditions of the citizens. We witnessed Holy Allah's grants and gifts as soon as he provided us with additional powers. No praise would be enough to thank Him. In this transitory world happiness and sorrow, and brilliant and ordinary days come one after another. Sometimes some of the tasks we undertake may end in failure. Even if the people of ill-will have time to think that these failures will do harm to us or will put unexpected obstacles before our wishes and will, there are many unimaginable sacred grants under the celestial secrets. The residents of this world know that whenever such grants are bestowed, being on our side results in safety and comfort; and being suspicious of us, and engaging in conspiracies against us ends in discomfort and regret. We have come to fulfilll our responsibilities before Allah for all that He gave us either secretly or openly. We have adopted the Qur'anic verse which runs, "Say, Allah is Compassionate and Merciful," as our principle. We witnessed the results of the verse, "If you praise me, I shall increase that which I bestow
" W
upon you. e always focused on the people's problems that
386
we were ordered by Allah to protect when we were fulfillling responsibilities. We did all that we could to disseminate justice. We appointed experienced and ethical representatives to every corner of the country. We ordered them to follow and organize the affairs of the Muslim community.

Whenever we witnessed someone engaging in a crime or in a deed not approved by us, we deemed it proper to change that which was being conducted; in this regard we caused no delays. With Allah's help and grace, state affairs are improving in a way to satisfy us. The affairs being conducted under our Sultanate have been arranged properly. Those whom we trained range from Governors presiding over the farthest points of Tirkistan to Indian princes and Soltans, and to other states Soltans and governors that rule in the terrain that stretches till the Greek and Western lands, and they are appointed by us and we impose taxes upon them. They are all subject to us.

The Emir Muhammed Yolabi was commissioned, trained and appointed by us. When we appointed him to the governor's office in Girgen, he showed that he was loyal to us and that he was after his subjects interests. He exhibited examples of wisdom, foresight, ethical standards, and discretion. He started with this office successfully and completed his duties in the same way. Our valuable traditions required us to do what the heritage of the dead instructed us to do and as such, and in consideration o his successful time in office,
!f
we commissioned his son to the same office. We thought he would follow the path led by his father in terms of loyalty, goodness and taking care of his subjects interests, and that he would imitate what he had heard and listened to from his father. Therefore we provided him with many privileges. For
387
a while he acted in the way we expected. He displayed progress and established

good relations. This continued until he saw himself as wealthier and more powerful than he actually was. He then started behaving arrogantly and enabled the Devil to create tensions, in the way decreed by the Qur'an: "No, the man became greedy for he saw his predictions came to be true." If an administrator enables the Devil to create tensions and his affairs do not proceed well, then his subjects will have to lead a life under cruelty and in misfortune since he digressed from the true path and led an unfavorable life. In that case punishing that administrator, taking back from him the lands and subjects under his office, overcoming the public unrest, and getting him to taste the sorrowful pain of his unfavorable deeds, and relieving people of their misfortune and his cruelty became a responsibility that had to be fulfillled. When we hoisted our flag in that region everyone saw what he was worth for what he had done. His armies and warriors he had been breeding for long could not even resist a single fist of our soldiers. Those who were present there saw for sure that he made a grave mistake by trusting his army as ever and that type of mistake would even cause the Devil to find a place to flee to.

Now that we had confidence in Allah's might and power, and in celestial patronage, this very numerous army of the traitor was ruined as decreed in the Holy Qur'an: "We made him like the reaped corn. It was as if he weren't rich the day before." When it was evident that the war followed a course to our benefit, those warriors who started fleeing and wandering to and fro, begged mercy everywhere and sought our commanders and soldiers compassion. After that, in line with the dignity granted to us by Allah and thanks to His Mercy (Highest of the Praises be to Him) we forgave them all in accordance with our virtues which tell us to assist those

who yielded to mishaps and to forgive the criminals, and as per the decree which ran, "You won't be condemned today." We declared to the residents of Girgen and its vicinities that we welcomed the peoples of amul and Tabarystan, and those urban residents and others living near the sea. We told them we shared their feelings. Thus, we paid them special respect, gave them privileges over other people under different governors. And we provided them with the comfort, safety and justice for which they have been longing for years.

We expressed thanks to Allah (He is the Almighty and the Great Allah) and held discussions where different viewpoints were expressed. We made a decision to subject the residents of certain towns, soldiers and civilians, all regional residents, castles and residences in those districts, treasures, plains, mountains, sites on the ground and the sea to the patronage and order of the new governor. I appointed my son Mdlik Gyyasetdin we'd-di-ny',j Mdlik'fl-I Islam Mesud (May he have a long life) as the new governor. He is of a pure Seljuk Turkmen generation. He agrees to be bound by our traditions and developed administrative skills; he intends to hoist the flag of the religion and establish the sacred law of Islam; he shows respect to Allah (May his name become famous); he is concerned over the elderly, and he is skilled at establishing proper relations with his subjects. So skilled is he that though he is young, even experienced old men who sufferedfrom the pains of life have much to learn from him. We trained him (May Allah give him long life, peace and may He protect him) so that he could preside over the whole world. We declaredpublicly that he would be the Soltan. This declaration is still valid.

Without regard to this declaration, and now that he has become extremely interested in the affairs of that country, we

ordered this decree. We confirm in practice that this decree and instruction will be valid in consideration of Allah's words in the sacred Qur'an: "We will release another verse in place of any other one that we lifted or made you forget, it will be similar to or better than the former one." This change in office has evidently nothing to do with former issues. When taken into careful consideration, this change gives us the opportunity to say, "We dethroned the giant and placed there Sile'man instead." Those who have common sense know that this sets a wise example and it will not cause any repentance. Praise be to Allah for He rewards those who correct, confirm, prove, resolve and judge. We are always indebted to Him. From now on my dear son's (may he always be glorious) orders and instructions will be valid whenever he wishes them to be valid. His decisions equal ours in that they will apply to detentions or releases, approvals and refusals, dismissal, forgiving or punishing criminals, sending Ifu or not sending to exile. We order that everyone should recognize this as such. We state that his orders and prohibitions will be deemed to be of ours in every respect and everywhere. We order him to obey Allah in all that he does either openly or secretly, and to follow the way of loyalty and fear toward Allah (He is High and Almighty) so that he may find peace in both worlds. For "He who fears from Allah will attain to superiority." With respect to the establishment of the sacred law of Islam, May Allah make him very respectful to the judges, religious leaders and men of letters (Allah be pleased with them all) who are responsible for the protection of the Prophet's heritage. He will help them in carrying out legal transactions and making decisions. He will display signs of persistence and faith to the infidel in battles against the infidel who live on the borders of Dehistan and Mi'ngyylak.

He will, when necessary , crush or destroy them as 390

decreed by Allah: "Obey him in the way you are to, it is Allah that chose you." He will give utmost importance to the safety of travellers and passages on the ground and the sea. He will be sensitive toward farther regions that require awareness all the time. He will punish those engaged in improper deeds, infidelity and theft in line with what Allah (He is the High and the Almighty) says: "Those who act contrary to Allah and His representatives will be punished in the following way: they will either be killed or crucified, or their hand and legs are cut, or they are sent to exile." He will appoint wise and experienced commanders who are loyal to castles and important locations. He will be sensitive on this issue and never forget that he should always keep it so. He will exhibit unlimited respect for administrators and men of reputation that live in Horasan, Iraq and Mesopotamia, according to the level of the posts they hold. He will listen to their advice. He will receive everybody's opinion carefully, analyse different viewpoints and do whatever is most beneficial according to him. He will comply with justice in all that he does. He will do every job to the full, without its remaining arbitrary or incomplete. He will consult experienced older people who are loyal before he does anything. He will adopt it as his main goal to win peoples hearts in administrative affairs and provide them with comfort. By the same token, he will never let the servants, slaves or the freed individuals become open or secret enemies to one another. For wishes and disputes among the public might result in violations, fights and bloodshed. He will fix various types of gifts and grants according to the type of service rendered by everyone, and he will give these gifts.

He will not immediately punish those people under his patronage if they commit a crime. He will not act in haste

391

and punish others. He will not punish soldiers and his officers in haste. Unless evident or proven, he will not decree a punishment for any crime. For sure, if he knows of the treachery and the evils of another person he will not forgive them since the greatness of a ruler depends on to what extent his orders are being confirmed and executed. He will tell his officers not to make citizens face unnecessary difficulties. He will order his officers to collect various types of taxes fixed by law (the Qur'an, 16: 92) in a polite manner, not to charge the public extra amounts, and to protect those who are subject to them under justice and law. "For sure, Allah orders that you be generous, just and lawful to those nearby. He prohibits badness, excessiveness and murders. He gives you the advice. He orders these so that maybe you could take examples from these." When he listens to the cases brought before the head of the court of Mazali, he will order him to pay all due attention, to listen to all the parties statements carefully, to take back the right of the oppressed from the oppressor, and give the oppressed their rights. He will warn him often so that he will not divert from truth, will avoid intolerance, hypocrisy, bigotry, and fraud.

Dear son, the greatest ruler is the one who will believe that our words in this instruction are compliant with Allah's order: "O David, Verily We rendered you our representative on earth. Judge then between people in justice." (The Qur'an, 38:25)

The decree follows: Girgen, Tabarystan, Dehistan, Bistam and Damgan's officers, tradesmen and residents, either slave or free, (May Allah grant them prosperity!) should recognize the great ruler as their Soltan and ruler. They should be honest when they submit to him. They should submit to whatever is ruled by him, and serve him frankly. They should try to fuyil his orders as soon as possible. They

392

should not avoid the instructions of their officers and find excuses. They should know that his decrees are the same as ours, and his approval of or anger toward a particular issue is the same as our approval of or anger toward that particular issue. They should consult his representatives for their wages and means of subsistence. All wealthy people, citizens and military leaders should consult the supreme court composed of trustworthy members. Taxes fixed upon his orders and decrees should be paid. We hope they will remember our administration as one that gave benefits to them.

Another decree:

Appointment to governor's office in Sarahs

The sustenance of the state and the regularity of its affairs depend on the fruits of justice and on how these fruits taste. The Soltan of the world will only have Allah's grace if he rules justly. Since we have started ruling this world by Allah's will, we have been spending every effort to provide an equal amount of protection for everyone and to approach everyone with mercy. This task upon us is an order from Allah. We take care of the residents of Sarahs, may Allah protect them, with due attention and mercy. Thus, the administrator who will lead these people must be experienced, persevering, persistent and to the fore in the virtues. He should know about the pleasures and sorrows of life. Nejmeddin yark bears all these qualities.

He spent the most beautiful times of his life at the disposal of his nation. He engaged in significant affairs, he assumed high posts and he proved to be successful. By Allah's will, we deemed it proper to appoint him as the governor of Sarahs and vicinities. This was a post that was always the share of selected people. We ordered Nejmeddin to stick to his duties with a pure heart and relaxed soul and

393

solve disputes in a confident manner. We ask him to act kindly and respectfully toward religious leaders and scientists, and care for all people with feelings of mercy. He will be responsible for their safety and peace. Poor men should not be subject to cruel acts as stated in a proverb, "The day belongs to he who has a strong hand." Foreign soldiers and commanders of armies should not be permitted to collect taxes from the public except upon displaying a document obtained from the supreme authorities.

He will prevent the citizens from paying arbitrarily fixed taxes, he will leave no room for privileges, he will protect peace and justice.

According to this decree, the tradesmen, religious leaders, sheikhs and the descendants of the Prophet and residents of Sarahs will show respect to Nejmeddin as long as he continues fulfillling his responsibilities, and will consult him in every matter. They will treat well his representative. Bahaiddin, Horasan's Governor, should support Nejmeddin in every respect. The two will join in maintaining the safety of citizens depending on law, and help the citizens carry out their transactions. The administrative office's representative will inform Nejmeddin's representative as to the affairs being conducted, and the two will protect the rights of the citizens. All Turkic people and Tajiks will be bound by this order and they should be respectful toward the administration of the governor. For this type of administration is totally different fro the state's administrations in other places. Nejmeddin's representative will be responsible for the fulfilllment of this order, and the wage and taxes that relate to him should be fixed upon the decision to be made. May Allah help and be with you!

My dear Turkmen!

Find below another decree, read and learn from it! It

394

belongs to your forefathers. But it is a guideline for us to select administrators even today.

Appointment to the vice-Chair's office in the Council of Merw

Merw is the place where the Sultanate is, where the official flag waves, and where Allah's grace and support embraces the Seljuk generation. Therefore, attention should be paid so that it is different from and more organized than other parts of the country. Our citizens who are far away from the center and its periphery, and those under our administration will always benefit from our mercy and compassion. We appoint our councils trustworthy, skilled, successful and experienced members who know much about the details of the taxation matters of the region and who were examined by us for the offices that need to be filled. The chair of that city's council was the famous scientist Zeyneddin Seyitfor a long time. By Allah's will and after his re-election to this office, we encumbered him with this duty again. We had confidence in his courage, his foresight, his skills and kind manners, his high level of scholarship and piety. He is an exceptional talent with all these qualities. So many and great are the services he rendered to his nation that no reward could be proper for him, for he deserves more than anything that could be granted to him. His excellent poems and prose praising the state and used as adornment in many books will live forever. They are such valuable pieces that they are beyond comparison. A man with such qualities will never lose his dignity. The office of the chair of the financial institutions was always assumed by his deputies. Zeyneddin (May Allah grant him more) was always at our disposal and he was responsible for the fulfilllment of a very important task in the palace. But we were informed of the fact at a time of

395

Zeyneddin's absence (May Allah grant him more power) that the supreme governor and his family were being made certain payments regarding some of their private property and securities and estates in a way that would not please the council and that would not provide comfort for the subjects. And following Zeyneddin's report, and in consideration of what was told to us, we ordered Zeyneddin (May Allah give him power) to deal with the case and to organize matters. Although our palace and council was devoid of the honor they would have had in the presence of Zeyneddin, we gave priority to the fulfilllment of this task, and gave him (May Allah protect him) the responsibilities relating to the taxation matters regarding the city of Mei-w and its vicinities, our property and other affairs of the year 43 together with the collection of production tax. We authorized him to pursue this task confidently and in a safe way, and to assess duly the former and recent payment relating to the previous governor's private property, securities and estates. He will send just, considerate, pious, and religiously observant collectors everywhere, and every collector will keep books in a proper way through following the true path, will determine payments to be made and submit the books to the council in a timely and tidy form, and inform the council of the course of events. We ordered Zeyneddin (May Allah help him always) to calculate the expenses that would be required for the allocations to seyyids (May Allah increase their number) and to find the rest of the taxes, and to fix the resources to be transferred to other famous people, and to find the administrative fees (relating to the permanent retirement pay of public officials and religious leaders). He will appoint a man in whom he has confidence to take care of the spending of these resources. If part of the fees or taxes are spent elsewhere, they should be returned and restored to their former status, they should be included within the amounts allocated for

396

work and restored to their previous condition. He should know everything about tax-related issues. He should provide information as to who recently started collecting taxes and the amount of tax and the debts to be paid by particular individuals. He should keep a record of those taxes and fees, review former accounts; should he notice that certain matters were not recorded and there were betrayals, then he will know that he has to correct these mistakes.

All representatives should pay due respect to Zeyneddin (May Allah elevate him in rank). He should be provided with the principles regarding the resolution of tax-related matters and guiding the collectors in how to approach the taxpayers: All collectors of the higher inspection board should report to him with respect to income taxes and fees that were deducted from calculations; he will then review these diligently, and later use them in the course of his duties. The representatives of the governor (May Allah help them) should continue respecting Zeyneddin and give him the necessary means with a view to helping him succeed in his office. The acting chairs (May Allah protect them) will give him all the due support they can, they will reach agreement with him in every respect, and convey to him and his staff their demands in line with the needs of his representatives. All deputies, savings personnel and public relations officers, aliens, subjects and others (May Allah protect them all) recognize him as the highest of the representatives. He will be given a monthly wage, and he will not be objected to in any respect, as indicated in the order and documents. The reputable and famous scientist Nasyheddin (May Allah help him) will use all available means with respect to the realization of this decree. Show respect to Zeyneddin, have confidence in what he issues, and help him gain personal comfort. By Allah's will obey him absolutely."

397

My dear Turkmen!

I think you will be able to understand after reading these decrees how our ancestors chose administrators for offices and how they fulfillled their responsibilities nine hundred years ago.

My dear Turkmen Nation!

The way I'm leading is that of freedom.

Freedom is the essential condition for one's self-esteem. In this context, as a social value, freedom was one of the main characteristics of all the ages that the Turkmens passed through. Freedom is inherent in the Turkmen.

However, freedom, an aspect of the everlasting Turkmen way, should have a more concrete and peculiar meaning in our age.

I am attempting to have a logical kind of freedom accepted and approved by this nation. Otherwise, freedom will turn into irregularity and destroy the essentials of the state and harm the society.

There should be a clear borderline between freedom and corruption.

Freedom is by definition dependent on law and it should comply with law. If there is no freedom, then there will be no good in this society. And the absence of law means the lack of society itself. The essential meaning of law is the individual's compliance with the will accepted by the major part of society.

The majority is the sum of thousands and millions of individuals. In other words, it is the individual himself that determines the destiny of the individual. This is the basic meaning that underlies freedom. The Turkmen has maintained his national values and traditions for centuries. These values and traditions mean the adoption of the majority's will as the social principle. The Turkmen nation is a people which has provided the best examples of living together. The ancestors of the Turkmens said, "Turn your face to the direction where the majority turn their faces." This is freedom.

The way of freedom is the way of the national perceptions and national spirit. The national principles relating to the establishment of the Turkmen nation's life depend on the experience of freedom and the essentiality of making use of it. Without taking into consideration the national culture, not every sociocultural development can be agreed by every individual. So such developments will only remain on paper. Therefore, it is most important for the Turkmen to lead the spiritual way. Walking along this way in consideration of contemporary needs, we will make progress more easily.

The way of freedom of the Turkmens is only co-existent with proper, lawful, deeds and spiritual power. Honesty is society's demand from the individual; freedom is the value of the individual that finds repetition in society.

In order that the nation could have self-confidence, trust in its power and future and be proud, the nation should be informed of the eminence of its past.

This is the first condition of not going to extremes.

For going to extremes means losing one's way, which means diverting from the way.

For the first time in Turkmen history, the Turkmen's past is praised as a whole.

For the first time in the nation's history, a Turkmen state has been established on the basis of its own moral and

399

national values, and a flag that displays these values has been formed. This is the sign of the independence of the sovereign state.

Our flag is sacred.

After centuries, our people have adopted the official flag in harmony with their national character and the traditions of their forefathers and have become the owner of their green flag.

The flag of the Turkmen state has become a source of national pride. This is the standard that makes our nation proceed and our spirits elevate.

The souls of our ancestors have been absorbed into our flag.

The placement of the Turkmen carpet motifs on our flag symbolizes the importance of national values and national unity.

On the Turkmen flag are those characteristics we share with our ancestors and their mistakes from which we take lessons. Many Turkmen states unfortunately did not pay due attention to the national language of the Turkmen.

The national language is an essential quality of our state and society. We have been using the Turkmen language as our official language. Otherwise, our essential quality, nationality, would not be able to penetrate into the meaning of our state and its properties.

The Turkmens have shown in the five ages they have survived that they are capable of living after overcoming many difficulties. The Turkmen who overcame these difficulties proved that he was the Turkmen. The way of the

400

Turkmens led from one summit to another. The way of the contemporary age unified the Turkmen nation and the individual. Therefore our way is one of unity and integration.

The Turkmens need a center of attraction that will hold them united in material and spiritual terms in the new age. It is only the state and its national principles that will meet this need.

Only one thing remains of the man, the tasks he accomplished. It is not the office we assume or the task we undertake, but the way we follow that matters.

It should be our main goal to leave a valuable memoir to future generations who will follow the Golden path we chose. We should work, live and produce in consideration of this aim.

The essence of the nation lies in its perception of the world.

All the material and spiritual wealth, language, religion, culture, state and society of the nation are founded on this essence. If this essence lacks, none of these can be properly established. For these do not depend on law, but rely upon their own course. An unguided course would bring about regression and dispersal.

The Ruhnama brings the national perception into a system and organization. From now on, the national future of the Turkmens will be completely guaranteed in practice.

My way is the way of our essential qualities; it is the way where spiritual qualities become guiding principles.

Setting principles means holding things united without releasing them or just saying, "Go find your own way."

401

My way is that of spiritual strength.

My way is the one which gives the will of history to the hand of the nation.

My way is one where national perceptions and spiritual power unite and become one with the future.

The tone of the future is to depend on the characteristics of the national perception and spiritual strength.

The Turkmen has a great future, a famous future, for he has his past and today.

The difference of my way lies in that it not only covers the past and this day but also understands the future and displays it in full to the nation.

My dear fellow countrymen!

There are different ideas and sources of wisdom in the world: Some are happy saying that the world is proceeding toward the Judgment Day and many catastrophes will take place soon (as if these will facilitate their own lives). And some say the old world is retreating to its previous course. Just as it is not us who set the world on its axis and caused the world to move round its orbit so too it is not us who will be able to change it altogether! The world is at the disposal of Allah Almighty, the Highest of the High and the One.

Peoples, nations, states, countries of the world are proceeding toward unification, becoming brothers, friends, prosperous and peaceful. The world is proceeding toward truth,

402

justice, peace and free labOULThe meaning of humanity is constitution, production, seeking, searching and establishing.

Dispersal has caused many problems for the world. The solution is solidarity and unity. The good and the bad, the light and darkness, benevolence and malevolence are almost intermingled, but the good will supersede the bad, and benevolence will preside over malevolence.

The world is proceeding toward a bright future. The people who have good will and who are honest believe so. Benevolence, good will and brightness come from Allah.

My beloved people!

We have set out on a noble way. The Turkmen said, "Listen to others but do what you will." Let us work, for when we do so, we do it for our nation and land! Let us build beautiful structures, for we do it for our sons, children and grandchildren!

Setting up, bringing into existence, creating and constructing is the way of Allah the Almighty and His Prophets. Up to now there is no fault with those who follow this way.

Let us establish ways of friendship, brotherhood, unity, justice and proper knowledge. Let us be friends and find benefits, for none will be harmed by brotherhood!

For the sake of our ancestors who founded great states and led prosperous lives, for the sake of brave men and heroes who died for this country, let us make independent and impartial Turkmenistan a great and powerful state.

403

For the sake of those who have miraculous powers, sacred people, men of wisdom, let us establish, produce, have access to information, for proper knowledge should be the foundation of our country!

Let us have the ability to foresee the future, for the sake of brave men like Gorkut Ata, for this ability should be our country's foundation!

Let us love one another for the sake of our forefathers who are like saints and our grandmothers who are like angels. Let us be brothers and confidantes to one another. May the nation be built of love and peace!

Let us make this land for which our ancestors spilled their blood and for which our mothers shed their tears a place where prosperity abounds together with happiness, smiles and joy; for this is a sacred land; for this is a holy land!

May our father Oguz Han, who is like a prophet, be a witness to what I say: the way I choose is one of justice!

May our father Gin Han, who spreads sacred lights from the skies, be a witness to what I say: the way I'm leading is the enlightened way of truth!

May our father Ay Han, who spreads silver lights all through the night, be a witness to what I say: the way led by the Turkmens is the Golden way!

May our father Yyldyz Han, who keeps a close eye on Turkmenistan as ever, be a witness to what I say: our way is the prophets way!

May our father Gik Han, who inspires our families and hearts today and tomorrow, be a witness to the Turkmen's

404

efforts to warm the heart of the world and spread its merciful light to the future!

May our father Deiiz Han, who sends rains to the Turkmen land from the North, be a witness to the Turkmen's enthusiasm, Turkmen's progress; the power of the people is like the power of the flood, no power can stand before us!

May our father Dag Han, who maintains a close eye on us as ever, be a witness to the Turkmen's wish to attain to the highest spiritual levels! The world may reside in our heart, and we are a nation that deserves to reside in the heart of the world!

See for yourselves my brothers, my elders, my grandfathers, my grandmothers, my sisters, my sons, my grandsons, Ruhnama is complete now: This is your book, although I am the one who wrote it. This book is your book; it is the Turkmen's book; it is a statement of the Turkmen's goals and desires.

Ruhnama is our way! Every Turkmen will know himself after reading Ruhnama. Peoples of our other nations who read the Ruhnama will understand and know the Turkmen!

My Turkmen nation, may you never be belittled before a great nation, and may you never grow greedy before a small nation. The Turkmens will maintain the balance in international relations. Let this balance be an unshakable pillar of the Turkmen policy!

405

May your ways be enlightened, your future be filled with the sacred light, your age be of gold, my eternal and immortal Turkmen!

May the Turkmen stand as long as the world stands. May Turkmenistan stand as long as the world stands. May the independent and impartial Turkmenistan last forever!

(Notes on edited and translating:
-The book often used the Turkic "i" which is dotless, which has been converted to a Latin dotted "i".
-Often in the original text there would be a "(;" in the text. This most often represented a Q or a C and was therefore replaced in this version with a Q.
-It appears that the original of this version was edited or translated on a computer, as its translation into English took place in the mid-2000s. Because of this there were many errors in letter confusion that needed to be fixed such as the letter m being mistaken for the letters r and n.
-You will notice odd numbers throughout the text- this represents page numbers for the large font text it originated from. The book was in large font to make it easier for the average or below average reader. Many of the numbers remain, but some were taken out in the editing process. It is important to keep some as reference to the original version.
-Finally there were many spelling errors in the text, that can only be attributed to errors by the translators. As many of these as possible have been removed.)

www.ingramcontent.com/pod-product-compliance
Lightning Source LLC
Chambersburg PA
CBHW062003280526
45787CB00005B/1981